T0229596

Chapman & Hall/CRC Innovations in Software Engineering and Software Development

Series Editor
Richard LeBlanc
Chair, Department of Computer Science and Software Engineering, Seattle University

AIMS AND SCOPE

This series covers all aspects of software engineering and software development. Books in the series will be innovative reference books, research monographs, and textbooks at the undergraduate and graduate level. Coverage will include traditional subject matter, cutting-edge research, and current industry practice, such as agile software development methods and service-oriented architectures. We also welcome proposals for books that capture the latest results on the domains and conditions in which practices are most effective.

PUBLISHED TITLES

Computer Games and Software Engineering
Kendra M. L. Cooper and Walt Scacchi

Software Essentials: Design and Construction
Adair Dingle

Software Metrics: A Rigorous and Practical Approach, Third Edition
Norman Fenton and James Bieman

Software Test Attacks to Break Mobile and Embedded Devices
Jon Duncan Hagar

Software Designers in Action: A Human-Centric Look at Design Work
André van der Hoek and Marian Petre

Fundamentals of Dependable Computing for Software Engineers
John Knight

Introduction to Combinatorial Testing
D. Richard Kuhn, Raghu N. Kacker, and Yu Lei

Building Enterprise Systems with ODP: An Introduction to Open Distributed Processing
Peter F. Linington, Zoran Milosevic, Akira Tanaka, and Antonio Vallecillo

Software Engineering: The Current Practice
Václav Rajlich

Software Development: An Open Source Approach
Allen Tucker, Ralph Morelli, and Chamindra de Silva

CHAPMAN & HALL/CRC INNOVATIONS IN
SOFTWARE ENGINEERING AND SOFTWARE DEVELOPMENT

Computer Games and Software Engineering

Edited by

Kendra M. L. Cooper

University of Texas
Dallas, USA

Walt Scacchi

University of California, Irvine
Irvine, USA

CRC Press
Taylor & Francis Group
Boca Raton   London   New York

CRC Press is an imprint of the
Taylor & Francis Group an **informa** business

A CHAPMAN & HALL BOOK

CRC Press
Taylor & Francis Group
6000 Broken Sound Parkway NW, Suite 300
Boca Raton, FL 33487-2742

Printed on acid-free paper
Version Date: 20150317

International Standard Book Number-13: 978-1-4822-2668-3 (Hardback)

Library of Congress Cataloging-in-Publication Data

Computer games and software engineering / edited by Kendra M. L. Cooper and Walt Scacchi.
     pages cm. -- (Chapman & Hall/CRC innovations in software engineering and software development series ; 9)
     "A CRC title, part of the Taylor & Francis imprint, a member of the Taylor & Francis Group, the academic division of T&F Informa PLC."
     Includes bibliographical references and index.
     ISBN 978-1-4822-2668-3 (hardcover : acid-free paper) 1. Computer games--Programming. I. Cooper, Kendra M. L. II. Scacchi, Walt.

QA76.76.C672C6635 2015
794.8'1526--dc23   2015008925

Visit the Taylor & Francis Web site at
http://www.taylorandfrancis.com

and the CRC Press Web site at
http://www.crcpress.com

Contents

Contributors, vii

CHAPTER 1 ▪ Introducing Computer Games and Software
Engineering   1

KENDRA M.L. COOPER AND WALT SCACCHI

SECTION I **The Potential for Games in Software
Engineering Education**

CHAPTER 2 ▪ Use of Game Development in Computer
Science and Software Engineering Education   31

ALF INGE WANG AND BIAN WU

CHAPTER 3 ▪ Model-Driven Engineering of Serious
Educational Games: Integrating Learning
Objectives for Subject-Specific Topics
and Transferable Skills   59

KENDRA M.L. COOPER AND SHAUN LONGSTREET

CHAPTER 4 ▪ A Gameful Approach to Teaching Software
Design and Software Testing   91

SWAPNEEL SHETH, JONATHAN BELL, AND GAIL KAISER

CHAPTER 5 ▪ Educational Software Engineering:
Where Software Engineering, Education,
and Gaming Meet   113

TAO XIE, NIKOLAI TILLMANN, JONATHAN DE HALLEUX,
AND JUDITH BISHOP

CHAPTER 6 ■ Adaptive Serious Games   133

BARBARA REICHART, DAMIR ISMAILOVIĆ, DENNIS PAGANO,
AND BERND BRÜGGE

SECTION II **Conducting Fundamental Software Engineering Research with Computer Games**

CHAPTER 7 ■ RESTful Client–Server Architecture: A Scalable Architecture for Massively Multiuser Online Environments   153

THOMAS DEBEAUVAIS, ARTHUR VALADARES, AND CRISTINA V. LOPES

CHAPTER 8 ■ Software Engineering Challenges of Multiplayer Outdoor Smart Phone Games   183

ROBERT J. HALL

CHAPTER 9 ■ Understanding User Behavior at Three Scales: The AGoogleADay Story   199

DANIEL M. RUSSELL

CHAPTER 10 ■ Modular Reuse of AI Behaviors for Digital Games   215

CHRISTOPHER DRAGERT, JÖRG KIENZLE, AND CLARK VERBRUGGE

CHAPTER 11 ■ Repurposing Game Play Mechanics as a Technique for Designing Game-Based Virtual Worlds   241

WALT SCACCHI

CHAPTER 12 ■ Emerging Research Challenges in Computer Games and Software Engineering   261

WALT SCACCHI AND KENDRA M.L. COOPER

INDEX, 285

Contributors

Jonathan Bell
Department of Computer Science
Columbia University
New York, New York

Judith Bishop
Microsoft Research
Redmond, Washington

Bernd Brügge
Computer Science Department
Technical University of Munich
Munich, Germany

Kendra M.L. Cooper
Department of Computer Science
University of Texas, Dallas
Richardson, Texas

Jonathan de Halleux
Microsoft Research
Redmond, Washington

Thomas Debeauvais
Department of Informatics
University of California, Irvine
Irvine, California

Christopher Dragert
School of Computer Science
McGill University
Montréal, Québec, Canada

Robert J. Hall
AT&T Labs Research
Florham Park, New Jersey

Damir Ismailović
Computer Science Department
Technical University of Munich
Munich, Germany

Gail Kaiser
Department of Computer Science
Columbia University
New York, New York

Jörg Kienzle
School of Computer Science
McGill University
Montréal, Québec, Canada

Shaun Longstreet
Center for Teaching and Learning
Marquette University
Milwaukee, Wisconsin

Cristina V. Lopes
Department of Informatics
University of California, Irvine
Irvine, California

Dennis Pagano
Computer Science Department
Technical University of Munich
Munich, Germany

Barbara Reichart
Computer Science Department
Technical University of Munich
Munich, Germany

Daniel M. Russell
Google, Inc.
Menlo Park, California

Walt Scacchi
Center for Computer Games and
    Virtual Worlds
University of California, Irvine
Irvine, California

Swapneel Sheth
Department of Computer Science
Columbia University
New York, New York

Nikolai Tillmann
Microsoft Research
Redmond, Washington

Arthur Valadares
Department of Informatics
University of California, Irvine
Irvine, California

Clark Verbrugge
School of Computer Science
McGill University
Montréal, Québec, Canada

Alf Inge Wang
Department of Computer and
    Information Science
Norwegian University of Science
    and Technology
Trondheim, Norway

Bian Wu
Department of Computer
    and Information Science
Norwegian University of Science
    and Technology
Trondheim, Norway

Tao Xie
University of Illinois at Urbana,
    Champaign
Champaign, Illinois

CHAPTER 1

Introducing Computer Games and Software Engineering

Kendra M.L. Cooper and Walt Scacchi

CONTENTS

1.1 Emerging Field of Computer Games and Software Engineering   1
1.2 Brief History of Computer Game Software Development   3
1.3 Topics in Computer Games and Software Engineering   6
     1.3.1 Computer Games and SEE   6
     1.3.2 Game Software Requirements Engineering   8
     1.3.3 Game Software Architecture Design   8
     1.3.4 Game Software Playtesting and User Experience   9
     1.3.5 Game Software Reuse   10
     1.3.6 Game Services and Scalability Infrastructure   11
1.4 Emergence of a Community of Interest in CGSE   12
1.5 Introducing the Chapters and Research Contributions   14
1.6 Summary   24
Acknowledgments   25
References   25

1.1 EMERGING FIELD OF COMPUTER GAMES AND SOFTWARE ENGINEERING

Computer games (CGs) are rich, complex, and often large-scale software applications. CGs are a significant, interesting, and often compelling software application domain for innovative research in software engineering (SE) techniques and technologies. CGs are progressively changing the everyday world in many positive ways (Reeves and Read 2009). Game developers, whether focusing on entertainment-market opportunities or game-based applications in nonentertainment domains such as education, health care, defense, or scientific research (serious games or games with a purpose), thus share a common community of interest in how to best engineer game software.

There are many different and distinct types of games, game engines, and game platforms, much like there are many different and distinct types of software applications, information systems, and computing systems used for business. Understanding how games as a software system are developed to operate on a particular game platform requires identifying what types of games (i.e., game genre) are available in the market. Popular game genres include action or first-person shooters, adventure, role-playing game (RPG), fighting, racing, simulations, sports, strategy and real-time strategy, music and rhythm, parlor (board and card games), puzzles, educational or training, and massively multiplayer online games (MMOGs). This suggests that knowledge about one type of game (e.g., RPGs such as *Dungeons and Dragons*) does not subsume, contain, or provide the game play experience, player control interface, game play scenarios, or player actions found in other types of games. Therefore, being highly skilled in the art of one type of game software development (e.g., building a turn-taking RPG) does not imply an equivalent level of skill in developing another type of game software (e.g., a continuous play twitch or action game). This is analogous to saying that if a software developer is skilled in payroll and accounting software application systems, this does not imply that such a developer is also competent or skilled in the development of enterprise database management or e-commerce product sales over the web systems. The differences can be profound, and the developers' skills and expertise narrowly specialized.

Conversely, similar games, such as card or board games, raise the obvious possibility for a single game engine to be developed and shared or reused to support multiple game kinds of a single type. Game engines provide a runtime environment and reusable components for common game-related tasks, which leaves the developers freer to focus on the unique aspects of their game. For example, the games checkers and chess are played on an 8 × 8 checkerboard; though the shape and appearance of the game play pieces differ and the rules of game play differ, the kinds of player actions involved in playing either chess or checkers are the same (picking a piece and moving it to a square allowed by the rules of the game). Therefore, being skilled in the art of developing a game of checkers can suggest the ability or competent skill in developing a similar game like chess, especially if both games can use the same game engine. However, this is feasible only when the game engine is designed to allow for distinct sets of game rules and distinct appearance of game pieces—that is, the game engine must be designed for reuse or extension. This design goal is not always an obvious engineering choice, and it is one that increases the initial cost of game engine development (Bishop et al. 1998; Gregory 2009). Subsequently, developing software for different kinds of games of the same type, or using the same game engine, requires a higher level of technical skill and competence in software development than designing an individual game of a given type.

Understanding how game software operates on a game platform requires an understanding of the game device (e.g., Nintendo GameBoy, Microsoft Xbox One, Apple iPhone) and the internal software run-time environment that enables its intended operation and data communication capabilities. A game platform constrains the game design in terms of its architectural structure, how it functions, how the game player controls the game device through its interfaces (keyboard, buttons, stylus, etc.) and video/audio displays, and how they affect game data transmission and reception in a multiplayer game network.

1.2 BRIEF HISTORY OF COMPUTER GAME SOFTWARE DEVELOPMENT

Game software researchers and developers have been exploring computer game software engineering (CGSE) from a number of perspectives for many years. Many are rooted in the history of CG development, much of which is beyond what we address here, as are topics arising from many important and foundational studies of games as new media and as cultural practice. However, it may be reasonable to anticipate new game studies that focus on topics such as how best to develop CGs for play across global cultures or through multisite, global SE practices.

The history of techniques for CG software development goes back many decades, far enough to coincide with the emergence of SE as a field of research and practices in the late 1960s. As CG software development was new and unfamiliar, people benefitted from publications of open source game software, often written in programming languages such as Fortran (Spencer 1968). Before that, interest in computer-based playing against human opponents in popular parlor games such as chess, checkers, poker, bridge, backgammon, and go was an early fascination of researchers exploring the potential of artificial intelligence (AI) using computers (Samuel 1960). It should be noted that these CG efforts did not rely on graphic interfaces, which were to follow with the emergence of video games that operated on general-purpose computer workstations, and later personal computers and special-purpose game consoles.

Spacewar!, PONG, Maze War, DOOM, SimCity, and thousands of other CGs began to capture the imagination of software developers and end users as opening up new worlds of interactive play for human player versus computer or player versus player game play to large public audiences, and later to end-user development or modification of commercial games (Burnett 2004).

Combat-oriented maze games such as *Maze War, Amaze* (Berglund and Cheriton 1985), *MiMaze* (Gautier and Dior 1998), and others (Sweeney 1998) helped introduce the development and deployment of networked multiplayer games. *BattleZone, Habitat,* and other game-based virtual worlds similarly helped launch popular interest in MMOGs (Bartle 1990), along with early social media capabilities such as online forums (threaded e-mail lists), multiuser chat (including Internet Relay Chat) and online chat meeting rooms (from multiuser dungeons), which would then be globally popularized within *Ultima Online, EverQuest, World of Warcraft,* and others. The emergence of the CG development industry, with major studios creating games for global markets, soon made clear the need for game development to embrace modern SE techniques and practices, or else likely suffer the fate of problematic, difficult-to-maintain or -expand game software systems, which is the common fate of software application systems whose unrecognized complexity grows beyond the conventional programming skills of their developers.

As many game developers in the early days were self-taught software makers, it was not surprising to see their embrace of practices for sharing game source code and play mechanic algorithms. Such ways and means served to collectively advance and disseminate game development practices on a global basis. As noted above, early game development books prominently featured open source game programs that others could copy, build, modify, debug, and redistribute, albeit through pre-Internet file sharing services such as those offered by CompuServe, though game-making students in academic settings might also share source code to games such as *Spacewar!, Adventure,* and *Zork* using Internet-accessible file servers via file transfer protocols.

The pioneering development of *DOOM* in the early 1990s (Hall 1992; Kushner 2003), along with the growing popularity of Internet-based file sharing, alongside of the emergence of the open source software movement, the World Wide Web, and web-based service portals and applications, all contributed in different ways to the growing realization that CGs as a software application could similarly exploit these new ways and means for developing and deploying game software systems. Id Software, through the game software developer John Carmack and the game designer John Romero, eventually came to realize that digital game distribution via file sharing (initially via floppy disks for freeware and paid versions of *DOOM*), rather than in-store retail sales, would also point the way to offload the ongoing development and customization of games such as *DOOM*, by offering basic means for end-user programming and modification of CGs that might have little viable commercial market sales remaining (Au 2002; Kushner 2003). The end users' ability to therefore engage in primitive CGSE via game modding was thus set into motion (cf. Au 2002; Burnett 2004; Morris 2003; Scacchi 2010). Other game development studios such as Epic Games also began to share their game software development tools as software development kits (SDKs), such as the UnrealEd game level editor and script development interface, and its counterpart packages with *Quake* from Id Software (QuakeEd) and *Half-Life* from Valve Software. These basic game SDKs were distributed for no additional cost on the CD-ROM media that retail consumers would purchase starting in the late 1990s. Similarly, online sharing of game software, as either retail product or free game mod, was formalized by Valve Software through their provision of the Steam online game distribution service, along with its integrated payment services (Au 2002; Scacchi 2010).

Finally, much of the wisdom to arise from the early and more recent days of CG development still focus attention on game programming and game design, rather than on CGSE. For example, the current eight-volume series *Game Programming Gems*, published by Charles River Media and later Cengage Learning PTR (2000–2010), reveals long-standing interest on the part of game makers to view their undertaking as one primarily focused on programming rather than SE; field of SE long ago recognized that programming is but one of the major activities in developing, deploying, and sustaining large-scale software system applications, but not the only activity that can yield high quality software products and related artifacts. Similarly, there are many books written by well-informed, accomplished game developers on how best to design games as *playful interactive media* that can induce fun or hedonic experiences (Fullerton et al. 2004; Meigs 2003; Rogers 2010; Salen and Zimmerman 2004; Schell 2008). This points to another gap, as many students interested in making CG choose to focus their attention toward a playful user experience, while ignoring whether SE can help produce better quality CG at lower costs with greater productivity. That is part of the challenge that motivates new research and practice in CGSE.

1.3 TOPICS IN COMPUTER GAMES AND SOFTWARE ENGINEERING

This book collects 11 chapters that systematically explore the CGSE space. The chapters that follow draw attention to topics such as CG and SE education (SEE), game software requirements engineering, game software architecture and design approaches, game software testing and usability assessment, game development frameworks and reusability techniques, and game scalability infrastructure, including support for mobile devices and web-based services. Here, a sample of earlier research efforts in CGSE that help inform these contemporary studies is presented in the following subsections.

1.3.1 Computer Games and SEE

Swartout and van Lent (2003) were among the earliest to recognize the potential of bringing CG and game-based virtual worlds into mainstream computer science education and system development expertise. Zyda (2006) followed by further bringing attention to the challenge of how best to educate a new generation of CG developers. He observes something of a conflict between programs that stress CG as interactive media created by artists and storytellers (therefore somewhat analogous to feature film production) and programs that would stress the expertise in computer science required of game software developers or infrastructural systems engineers. These pioneers in computer science research recognized the practical utility of CG beyond entertainment that could be marshaled and directed to support serious game development for training and educational applications. However, for both of these visions for undergraduate computer science education, SE has little role to play in their respective framings. In contrast, SE faculty who teach project-oriented SE courses increasingly have sought to better motivate and engage students through game software development projects, as most computer science students worldwide are literate in CG and game play. Building from this insight, Oh Navarro and van der Hoek (2005, 2009), the Claypools (Claypool and

Claypool 2005), and Wang and students (Wang 2011; Wang et al. 2008) were among the earliest to call out the opportunity for focusing on the incorporation of CG deep into SEE coursework.

Oh Navarro and van der Hoek started in the late 1990s exploring the innovative idea of teaching SE project dynamics through a simulation-based SE RPG, called *SimSE*. Such a game spans the worlds of software process modeling and simulation, team-based SE, and SE project management, so that students can play, study, and manipulate different SE tasking scenarios along with simulated encounters with common problems in SE projects (e.g., developers falling behind schedule, thus disrupting development plans and inter-role coordination). In this way, SE students could play the game before they undertook the software development project, and thus be better informed about some of the challenges of working together as a team, rather than just as skilled individual software engineers.

The Claypools highlight how SE project or capstone courses can focus on student teams conducting game development projects, which seek to demonstrate their skill in SE, as well as their frequent enthusiastic interest in CG culture and technology. The popularity of encouraging game development projects for SE capstone project courses is now widespread. However, the tension between CG design proffered in texts that mostly ignore modern SE principles and practices (Fullerton et al. 2004; Meigs 2003; Rogers 2010; Salen and Zimmerman 2004; Schell 2008) may sometimes lead to projects that produce interesting, playful games but do so with minimal demonstration of SE skill or expertise.

Wang et al. (2008) have demonstrated how other CG and game play experiences can be introduced into computer science or SEE coursework through gamifying course lectures that facilitate faculty–student interactions and feedback. Wang (2011) along with Cooper and Longstreet (2012) (and in Chapter 3) expand their visions for SEE by incorporating contemporary SE practices such as software architecture and model-driven development. More broadly, Chapters 2 through 6 all discuss different ways and means for advancing SEE through CG.

Finally, readers who teach SEE project courses would find it valuable to have their students learn CGSE through their exposure to the history of CG software development, including a review of some of the pioneering papers or reports cited earlier in this introductory chapter. Similarly, whether to structure the SEE coursework projects as massively open online courses or around competitive, inter-team game jams also merits consideration. Such competitions can serve as test beds for empirical

SE (or SEE) studies, for example, when project teams are composed by students who take on different development roles and each team engages members with comparable roles and prior experience. Such ideas are discussed in Chapter 12.

1.3.2 Game Software Requirements Engineering

Understanding how best to elicit and engineer the requirements for CG is unsurprisingly a fertile area for CGSE research and practice (Ampatzoglou and Stamelos 2010; Callele et al. 2005), much like it has been for mainstream SE. However, there are still relatively few game development approaches that employ SE requirements development methods such as use cases and scenario-based design (Walker 2003).

Many game developers in industry have reviewed the informal game "postmortems" that first began to be published in *Game Developer* magazine in the 1990s (Grossman 2003), and more recently on the Gamasutra. com online portal. Grossman's (2003) collection of nearly 50 postmortems best reveals common problems that recur in game development projects, which cluster around project software and content development scheduling, budget shifts (generally development budget cuts), and other nonfunctional requirements that drift or shift in importance during game development projects (Alspaugh and Scacchi 2013; Petrillo et al. 2009). None of this should be surprising to experienced SE practitioners or project managers, though it may be "new knowledge" to SE students and new self-taught game developers. Similarly, software functional requirements for CG most often come from the game producers or developers, rather than from end users. However, nonfunctional requirements (e.g., the game should be fun to play but hard to master and it should be compatible with mobile devices and the web) dominate CG development efforts, and thus marginalize the systematic engineering of functional game requirements. Nonetheless, the practice of openly publishing and sharing postproject descriptions and hindsight rationalizations may prove valuable as another kind of empirical SE data for further study, as well as something to teach and practice within SEE project courses.

1.3.3 Game Software Architecture Design

CGs as complex software applications often represent configurations of multiple software components, libraries, and network services. As such, CG software must have an architecture, and ideally such an architecture is explicitly represented and documented as such. Although such architecture may be proprietary and thus protected by its developers as intellectual property covered by trade secrets and end-user license agreements, there is substantial educational value in having access to such architectural renderings as a means for quickly grasping key system design decisions and participating modules in game play event processing. This is one reason for interest in games that are open to modding (Seif El-Nasr and Smith 2006; Scacchi 2010). However, other software architecture concerns exist. For instance, there are at least four kinds of CG software architecture that arise in networked multiplayer games: (1) the static and dynamic run-time architectures for a game engine; (2) the architecture of the game development frameworks or SDKs that embed a game's development architecture together with its game engine (Wang 2011); (3) the architectural distribution of software functionality and data processing services for networked multiplayer games; and (4) the informational and geographical architecture of the game levels as designed play spaces. For example, for (3) there are four common alternative system configurations: single server for multiple interacting or turn-taking players, peer-to-peer networking, client–server networking for end-user clients and playspace data exchange servers, and distributed, replicated servers for segmented user community play sessions (via *sharding*) (Alexander 2003; Bartle 1990; Berglund and Cheriton 1985; Bishop et al. 1998; Gautier and Dior 1998; Hall 1992; Sweeney 1998).

In contrast, the focus on CG as interactive media often sees little or no software architecture as being relevant to game design, especially for games that assume a single server architecture or PC game run-time environment, or in a distributed environment that networking system specialists, it is assumed, will design and provide (Fullerton et al. 2004; Meigs 2003; Rogers 2010; Salen and Zimmerman 2004; Schell 2008). Ultimately, our point is not to focus on the gap between game design and game software (architecture) design as alternative views but to draw attention to the need for CGSE to find ways to span the gap.

1.3.4 Game Software Playtesting and User Experience

CGs as complex software applications for potentially millions of end users will consistently and routinely manifest bugs (Lewis 2010). Again, this is part of the puzzle of any complex SE effort, so games are no exception. However, as user experience and thus user satisfaction may be key to driving viral social media that helps promote retail game sales and adoption, paying close attention to bugs and features in CG development and usability (Pinelle et al. 2008) may be key to the economic viability of a game development studio. Further, on the basis of decades of experience in developing large-scale software applications, we believe that most end users cannot articulate their needs or requirements in advance but can assess what is provided in terms of whether or not it meets their needs. This in turn may drive the development of large-scale, high-cost CGs that take calendars to produce and person-decades (or person-centuries) of developer effort away from monolithic product development life cycles to ones that are much more incremental and driven by user feedback based on progressively refined or enhanced game version (or prototype) releases. Early and ongoing game playtesting will likely come to be a central facet of CGSE, as will tools and techniques for collecting, analyzing, and visualizing game playtesting data (Drachen and Canossa 2009; Zoeller 2013). This is one activity where CGSE efforts going forward may substantially diverge from early CG software development approaches, much like agile methods often displace *waterfall* software life cycle development approaches. Therefore, CG developers, much like mainstream software engineers, are moving toward incremental development, rapid release, and user playtesting to drive new product release versions.

1.3.5 Game Software Reuse

Systematic software reuse could be considered within multiple SE activities (requirements, architecture, design, code, build and release, test cases) for a single game or a product line of games (Furtado et al. 2011). For example, many successful CGs are made into *franchise brands* through the production and release of extension packs (that provide new game content or play levels) or product line sequels (e.g., *Quake, Quake II, and Quake III; Unreal, Unreal Tournament 2003, and Unreal Tournament 2007*). Whether or how the concepts and methods of software product lines can be employed in widespread CG business models is unclear and underexplored. A new successful CG product may have been developed and released in ways that sought to minimize software production costs, thus avoiding the necessary investment to make the software architecture reusable and extensible and the component modules replaceable or upgradable without discarding much of the software developed up to that point. This means that SE approaches to CG product lines may be recognized in hindsight as missed opportunities, at least for a given game franchise.

Reuse has the potential to reduce CG development costs and improve quality and productivity, as it often does in mainstream SE. Commercial

CG development relies often on software components (e.g., game engines) or middleware products provided by third parties (AI libraries for non-player characters [NPCs]) as perhaps its most visible form of software reuse practice. Game SDKs, game engines, procedural game content generation tools, and game middleware services all undergo active R&D within industry and academia. Game engines are perhaps the best success story for CG software reuse, but it is often the case that commercial game development studios and independent game developers avoid adoption of such game engines when they are perceived to overly constrain game development patterns or choice of game play mechanics to those characteristic of the engine. This means that game players may recognize such games as offering derivative play experience rather than original play experience. However, moving to catalogs of pattern or antipatterns for game requirements, architecture and design patterns for game software product lines (Furtado et al. 2011), and online repositories of reusable game assets organized by standardized ontologies may be part of the future of reusable game development techniques. As noted earlier, such topics are explored in Chapters 10 and 11.

Other approaches to software reuse may be found in free or open source software for CG development (Scacchi 2004), and also in AI or computational intelligence methods for semiautomated or automated content generation and level design (IEEE 2014).

1.3.6 Game Services and Scalability Infrastructure

CGs range from small-scale, stand-alone applications for smart phones (e.g., app games) to large-scale, distributed, real-time MMOGs. CGs are sometimes played by millions of end users, so that large-scale, *big data* approaches to game play analytics and data visualization become essential techniques for engineering sustained game play and deployment support (Drachen and Canossa 2009; Zoeller 2013). Prior knowledge of the development of multiplayer game software systems and networking services (cf. Alexander 2003; Berglund and Cheriton 1985; Gautier and Dior 1998; Sweeney 1998) may be essential for CGSE students focusing on development of social or mobile MMOGs. In order to engage the users and promote the adoption and ongoing use of such large and upward or downward scalable applications, CGSE techniques have significant potential but require further articulation and refinement. Questions on the integration of game playtesting and end-user play analytic techniques together with large-scale, big-data applications are just beginning to emerge. Similarly, how best to design back-end game data management capabilities or remote middleware game play services also points to SE challenges for networked software systems engineering, as has been recognized within the history of networked game software development (Alexander 2003, Bartle 1990, Berglund and Cheriton 1985; Gautier and Dior 1998; Sweeney 1998). Whether or how cloud services or cloud-based gaming has a role in CGSE may benefit by review of the chapters that follow.

The ongoing emphasis on CGs that realize playful, fun, social, or learning game experiences across different game play platforms leads naturally to interdisciplinary approaches to CGSE, where psychologists, sociologists, anthropologists, and economists could provide expertise on defining new game play requirements and experimental designs to assess the quality of user play experiences. Further, the emergence of online fantasy sports, along with eSports (e.g., team/player vs. team/player competitions for prizes or championship rankings) and commercial endeavors such as the National Gaming League for professional-level game play tournaments, points to other CGSE challenges such as cheat prevention, latency equalization, statistical scoring systems, complex data analytics (DsC09), and play data visualizations (Zoeller 2013), all of which support game systems that are balanced and performance (monitoring) equalized for professional-level tournaments. The social sciences could provide insight into how to attract, engage, and retain players across demographic groups (e.g., age, gender, geographic location), much like recent advances in the Cooperative and Human Aspects in Software Engineering workshop and ethnographic studies of users in contemporary SE research.

With this background in mind, we turn to explain the motivating events that gave rise to the production of this book on CGSE.

1.4 EMERGENCE OF A COMMUNITY OF INTEREST IN CGSE

At the core of CGs are complex human–software platform interactions leading to emergent game play behaviors. This complexity creates difficulties architecting game software components, predicting their behaviors, and testing the results. SE has not yet been able to meet the demands of the CG software development industry, an industry that works at the forefront of technology and creativity, where creating a fun experience is the most important metric of success. In recognition of this gap, the first games and software engineering workshop (GAS 2011) was held at the International Conference on Software Engineering (ICSE 2011), initiated through the efforts of Chris Lewis and E. James Whitehead (both from UC Santa Cruz). Together with a committee of like-minded others within the SE community, Lewis and Whitehead sought to bring together SE researchers interested in exploring the demands of game creation and ascertain how the SE community can contribute to this important creative domain. GAS 2011 participants were also challenged to investigate how games can help aid the SE process or improve SEE. Research in these areas has been exciting and interesting, and GAS 2011 was envisioned to be the first time practitioners from these fields would have the opportunity to come together at ICSE to investigate the possibilities of this innovative research area. The content of Chapters 4 and 8 was originally presented at GAS 2011, in simpler form.

The GAS 2012 workshop explored issues that crosscut the SE and the game engineering communities. Advances in game engineering techniques can be adopted by the SE community to develop more engaging applications across diverse domains: education, health care, fitness, sustainable activities (e.g., recycling awareness), and so on. Successful CGs feature properties that are not always found in traditional software: they are highly engaging, they are playful, and they can be fun to play for extended periods of time. Engaging games enthrall players and result in users willing to spend increasing amounts of time and money playing them. ICSE 2012 sought to provide a forum for advances in SE for developing more sustainable (*greener*) software, so GAS 2012 encouraged presentation and discussion of ways and means through green game applications. For example, approaches that support adapting software to trade off power consumption and video quality would benefit the game community. SE techniques spanning patterns (requirements, design), middleware, testing techniques, development environments, and processes for building sustainable software are of great interest. Chapters 6 and 10 were both initially presented in simpler form at GAS 2012.

GAS 2013 explored issues that crosscut the SE and the game development communities. Advances in game development techniques can be adopted by the SE community to develop more engaging applications across diverse domains: education, health care, fitness, sustainable activities (e.g., recycling awareness), and so on. GAS 2013 provided a forum for advances in SE for developing games that enable progressive societal change through fun, playful game software. SE techniques spanning patterns, middleware, testing techniques, development environments, and processes were in focus and consumed much of participant interest, including a handful of live game demonstrations. Chapters 9 and 5 were initially presented in simpler form at GAS 2013. Chapters 2, 7, and Chapter 11 are new and were prepared specifically for this book. Finally, it should be noted that Cooper, Scacchi, and Wang were the co-organizers of GAS 2013.

The topic of how best to elevate the emerging results and discipline of CGSE was put into motion at the end of GAS 2013; this book is now the product of that effort. Many participants at the various GAS workshops were invited to develop and refine their earlier contributions into full chapters. The chapters that follow are the result. Similarly, other research papers that speak to CGSE topics that appeared in other workshops, conferences, or journals were reviewed for possible inclusion in this book. Therefore, please recognize the chapters that follow as a sample of recent research in the area of CGSE, rather than representing some other criteria for selection. However, given more time and more pages to fill for publication, others who were not in a position to prepare a full chapter of their work would have been included.

As such, we turn next to briefly introduce each of the chapters that were contributed for this book on CGSE. The interested reader is encouraged to consider focusing on topics of greatest interest first and to review the other chapters as complementary issues found at the intersection of CG and SE covered across the set of remaining chapters.

1.5 INTRODUCING THE CHAPTERS AND RESEARCH CONTRIBUTIONS

A comprehensive literature review of CG in software education is presented in Chapter 2 by Alf Inge Wang and Bian Wu. They explore how CG development is being integrated into computer science and SE coursework. The survey is organized around three research questions:

- The first question focuses on discovering the topics where game development has been used as a teaching method. These results are presented in three categories: computer science (37 articles), SE (16 articles), and applied computer science (13 articles). For computer science, a variety of topics (e.g., programming, AI, algorithms) are being taught at different levels (university and elementary, middle, and high school). Game development approaches in university courses on programming dominate the findings, followed by AI. For SE, a variety of topics (e.g., architecture, object-oriented analysis and design, and testing) are being taught in university courses. Game development approaches in design topics (architecture and object-oriented) lead the findings, followed by testing. For applied computer science a variety of topics (e.g., game design, game development with a focus on game design, and art design) are being taught in pre-college/university and university courses. These approaches focus on creating or changing games through graphical tools to create terrains, characters, game objects, and populate levels. Applied courses on game design and development dominate the findings, followed by art design; approximately half the findings were for courses at the pre-college/university level.

- The second research question focuses on identifying the most common tools used and any shared experiences from using these tools. The articles reveal a plethora of game development frameworks and languages in use. Interestingly, the most commonly used frameworks include the educators' own framework, XNA, or a Java game development framework; Unity has not been reported in the articles reviewed. With respect to programming languages, visual programming languages and Java dominate, followed by C#. Visual languages have worked well for introducing programming concepts, promoting the field of computer science. Often, students are asked to create simple 2D games from scratch; an alternative approach reported is to use game modding, in which the existing code is changed, modifying the behavior and presentation of a game.

- The third research question focuses on identifying common experiences from using game development to teach computer science and SE subjects. Most studies in the survey report that game development improves student motivation and engagement, as the visualization makes programming fun. However, only a few studies report learning improvements in terms of better grades; there is a tendency for some students to focus too much on game development instead of the topic being taught. In addition, many articles reported that game development positively supported recruiting and enrolment efforts in computer science and SE.

Based on the results of this survey, the authors propose a set of recommendations for choosing an appropriate game development framework to use in a course. The recommendations include the consideration of the educational goals, subject constraints, programming experience, staff expertise, usability of the game development platform, and the technical environment.

A model-driven SE approach to the development of serious educational games (SEGs) is presented in Chapter 3 by Kendra Cooper and Shaun Longstreet. SEGs are complex applications; developing new ones has been time consuming and expensive, and has required substantial expertise from diverse stakeholders: game developers, software developers, educators, and players. To improve the development of SEGs, the authors present a model-driven engineering (MDE)-based approach that uniquely integrates elements of traditional game design, pedagogical content, and SE. In the SE community, MDE is an established approach for systematically developing complex applications, where models of the application are created, analyzed (validated/verified), and subsequently transformed to lower levels of abstraction.

The MDE-based approach consists of three main steps to systematically develop the SEGs:

- The first step is to create an informal model of the SEG captured as a storyboard with preliminary descriptions of the learning objectives, game play, and user interface concepts. The learning objectives cover specific topics (e.g., design patterns, grade 4 reading) as well as transferable skills (e.g., problem solving, analysis, critical thinking). Storyboards are an established, informal approach used in diverse creative endeavors to capture the flow of events over time using a combination of graphics and text. The SimSYS storyboard is tailored to explicitly include the learning objectives for the game.

- The second step is to transform the informal model into a semiformal, tailored unified modeling language (UML) use case model (visual and tabular, template-based specifications). Here, the preliminary description is refined to organize it into acts, scenes, screens, and challenges; each of these has a tabular template to assist in the game development. The templates include places for the learning objectives; they can be traced from the highest level (game template) down to specific challenges. More detailed descriptions of the game play narrative, graphics, animation, music and sound effects, and challenge content are defined.

- The third step is to transform the semiformal model into formal, executable models in statecharts and extensible markup language (XML). A statechart can undergo comprehensive simulation or animation to verify the model's behavior using existing tool support; errors can be identified and corrected in both the statechart model and the semiformal model as needed. XML is the game specification, which can be loaded, played, and tested using the SimSYS game play engine; the XML schema definition for the game is defined.

A key feature of the MDE approach is the meta-model foundation, which explicitly represents traditional game elements (e.g., narrative, characters), educational elements (e.g., learning objectives, learning taxonomy), and their relationships. The approach supports the wide adoption across curricula, as domain-specific knowledge can be plugged in across multiple disciplines (e.g., science, technology, engineering and mathematics [STEM], humanities) and the thorough integration of learning objectives. This approach is flexible, as it can be applied in an agile, iterative development process by describing a part of the game informally, semiformally, and formally (executable), allowing earlier assessment and feedback on a running (partial) game.

In Chapter 4, Swapneel Sheth, Jonathan Bell, and Gail Kaiser present an experience report describing their efforts in using game play motifs, inspired from online RPGs, and competitive game tournaments to introduce students to software testing and design principles. The authors draw upon the reported success of gamifying another topic in SE (formal verification) by proposing a social approach to introduce students to software testing using their game-like environment HALO (highly addictive, socially optimized) SE. HALO can make the software development process, and in particular, the testing process, more fun and social by using themes from popular CGs. HALO represents SE tasks as quests; a storyline binds multiple quests together. Quests can be individual, requiring a developer to work alone, or in groups, requiring a developer to form a team and work collaboratively toward an objective. Social rewards in HALO can include titles—prefixes or suffixes of players' names—and levels, both of which showcase players' successes in the game world. These social rewards harness a model, operant conditioning, which rewards players for good behavior and encourages repeating good behavior.

HALO was introduced into the course as an optional part of two assignments and as a bonus question in a third assignment. The student evaluations on using HALO in their assignments revealed that the approach may be more effective if the HALO quests had a stronger alignment with all the students doing well in the assignment, not as an optional or bonus question that may only appeal to some of the students. The ability to embrace a broader range of students, perhaps by providing some adaptability to adjust the level of difficulty based on what the students would find it most useful, was recommended by the authors. For example, students who are struggling with the assignment might want quests covering more basic aspects of the assignment, whereas students who are doing well might need quests covering more challenging aspects.

To instill good software design principles, a programming assignment using a game was used in combination with a competitive game tournament in an early course. The assignment and tournament centered on developing the game *Battleship*. The students were provided with three interfaces as a starting point for the assignment: game, location, and player. As long as the students' code respected the interfaces, they would be able to take part in the tournament. The teaching staff provided implementations of the game and location interfaces; each student's automated computer player implementation was used. Extra credit was used as an incentive; even though the extra credit was modest, the combination of the extra credit and the competitive aspect resulted in almost the entire class participating in the tournament: a remarkable 92% of the class had implementations that realized the defined interfaces and were permitted to compete in the tournament. The authors note that the competitive tournaments require substantial resources (e.g., time, automated testing frameworks, equipment), in particular for large classes.

In Chapter 5, Tao Xie, Nikolai Tillmann, Jonathan de Halleux, and Judith Bishop focus on the gamification of online programming exercise systems through their online CG, Pex4Fun, and its successor, Code Hunt. These game-based environments are designed to address educational tasks of teaching and learning programming and SE skills. They are open, browser based, interactive gaming-based teaching and learning platforms for .NET programming languages such as C#, Visual Basic, and F#. Students play coding-duel game play sessions, where they need to write code to implement the capabilities of a hidden specification (i.e., sample solution code not visible to the student). The Pex4Fun system automatically finds discrepancies in the behavior between the student's code and the hidden specification, which are provided as feedback to the student. The students then proceed to correct their code. The coding-duel game type within Pex4Fun is flexible and can be used to create games that target a wide range of skills such as programming, program understanding, induction, debugging, problem solving, testing, and specification writing, with different degrees of difficulty. Code Hunt offers additional gaming aspects to enhance the game play experience such as audio support, a leaderboard, and visibility to the coding duels of other players to enhance the social aspect; games can also be organized in a series of worlds, sectors, and levels, which become increasingly challenging. Pex4Fun has been adopted as a major platform for assignments in a graduate SE course, and a coding-duel contest has recently been held at the ICSE 2011 for engaging conference attendees to solve coding duels in a dynamic social contest. The response from the broader community using the Pex4Fun system has been positive and enthusiastic, indicating the gamification of online programming exercise systems holds great promise as a tool in SEE.

An exploratory study on how human tutors interact with learners playing serious games is presented by Barbara Reichart, Damir Ismailović, Dennis Pagano, and Bernd Brügge in Chapter 6. In traditional educational settings, a professional human tutor observes a student's skills and uses those observations to select learning content, adapting the material as needed. Moving into a serious game educational setting, this study investigates how players can be characterized and how to provide them with help in this new environment. The study uses four small serious games with focus on elementary-school mathematics. The authors created these over a span of 2 years; the new games were needed to retain very high control over the game elements (content, difficulty level, and game speed), which would not be possible with games already available. Interviews with experts and observing children at play provided qualitative data for the first part of the study. Here, the results reveal that the human tutor observes the correct and incorrect execution of the tasks in the game as well as the motorical execution (hand–eye coordination, timing); tutors rate the skills of the learners in a fuzzy way. In the second part of the study, interviews with experts provided qualitative data; here, experts observed the recordings of children playing. The experts defined different levels of difficulty that they considered reasonable for each game. To provide the different levels of difficulty, a detailed description of the data (content) that can be changed in each of the developed serious games was defined. In addition to changes in the content, changes to some properties of the game elements are identified to affect specific skills. For example, adapting the speed of a game element has a direct effect on some skills necessary for mathematics, such as counting. Therefore, adapting the game element properties to change the level of difficulty is an option—a change in the learning content is not always necessary. Using the results of these studies, the authors also propose a definition for the adaptivity process in a serious game consisting of four stages: monitoring players (A1), learner characterization (A2), assessment generation (B1), and adaptive intervention (B2). This thorough, extensive study provides a strong foundation for the community to build upon in the investigation of adapting serious games, with respect to research methodologies and the results reported.

A scalable architecture for MMOGs is presented by Thomas Debeauvais, Arthur Valadares, and Cristina V. Lopes in Chapter 7. The research considers how to harmonize the representational state transfer principles, which have been used very successfully for scaling web applications, with the architecture-level design of MMOGs. The proposed architecture, restful client–server architecture (RCAT), consists of four tiers: proxies, game servers, caches, and database. Proxies handle the communication with clients, game servers handle the computation of the game logic, and the database ensures data persistence. RCAT supports the scalability of MMOGs through the addition of servers that provide the same functionality. The authors developed a reference implementation of RCAT as a middleware solution, and then conducted experiments to characterize the performance and identify bottlenecks.

Two quantitative performance studies are reported. The first uses a simple MMOG to analyze the impact of the number of clients on the bandwidth: from the proxy to the clients and from the server to the database, with and without caching. The experiments show that the bandwidth from the proxy to the clients increases quadratically; the database can be a central bottleneck, although caching can be an effective strategy for this component. The second experiment evaluates the performance impact of scaling up the number of players using an RCAT reference application, which is a multiplayer online jigsaw puzzle game. These experiments are designed to quantify how the number of proxies and the number of game servers scale with the number of players (bots) for different message frequencies. The quantitative results summarize (1) the behavior of CPU utilization and round trip time (latency) as the number of clients increases, (2) CPU utilization and context switches per second as the number of clients increases, (3) the maximum number of clients supported under alternative core/machine scenarios and message frequencies, and (4) CPU utilization when the maximum capacity is reached.

The authors' proposal of the RCAT architecture, the development of a reference implementation, the development of a reference application, and a quantitative performance study provides the community with a scalable architectural solution with a rigorous validation. The game-agnostic approach to the RCAT architecture, modularizing the game logic in one tier, means that it can be applied broadly, supporting the development of diverse MMOGs.

The challenges in developing multiplayer outdoor smart phone games are presented in five core areas of SE (requirements, architecture, design, implementation, and testing) by Robert Hall in Chapter 8. The games, part of the Geocast Games Project, incorporate vigorous physical activity outdoors and encourage multiplayer interactions, contributing to worthwhile social goals. Given the outdoor environment these games are played in, such as parks or beaches, the games need to be deployed solely on equipment people are likely to carry anyway for other purposes, namely, smart phones and iPods, and they need to rely on device-to-device communication, as network access may not be available. These two characteristics have profound impacts on SE activities. One challenge in the requirements engineering area is the definition of domain-specific set of meta-requirements applicable to outdoor game design, providing domain-specific guidelines and constraints on requirements models to help developers better understand when they are posing impossible or impractical requirements for new games. The architectural challenges include defining solutions that support full distribution (no central server) and long-range play (seamless integration with networks when they are available). The design challenges include the need to allow coherent game behavior to be implemented at the top of a fully distributed architecture, subject to sporadic device communication. A collection of design issues falls under this distributed joint state problem: when devices have been out of communication, they need to resynchronize in a rapid and fair way when they reestablish a connection. The implementation challenges include the need to run the games on a broad range of smart phone brands and models; cross-platform code development frameworks are needed to provide cross-compilation of source code and help the developer compensate for differences in hardware performance, sensor capabilities, communications systems, operating system, and programming languages. Testing challenges include validating requirements relative to the distributed joint state of the system, which allows temporary network partitions that lead to inconsistent state views and the need to involve many to tens of different devices.

The author has implemented three multiplayer games promoting outdoor activity and social interactions; these have allowed experimentation with the concepts and provided initial trials of a Geocast Games Architecture and rapid recoherence design.

Multilevel data analytic studies are used to support user experience assessments during the development of a serious game, AGoogleADay.com, by Daniel Russell in Chapter 9. The game is a *trivia question*-style game that is intended to motivate the more sophisticated use of the Google search engine. The studies are designed to understand the overall user experience by analyzing game player behavior at three different timescales: micro-, meso-, and macroscale. The microscale studies measure behaviors from milliseconds up to minutes of behavior, usually with a small number of people in a laboratory setting. These studies provide insight into the mechanics of the game—where players look, how they perceive the game elements, and what is left unnoticed and unexplored. Eye tracking is used to understand how a player visually scans the display and the results are visualized in heat maps. A sample heat map is presented, which shows a player spent most of his or her time toward the bottom of the display (reading the question) and near the top (at the search query).

The mesoscale studies measure behaviors from minutes to hours, observing people playing the game in natural settings. These provide insights into why people choose to play, why they stop their play, as well as understanding what makes the game engaging. The players are interviewed to acquire data in these studies. The players have almost no learnability issues with the game—it is straightforward to learn and play. When presented with questions on unfamiliar topics, some players prefer to move on to another question; other reported greater satisfaction when they could accomplish the task on their own, without any hints of the solution. These results lead to the introduction of a Skip feature and a modification to the existing Clue feature in the game.

The macroscale measures behaviors from days to weeks and months. Typically, this involves large numbers of players and is usually an analysis of the logs of many people playing the game over time. These studies reveal unexpected behaviors, such as the cumulative effect of people returning to the game, and then backing up to play previous days' games; in addition, a significant drop in participation is identified and traced to an error in advertising the game.

Overall, Russell's approach of understanding complex user behavior at three different timescales, using three different kinds of studies, provides the community with a broadly applicable framework for assessing software systems with complex user interfaces.

A formal, structured approach to effectively reuse AI components in game development to create interesting behavior is presented by Christopher Dragert, Jörg Kienzle, and Clark Verbrugge in Chapter 10. The approach is based on a layered statechart, which provides inherent modularity with nesting capabilities. Each statechart defines a single behavioral concern, such as sensing data. The individual statecharts are used to create more complex, higher level groups of intelligent behavior; the exhibited behavior is a function of the superposition of states. Under this model, the lowest layer contains *sensors*, which read events created as the game state changes. Events are passed up to *analyzers* that interpret and combine diverse data from sensors to form a coherent view of the game state. The next layer contains *memorizers* that store analyzed data and complex state information. The highest layer is the *strategic decider*, which reacts to analyzed and memorized data and chooses a high-level goal. The high-level goal triggers a *tactical decider* to determine how it will be executed. Ultimately, *executors* contained in another layer enact decisions in order to translate goals into actions. Depending on the current state of the NPC, certain commands can cause conflicts or suboptimal courses of action, which are corrected by *coordinators*. The final layer contains *actuators*, which modify the game state.

The reuse approach is illustrated by creating a garbage collector NPC through the reuse of large portions of the AI designed for a squirrel NPC. By treating the AI as a collection of interacting modules, many behavioral similarities emerge; two-thirds of the AI modules in the garbage collector are reused from the squirrel. The authors have also created tool support to demonstrate the practical potential of their approach. The tool directs and facilitates the development process, taking in statecharts and associated classes, providing an interface for producing novel AIs from a library of behaviors, and exporting code that can be directly incorporated into a game. By formally representing and understanding the game code associated with specific behaviors, the constructed AI can be rigorously analyzed, ensuring that code and functional group dependencies are properly satisfied.

A collection of five case studies exploring the issue of reuse in game play mechanics from a repurposing perspective on the design of CGs and game-based virtual worlds is presented by Walt Scacchi in Chapter 11. The case studies are research and development projects that have been created with diverse purposes, target audiences, and external collaborators over an extended period of time. The projects include a K-6 educational game on informal life science education; training for technicians in advanced, semiconductor manufacturing; training for newly hired personnel on business processes; training for state employees on sexual harassment; multiplayer mission planning; and games on science mission research projects. In their creation, designers have drawn upon design-level, game play mechanics to reuse from the existing games; here the collection of case studies is analyzed from this repurposing perspective. For example, the first case study focuses on games for students in grade K-6 on informal life science education. The games were on dinosaurs and their ecology, encompassing fundamental relationships that evolve over time including prey–predator food chains and the *circle of life* (mulch contributes to the plants, plants to herbivores, herbivores to carnivores, and carnivores to mulch). The design of the game play mechanics to highlight these relationships was drawn from tile-matching puzzle games, *Tetris* and *Dr. Mario*, where game play is motivated by time: the patterns fall into and progress across the playing field at a certain pace. In the new game, tiles for mulch, plants, herbivores, and carnivores are used. When carnivores (predators) align with herbivores (prey), they form a simple food chain, allowing the survival of the carnivores and the consumption of the prey.

The analysis of these case studies identifies five ways to repurpose game play mechanics: (1) appropriating play mechanics from functional similar games, as briefly described above; (2) modding game play levels, characters, and weapons through a game-specific SDK; (3) substituting in-game character/NPC dialogs along with adopting multiplayer role-playing scenarios; (4) employing play mechanisms for resource allocation with uncertainty that reenact classic game theory problems; and (5) identifying game design patterns (quests, multiplayer role-playing) that can be used to develop families of games across science research problem-solving domains.

This study provides the community with a foundation to systematically observe, identify, conceptually extract, generalize, and then specialize or tailor game play mechanics that are provided in the existing games. Such study can also inform how best to design or generate game content assets (e.g., NPCs, behavioral objects, extensible rule sets for modifying game play mechanics) for modding or repurposing, along with how software domain analysis and modeling techniques can support them.

Finally, in Chapter 12, Walt Scacchi and Kendra Cooper review the follow-on ideas and suggestions identified in the preceding chapters to serve as an outline for identifying an agenda for the future of research in CGSE.

1.6 SUMMARY

This chapter serves as an introduction to this collection of research papers in the area of CGs and SE—a first. It starts with a brief recapitulation of the history of CG software development that helps set the stage for the introduction of the research contributions in the chapters that follow. Chapters 2 through 11 are the core of this book, which is followed by a brief outlook on the future of research in CG and SE, as both are identified within the contributing chapters, as well as with respect to some of the grand challenges in SE, and other complementary R&D opportunities for CGSE.

ACKNOWLEDGMENTS

The research of Walt Scacchi was supported by grants #0808783, #1041918, and #1256593 from the U.S. National Science Foundation. No review, approval, or endorsement is implied. The authors of this chapter are responsible for statements and recommendations made herein.

REFERENCES

Alexander, T. (Ed.) (2003). *Massively Multiplayer Game Development.* Charles River Media, Hingham, MA.

Alspaugh, T.A. and Scacchi, W. (2013). Ongoing software development without classical functional requirements, *Proceedings of the 21st IEEE International Conference Requirements Engineering*, Rio de Janeiro, Brazil, pp. 165–174.

Ampatzoglou, A. and Stamelos, I. (2010). Software engineering research for computer games: A systematic review. *Information and Software Technology*, 52(9), 888–901.

Au, J.W. (2002). Triumph of the mod. *Salon.* April 16. http://www.salon.com/tech/feature/2002/04/16/modding. Accessed June 10, 2014.

Bartle, R. (1990). Interactive multi-user computer games. Technical report, British Telecom, London, June. http://www.mud.co.uk/richard/imucg.htm.

Berglund, E.J. and Cheriton, D. (1985). Amaze: A multiplayer computer game. *IEEE Software*, 2, 30–39.

Bishop, L., Eberley, D., Whitted, T., Finch, M., and Shantz, M. (1998). Designing a PC game engine. *IEEE Computer Graphics and Applications*, 18(1), 46–53.

Burnett, M., Cook, C., and Rothermel, G. (2004). End-user software engineering. *Communications of the ACM*, 47(9), 53–58.

Callele, D., Neufeld, E., and Schneider, K. (2005). Requirements engineering and the creative process in the video game industry. *Proceedings of the 13th International Conference on Requirements Engineering*, Paris, France, August, pp. 240–250.

Claypool, K. and Claypool, M. (2005). Teaching software engineering through game design. *Proceedings of the 10th SIGCSE Conference on Innovation and Technology in Computer Science Education*, Caparica, Portugal, June, pp. 123–127.

Cooper, K. and Longstreet, S. (2012). Towards model-driven game engineering for serious educational games: Tailored use cases for game requirements. *Proceedings of the 17th International Conference on Computer Games*, IEEE Computer Society, Louisville, KY, July, pp. 208–212.

Drachen, A. and Canossa, A. (2009). Towards gameplay analysis via gameplay metrics. *Proceedings of the International MindTrek Conference*, Tampere, Finland, September, pp. 202–209.

Fullerton, T., Swain, C., and Hoffman, S. (2004). *Game Design Workshop: Designing, Prototyping and Playtesting Games*. CMP Books, San Francisco, CA.

Furtado, A.W.B., Santos, A.L.M., Ramalho, G.L., and de Almeida, E.S. (2011). Improving digital game development with software product lines. *IEEE Software*, 28(5), 30–37.

Gautier, L. and Dior, C. (1998). Design and evaluation of MiMaze, a multi-player game on the Internet. *Proceedings of the IEEE International Conference on Multimedia Computing and Systems*, Austin, TX, July, pp. 233–236.

Gregory, J. (2009). *Game Engine Architecture*. AK Peters/CRC Press, Boca Raton, FL.

Grossman, A. (Ed.) (2003). *Postmortems from Game Developer: Insights from the Developers of Unreal Tournament, Black and White, Age of Empires, and Other Top-Selling Games*. Focal Press, Burlington, MA.

Hall, T. (1992). *DOOM Bible*. Revision Number.02, ID Software, Austin, TX, November 11, 1992. http://5years.doomworld.com/doombible/doombible.pdf.

IEEE (2014). *IEEE Transactions on Computational Intelligence and AI in Games*. IEEE Computational Intelligence Society, New York.

Kushner, D. (2003). *Masters of Doom: How Two Guys Created an Empire and Transformed Pop Culture*. Random House, New York.

Lewis, C., Whitehead, J. and Wardrip-Fruin, N. (2010). What went wrong: A taxonomy of video game bugs. *Proceedings of the 5th International Conference on Foundations of Digital Games*, Monterey, CA, ACM, New York, June, pp. 108–115.

Meigs, T. (2003). *Ultimate Game Design: Building Game Worlds*. McGraw-Hill, New York.

Morris, S. (2003). WADs, bots, and mods: Multiplayer FPS games and co-creative media. *Level Up Conference Proceedings: 2003 Digital Games Research Association Conference*, Utrecht, the Netherlands. http://www.digra.org/dl/db/05150.21522.

Oh Navarro, E. and Van der Hoek, A. (2005). Software process modeling for an educational software engineering simulation game. *Software Process Improvement and Practice*, 10(3), 311–325.

Oh Navarro, E. and Van der Hoek, A. (2009). Multi-site evaluation of SimSE. *SIGCSE Bulletin*, 41(1), 326–330.

Petrillo, F., Pimenta, M., Trindade, F., and Dietrich, C. (2009). What went wrong? A survey of problems in game development. *Computers in Entertainment*, 7(1), Article 13. doi:10.1145/1486508.1486521.

Pinelle, D., Wong, N., and Stach, T. (2008). Heuristic evaluation for games: Usability principles for video game design. *Proceedings of the SIGCHI Conference on Human Factors in Computing Systems*, Florence, Italy, ACM, New York, April, pp. 1453–1462.

Reeves, B. and Read, J.L. (2009). *Total Engagement: Using Games and Virtual Worlds to Change the Way People Work and Businesses Compete*. Harvard Business Press, Boston, MA.

Rogers, S. (2010). *Level Up!: The Guide to Great Video Game Design*. Wiley, New York.

Salen, K. and Zimmerman, E. (2004). *Rules of Play: Game Design Fundamentals.* MIT Press, Cambridge, MA.

Samuel, A. (1960). Programming computers to play games. In Alt, F. (Ed.), *Advances in Computers*, vol. 1, pp. 165–192. Academic Press, New York.

Scacchi, W. (2004). Free/open source software development practices in the game community. *IEEE Software*, 21(1), 59–67.

Scacchi, W. (2010). Computer game mods, modders, modding, and the mod scene. *First Monday*, 15(5). http://firstmonday.org/ojs/index.php/fm/article/view/2965/2526.

Schell, J. (2008). *The Art of Game Design: A Book of Lenses.* Morgan Kauffman Elsevier, Burlington, MA.

Seif El-Nasr, M. and Smith, B.K. (2006). Learning through game modding. *Computers in Entertainment*, 4(1), Article 7. doi:10.1145/1111293.1111301.

Spencer, D.D. (1968). *Game Playing with Computers.* Spartan Books, New York.

Swartout, W. and van Lent, M. (2003). Making a game of system design. *Communications of the ACM*, 46(7), 32–39.

Sweeney, T. (1998). Unreal networking architecture. Epic MegaGames Inc., July 21. https://web.archive.org/web/20100728233924; http://unreal.epicgames.com/Network.htm.

Walker, M. (2003). Describing game behavior with use cases. In Alexander, T. (Ed.), *Massively Multiplayer Game Development*, pp. 49–70. Charles River Media, Hingham, MA.

Wang, A.I. (2011). Extensive evaluation of using a game project in a software architecture course. *ACM Transactions on Computing Education*, 11(1), 1–28.

Wang, A.I., Ofsdahl, T., and Morch-Storstein, O.K. (2008). An evaluation of a mobile game concept for lectures. *Proceedings of the 21st Conference on Software Engineering Education and Training.* IEEE Computer Society, Washington, DC, April, pp. 197–204.

Zoeller, G. (2013). Game development telemetry in production. In Seif El-Nasr, M., Drachen, A., and Canossa, A. (Eds.), *Game Analytics: Maximizing the Value of Player Data*, pp. 111–135. Springer-Verlag, New York.

Zyda, M. (2006). Educating the next generation of game developers. *Computer*, 39(6), 30–34.

I

The Potential for Games in Software Engineering Education

CHAPTER 2

Use of Game Development in Computer Science and Software Engineering Education

Alf Inge Wang and Bian Wu

CONTENTS

2.1	Introduction	32
2.2	Experiences from Using Game Development in a Software Architecture Course	33
	2.2.1 Software Architecture Course	33
	2.2.2 How Game Development Was Introduced in the Software Architecture Course	35
	2.2.3 Experiences Gained	37
2.3	Survey of the Use of Game Development in CS and SE Education	38
	2.3.1 Answer to RQ1: In What Context/Topics Is Game Development Used in CS/SE Education?	39
	2.3.1.1 CS Topics/Subjects Where Game Development Is Being Used	39
	2.3.1.2 SE Topics/Subjects Where Game Development Is Being Used	43
	2.3.1.3 Applied CS Topics/Subjects Where Game Development Is Being Used	43

2.3.2 Answer to RQ2: What GDFs Are Used in CS/SE
        Education?   45
2.3.3 Answer to RQ3: What Are the Experiences from
        Using Game Development in CS/SE Education?   49
2.4 Recommendations for the Use of GDFs   50
2.5 Conclusion   52
Acknowledgment   53
References   53

Abstract: This chapter presents the results of a literature survey on the use of game development in software engineering (SE) and computer science (CS) education. Games and game development have been used in recent years to increase motivation, engagement, and learning, and to promote careers in software and computers. The authors present a bird's eye perspective on how game development has been used in recent years to teach other things than just game development.

The literature survey includes research articles from the period 2004 to 2012, and it investigates among other things in what context game development has been used, the subjects and topics taught through game development, and what tools and frameworks are being used for game development to learn SE and CS. Further, this chapter includes a description of how game development was used in our software architecture course at the Norwegian University of Science and Technology (NTNU) and the experiences gained from running this course. Finally, we provide our recommendations for choosing an appropriate game development framework for teaching SE and CS.

2.1 INTRODUCTION

Games are increasingly being used in education to improve academic achievement, motivation, and classroom dynamics (Rosas et al. 2003). Games are not only used to teach young school children, but also used to improve the quality of university education (Sharples 2000). There are many good examples of SE and CS education benefiting from use of games and game development for teaching (Baker et al. 2003; Natvig et al. 2004; Navarro and Hoek 2004; El-Nasr and Smith 2006; Foss and Eikaas 2006; Distasio and Way 2007; Sindre et al. 2009). Over the years, several papers have been published that describe how game development has been used to promote, motivate, or teach SE and CS. The goal of this chapter is to present results from this research through a literature study ranging from the years 2004 to 2012.

Further, some of our own experiences from teaching software architecture through game development from 2008 to 2013 have been included. One very important factor when incorporating game development into a CS/SE course is the choice of an appropriate game development framework (GDF) and tools. We have included six recommendations that should be considered when choosing a GDF for a CS/SE course have been included.

This chapter answers the following research questions:

- *RQ1: In what context/topics is game development used in CS/SE education?* The focus of this research question is to find the topics or domains where game development has been used as a teaching method documented in the research literature.

- *RQ2: What GDFs are used in CS/SE education?* The focus of this research question is to find the most common tools used, and possibly see if there are any shared experiences from using these tools.

- *RQ3: What are the experiences from using game development in CS/SE education?* The focus here is to see if there are any common experiences from using game development to teach CS/SE subjects.

The rest of the chapter is organized as follows: Section 2.2 describes experiences from using game development in a software architecture course, Section 2.3 presents a literature survey on how game development has been used in CS/SE education, and Section 2.4 discusses recommendations for how to select an appropriate GDF; Section 2.5 concludes this chapter.

2.2 EXPERIENCES FROM USING GAME DEVELOPMENT IN A SOFTWARE ARCHITECTURE COURSE

To demonstrate how game development can be used in SE education, we included a section that describes how game development was introduced in a software architecture course and the results of doing so.

2.2.1 Software Architecture Course

The software architecture course at the NTNU is for postgraduate CS and SE students where the workload is 12 hours per week for one semester. About 70–130 students attend the course every spring. Most of the students are Norwegian students, but about 20% come from EU countries and other continents. The textbook used is *Software Architecture in Practice* (Clements and Kazman 2003) and additional articles are used to cover topics such as design patterns (Coplien 1998), software architecture documentation standards (Maier et al. 2004), and view models (Kruchten 1995). The learning outcomes from the course are as follows:

> The students should be able to *define* and *explain* central concepts in software architecture literature, and be able to *use* and *describe* design/architectural patterns, methods to design software architectures, methods/techniques to achieve software qualities, methods to document software architecture, and methods to evaluate software architecture.

The course is mainly taught in three ways:

1. Ordinary lectures (in English)

2. Invited guest lectures from professionals in the software industry

3. A software development project that focuses on software architecture

The software architecture course at the NTNU is taught differently than at most other universities, as the students also have to implement their designed architecture in groups of four to six. The motivation for doing so is to make the students understand the relationship between the architecture and the implementation, and to be able to perform real evaluation of whether the architecture and the resulting implementation fulfill the quality requirements specified for the application. In the first phase of the project, the students get familiar with the commercial-of-the-shelf (COTS) to be used through developing some simple applications. In the second phase, the students are asked to implement a selection of design and architectural patterns in the chosen COTS. The third phase focuses on producing a complete requirement specification, including quality requirements, as well as designing and documenting the architecture according to the specified quality requirements and architectural drivers. In the fourth phase, the groups evaluate each other's software architectures against the described quality requirements using the architecture tradeoff analysis method (Kazman et al. 1998). In the fifth phase, the students carry out a detailed design, implement the application according to the software architecture, and finally test the application. The sixth and final phase involves a postmortem analysis of the whole project to learn from successes and mistakes (Bjørnson et al. 2009). The student groups deliver reports from all the phases, and the code and the executable for the first, second, and fifth phases. The grade awarded is based on the grading of the project (30%) and a final written examination (70%). The project will not be graded until the final delivery in the sixth phase, and the students are encouraged to improve and update deliveries during the whole project cycle.

2.2.2 How Game Development Was Introduced in the Software Architecture Course

Before 2008, the project in software architecture course at the NTNU asked the students to develop an autonomous robot controller for the Khepera robot simulator in Java. The reason a robot controller was chosen for the project was that this domain had many well-documented architectural patterns with described software qualities (Elfes 1990; Lumia et al. 1990; Simmons 1992; Toal et al. 2005). Many students, however, found the robot domain difficult and not very interesting.

In 2009, the course staff decided to add video game as a domain to the software architecture project to boost motivation and interest in the course. To be able to do this, we had to do four changes to the course to be able to provide a game development project with emphasis on software architecture (Wang and Wu 2011).

1. *First*, we had to do some *course preparations* that involved choosing a GDF and making the necessary preparation to use it in the project. To do this, we searched for existing GDFs and evaluated how well they were suited for teaching software architecture, what GDF resources (manuals, guides, examples, tutorials, etc.) were available, and how to introduce the GDF to the students. Our choice landed on XNA from Microsoft due to its good documentation, its tutorials and examples, its high-level application programming interface (API), a programming language that was close to Java (C#), as well as the motivating factor of deploying games on PCs, Xbox, and mobile devices. Although XNA provides a high-level API, we decided to develop the XQUEST framework to make it even easier to create games in XNA (Wu et al. 2009). The reason for doing this was to allow the students to focus more on software architecture than on technical and game-specific matters.

2. *Second*, we had to *change the syllabus*. For the students to be able to create software architectures for the game domain, they needed some theoretical backing on design and architectural patterns for

the game domain, how to design game architectures, and how to specify quality attributes for games. It turned out that this task was rather difficult. In contrast to the autonomous robot domain, there was not much mature literature on game architecture or patterns. The result was that we added some chapters from the book *Game Architecture and Design* (Rollings and Morris 2004) to the syllabus, which was supported by a set of own composed slides with descriptions of relevant design and architectural patterns for games and how to specify quality attributes for games.

3. *Third, changes to the project* were made. The course staff decided to let the student teams themselves choose between the robot and the game project. The main structure of the project had to remain the same, but we had to support two domains and two different COTSs. One major difference between the two domains was that for the robot controller project, the variation in what you could do with the application was limited, whereas for the game project we wanted to encourage creativity. Thus, the functional requirements for the robot version of the project were fixed, although they were not fixed for the game version. Another thing we had to change was how to grade the project. The grading of the project has emphasis on quality and completeness of documentation and code, and the relationship between the code and the architecture. The main difference in grading the two variants was that to get the top grade (A) in the robot version, the robot had to solve its task efficiently and elegantly, whereas for the game version it was required to be impressive in some way. It was also a requirement that both the robot controller and the game had to have a certain level of complexity in terms of the number of classes and its structure of components.

4. *Fourth, changes were made to the schedule and the staff.* The change of course staff was basically that we had to hire one extra teaching assistant (TA) to provide technical support on the XNA framework. The main changes in the schedule were to add an extra 2-hour COTS introduction lecture to give an introduction of both the robot controller and C# and XNA (in parallel), changing and extending a lecture on design and architectural patterns to include the game domain, and to add one more lecture on software architecture in games.

All in all, the chances were not major, but it required quite a lot of effort from the course staff. Most of the effort went into getting familiar with the XNA framework, adapting the project, and creating and finding the theoretical foundation to be used in lectures on game architectures.

2.2.3 Experiences Gained

Since 2009, we have collected data on the game development project in the software architecture course at the NTNU. Most of the experiences we have gained are positive, but we have also identified some challenges. One clear indication that the students welcomed a game project was that 73% of the students chose the game project whereas 27% chose the robot project. Since 2009, the percentage of students choosing the robot project has further decreased. Further, the amount of students attending the course has increased from around 70 students in 2008 to over 150 in 2013. The course evaluations between 2009 and 2013 clearly show that game development is popular among the students and motivates and engages the students to learn software architecture. The four most popular game genres developed by students in these projects are shooter (38%), strategy (25%), board (13%), and platform games (12%). All the games developed so far have been 2D games. The course staff recommend the development of 2D games to avoid too much focus on technical challenges. Some students groups admit that they focus too much on the game itself and less on the software architecture. Another comment from the students is that they spend way too much time on the game project, so it hurts their effort in other courses. Figure 2.1 shows screenshots from the game *BlueRose* developed by one student group in XNA.

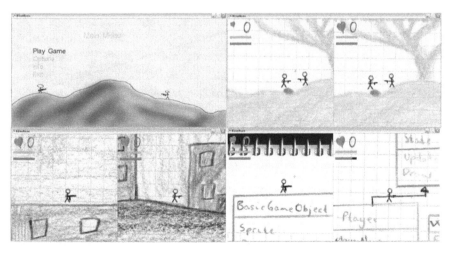

FIGURE 2.1 **(See color insert.)** Screenshots from the *BlueRose* XNA game.

From a teacher perspective, we have found that it is necessary to have good insight into both the GDF (XNA) and the domain of game architecture to enable the students to learn well from a game development project. A noticeable difference in the students' attitude seen by the teacher is that the students are interested in learning the XNA framework, whereas they are more reluctant to learn about the Khepera robot simulator.

In the work of Wang (2011), we performed an extensive evaluation of the software architecture course, where we compared the effect of the robot controller with that of the game project. The main conclusion was that game development projects can be used successfully to teach software architecture. Further, the results showed that students who chose the game project produced software architectures with higher complexity and put more effort into the project than students who chose the robot project. We found no statistically significant differences in the final grades awarded between the two variants of projects. However, the students who completed the game project obtained on average a higher grade on their project than on their written examination, whereas the students who completed the robot project on average scored a higher grade on their written examination than on their project. Although not significant, the students who completed the game project on average got a higher grade on the project compared to those who completed the robot project.

2.3 SURVEY OF THE USE OF GAME DEVELOPMENT IN CS AND SE EDUCATION

This section presents the results from a literature survey on the use of game development in CS and SE in articles between 2004 and 2012. The review followed the established method of systematic review (Khan et al. 2001; Higgins and Green 2008), undertaking the following stages: (1) protocol development, (2) data source and search strategy, (3) data extraction with inclusion and exclusion criteria, and (4) synthesis of findings. The search for literature was carried out on the digital research article databases such as Association for Computing Machinery (ACM), Institute of Electrical and Electronics Engineers (IEEE) Xplore, Springer, and ScienceDirect. The search string being used was "game AND (learning OR Teaching) AND (lecture or curriculum or lesson or course or exercise)." In addition, we searched the Google Scholar database with the search string "(game development) and (lecture or teaching or learning)" to pick up those we had missed.

The screening process of relevant articles was carried out in two steps. First, the abstracts were checked, and those articles that did not describe use of game development to learn or motivate for CS or SE were rejected. Articles rejected were typically about game theory or business games, or articles with words such as *game, learning,* and *development* but focused on something else. The second step was to read through the whole text of the remaining articles and exclude those that were too vague or outside the scope of the survey. Sixty-six articles relevant to game development and CS/SE education were found from the period 2004–2012. We noticed that there has been an increase in the number of articles published on this topic since the year 2004 up to 2009. Between 2009 and 2012, on average, 12 articles per year have been published on this topic. Further, out of the 66 articles, 65% were published by ACM, 26% by IEEE, and the remaining 9% equally divided between Springer, Elsevier, and Hindawi. Another interesting fact is that 59% of the relevant articles were U.S. studies, 24% were European studies, 12% were Asian studies, and 5% were international studies, that is, involving studies across continents and countries.

2.3.1 Answer to RQ1: In What Context/Topics Is Game Development Used in CS/SE Education?

To answer RQ1, we carried out an analysis of the 66 relevant articles. The first step of the analysis was to group the articles into the three main categories: SE, CS, and applied CS. Articles that ended up in the applied CS category were articles where CS was applied (e.g., using computer tools such as Alice or Scratch) but the main focus of the course was something else (e.g., art). Of the 66 articles, 55% of the articles were about game development in CS subjects, 26% in SE subjects, and 19% in applied CS subjects. Another interesting finding was that 81% of the articles described the use of game development at colleges and universities, 9% in high schools, 9% in middle schools, and 1% in an elementary school (one article).

The second step of the analysis was to identify the specific topics or domains where game development was used as a teaching aid. The following subsections describe the results from this analysis grouped according to CS, SE, and applied CS.

2.3.1.1 CS Topics/Subjects Where Game Development Is Being Used

Figure 2.2 shows the distribution of topics/subjects found in the articles where game development was used to teach CS. The figure clearly illustrates that for CS, game development is mainly used to teach programming (77%).

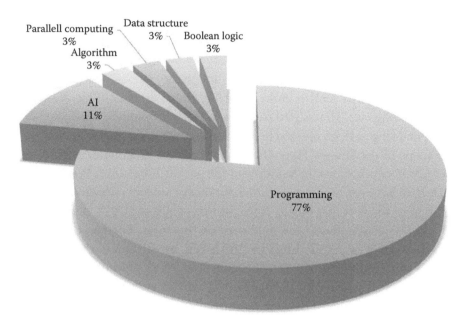

FIGURE 2.2   Distribution of topics taught using game development in CS.

Most of the articles within this category describe how game development was used as an introduction to CS and programming. There were few articles that described game development used for advanced programming courses. The second largest topic was found to be artificial intelligence (AI) (11%). In these articles, students were typically asked to program AI for nonplayable characters in a game or create or change the AI in a strategy game. Other topics in CS where game development has been used are algorithm, parallel computing, data structures, and Boolean logic.

Table 2.1 gives an overview of the articles in which game development was used in CS education at a college/university level. The table describes the main topics/subjects taught and briefly how game development was used in the course.

Table 2.1 shows that most articles are about programming courses using game development to motivate students. However, there is a great variety in how game development is used in different studies. In some studies, game development was only used in one or a few student assignments. Other articles describe approaches where the whole course was designed around a large game development project. The typical games developed in these projects and assignments are simple classical 2D games such as *Pacman, Bomberman,* or board games.

TABLE 2.1 Articles in Which Game Development Was Used in CS Education at the University Level

Article	How Game Development Is Used in Course	Topic
McGovern and Fager (2007)	Introduce the addition of AI code to games	AI
van Delden (2010)	Create games in robot simulation	AI
Timm et al. (2008)	Learn the addition of AI code to board game	AI
Barella et al. (2009)	Use multiplayer game framework to learn AI	AI
Weng et al. (2010)	Learn logic through changing *Pacman* code in *Scratch*	Logic
Detmer et al. (2010)	Develop learning through games for high-school teachers	Programming
Hundhausen et al. (2010)	Develop the game battleship as an assignment	Programming
Carter et al. (2011)	Improve motivation and learning through game development	Programming
Rick et al. (2012)	Use Greenfoot for simulations	Programming
Alvarado et al. (2012)	Introduce games to make CS more attractive for women	Programming
Coleman and Lang (2012)	Meta-study of use of game and game development in courses	Programming
Greenberg et al. (2012)	Learn CS using the context of art and creative coding	Programming
Anewalt (2008)	Learn programming, math, and logic in Alice	Programming
Eagle and Barnes (2009)	Change loops and arrays in the game *Wu's Castle* to learn programming	Programming
Chaffin and Barnes (2010)	Teach students to develop serious games	Programming
Williams and Beaubouef (2012)	Create simple games in assignments such as *Tic-Tac-Toe* to learn programming	Programming
Sung et al. (2011)	Learn programming through developing games in XNA	Programming
Angotti et al. (2010)	Learn programming through developing games in XNA	Programming
Goldweber et al. (2013)	Motivate CS through game programming	Programming
Fesakis and Serafeim (2009)	Learn programming through developing games in *Scratch*	Programming
Kurkovsky (2009)	Survey on the use of various mobile development platforms	Programming
Garrido et al. (2009)	Use games and visual programming to learn C++	Programming
Jiau et al. (2009)	Learn to program using game-based simulations and metrics	Programming

(*Continued*)

TABLE 2.1 (*Continued*)   Articles in Which Game Development Was Used in CS Education at the University Level

Article	How Game Development Is Used in Course	Topic
Chang and Chou (2008)	Learn programming by adding code to *Bomberman* game in C	Programming
Tan et al. (2009)	Learning programming through contributing to game design components	Programming
Stuurman et al. (2012)	Develop snake game as an introduction to programming	Programming
Ambrósio and Costa (2010)	Implement simple naval battle game as an assignment to learn about algorithms	Algorithm
Lawrence (2004)	Teach data structures through advanced game intelligence programming	Data structure
Bierre and Phelps (2004)	Learn programming through the development of 3D objects and games	Programming

Table 2.2 presents articles where game development is used for promoting or teaching CS courses in middle and high schools. The articles reporting from middle- and high-school experiences mainly focus on how to motivate for CS using a visual programming environment to create games. All articles but one focused on programming. Interestingly, the nonprogramming article gave an example of how parallel computing can be introduced to high-school students through games and game software. Parallel computing is a challenging and difficult topic, but through examples from games the students were able to learn and engage in the topic.

TABLE 2.2   Articles in Which Game Development Is Used for Promoting or Teaching CS in Middle and High Schools

Article	How Game Development Is Used in Course	Topic
Wang et al. (2006)	Teach ninth graders basic CS through game programming in StarLogo TNG	Programming
Goldberg et al. (2012)	Promote CS in middle schools through creating games such as Frogger and Space Invaders	Programming
Rodger et al. (2012)	Promote CS in middle schools through creating games in Alice	Programming
Webb and Rosson (2011)	Promote CS for the eighth-grade girls through game programming in Alice	Programming
Chesebrough and Turner (2010)	Demonstrate parallel computing in high schools through games and game software	Parallel computing
Al-Bow et al. (2009)	Use game creation to teach programming to both students and teachers in high schools	Programming
Jenkins et al. (2012)	Promote active learning and collaboration in high schools through game programming	Programming

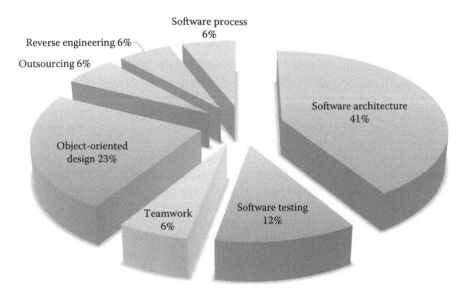

FIGURE 2.3   Distribution of topics taught using game development in SE.

2.3.1.2 *SE Topics/Subjects Where Game Development Is Being Used*

Figure 2.3 presents an overview of the topics/subjects being taught in SE where game development was a part of the course. The most recurring topic is software architecture (41%). However, it is important to note that most of these articles come from the same source. Object-oriented design (23%) and software testing (12%) are two other popular SE topics where game development is used. Other SE topics we identified are teamwork, outsourcing, reverse engineering, and software process (all of them 6%).

Table 2.3 presents an overview of the articles that describe how game development is used to teach SE. Similar to the articles related to CS, some describe how game development was a minor part of the exercises (one or two assignments), whereas other courses were designed around a game development project that motivated the students to learn about an SE topic. We also discovered a variety in how the game development was carried out. Some articles described projects where students modified code from existing games, whereas others describe projects going through a complete development cycle and the games are developed from scratch.

2.3.1.3 *Applied CS Topics/Subjects Where Game Development Is Being Used*

Figure 2.4 shows the distribution of articles on topics within applied CS where game development was used. The two most recurring topics were

TABLE 2.3   Articles Describing Game Development in SE Education

Article	How Game Development Is Used in Course	Topic
Chen and Cheng (2007)	Learn OO design and design through game programming	OO design
Jun (2010)	Use game development to improve teamwork skills	Teamwork
Wang and Wu (2009)	Learn design/architectural patterns and quality attributes through game development	Software architecture
Adipranata (2010)	Learn OO design/programming using GameMaker and Warcraft	OO design
Ryoo et al. (2008)	Learn OO design/programming and rational unified process (RUP) through game development and GUI programming	OO design
Mahoney and Gandhi (2012)	Learn reverse engineering by reverse engineering the executables of a *Tetris* game	Reverse engineering
Nordio et al. (2011)	Learn distributed and outsourced programming through the DOSE game platform	OO Design
Wang (2009)	Learn software architecture through game development in XNA	Software architecture
Wu et al. (2009)	Use high-level API in XNA to let students' focus more on software architecture than on game development	Software architecture
Wu et al. (2010)	Use high-level API in Android SDK to let students' focus more on software architecture than on game development	Software architecture
Wang (2011)	Compare the effect of using development of robot controller versus game in software architecture course	Software architecture
Wang and Wu (2011)	Learn software architecture through game development	Software architecture
Wu and Wang (2012)	Compare the effect of using development of applications versus games in software architecture course	Software architecture
Honig and Prasad (2007)	Learn outsourcing through development of various board games	Outsourcing
Smith et al. (2012)	Develop the games *Tetris* and *Boogle* as assignments to learn software testing	Software testing
Schild et al. (2010)	Learn scrum through game development in XNA	Software process

game design (46%) and game development (31%). One could argue that game development should be a part of CS, but in the articles described here game development was typically a course that focused on game design that also involved game programming, 3D modeling, and similar topics. The other two identified topics were art design (15%) and literacy (8%).

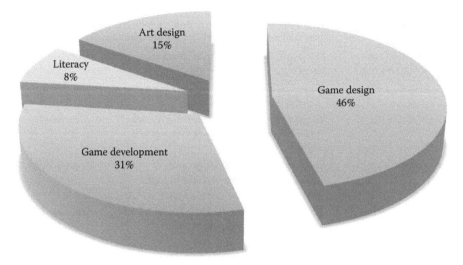

FIGURE 2.4   Distribution of topics taught using game development in applied CS.

The main difference between game design and art design is that art design has stronger emphasis on esthetics and artistic style and expression.

Table 2.4 presents an overview of the 12 articles in which game development was used to teach applied CS. These articles displayed a much stronger emphasis on creating or changing games through graphical tools with less emphasis on programming. Typically, many of the articles focused on creating game levels using editors and tools to create terrains, game characters, game objects, and populate levels with game objects. Half of the articles describe the use of game development at a precollege/university level.

2.3.2 Answer to RQ2: What GDFs Are Used in CS/SE Education?

To answer RQ2, we analyzed the 66 relevant articles with respect to the tools, frameworks, and programming languages used to develop games. Figure 2.5 shows the distribution of GDFs used for game development in the articles in the survey. The Others category (15%) includes development frameworks or tools such as CeeBot series, Maya, Neverwinter Nights 2 editor, OpenGL, OpenSceneGraph, Photoshop, processing, robot simulation framework (unspecified), Scala, StarLogo TNG, Torque, VPython 3D, and Windows binary. Figure 2.5 shows that many uses their own frameworks for developing games in their courses. Many of these frameworks were developed in Java. One reason for using their own frameworks is to adapt the development to fit the educational goals

TABLE 2.4   Articles in Which Game Development Was Used to Teach Applied CS

Article	How Game Development Is Used in Course	Topic
van Langeveld and Kessler (2009)	Promote CS to create digital characters in 3D	Art design
Rankin et al. (2008)	Learn CS through game design and development in GameMaker	Game design
Estey et al. (2010)	Use game design in Flash and GameMaker to learn communication and teamwork skills	Game design
Seaborn et al. (2012)	Teach CS using game design and development in GameMaker in high schools	Game design
Huang et al. (2008)	Teach integration of programming and art design through game development	Game design
Wynters (2007)	Motivate/create CS through modification in Unreal, Photoshop, and 3ds Max	Art design
Robertson and Howells (2008)	Learn game design through Neverwinter Nights 2 in middle schools	Game design
El-Nasr and Smith (2006)	Learn CS, math, and programming through changing code in Warcraft 3 and Unreal in high schools and universities	Game design
Ritzhaupt (2009)	Use free or cheap game development tools such as Torque, MilkShape 3D, Audacity, and GIMP to teach game development	Game development
Sullivan and Smith (2011)	Teach high-school students CS and programming skills through game development	Game development
Werner et al. (2009)	Learn programming through game development in Alice in middle schools	Game development
Owston et al. (2007)	Motivate and engage students in literacy activities in elementary schools through game development	Literacy

of the course. Two other popular GDFs are XNA and Java (both 11%). Many chose XNA because of the flexible and high-level API and good documentation, whereas many chose Java because it was familiar to the student or that the context was a Java programming course. Other popular GDFs are Alice, Android SDK, C++, GameMaker, Flash, and Scratch. It is interesting to note that the use of the currently very popular indie game engine Unity 3D was not found in any article. This picture is likely to change over the years. For example, Microsoft has decided to

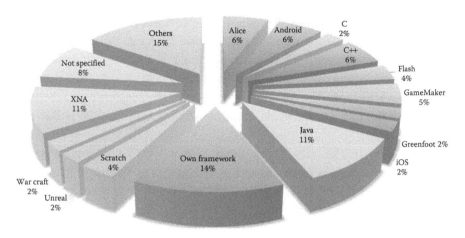

FIGURE 2.5   GDFs used in CS, SE, and applied CS.

stop all support for XNA, which will force many developers over to new platforms.

Figure 2.6 shows the distribution of programming languages used to teach SE, CS, and applied CS through game development. In the articles in the survey, 27% use some kind of a visual programming/editing to develop games. The visual programming category includes Alice, GameMaker,

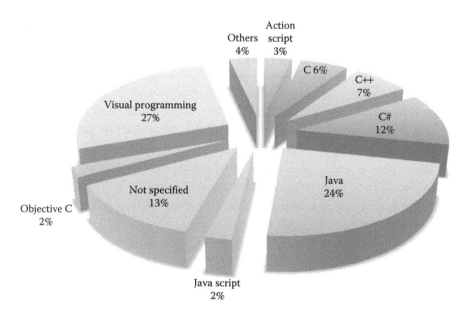

FIGURE 2.6   Programming languages used to teach SE, CS, and applied CS through game development.

Maya, Neverwinter Nights 2 (editor), OpenSceneGraph, Photoshop, Scratch, StarLogo TNG, Torque, Unreal Editor, Warcraft Editor, and Wu's Castle (own framework). The most common programming language is Java with 24%, where many articles describe the usage of additional framework in Java to make the game development faster, easier, and a better match with the educational goals. C# is also being used frequently due to the XNA GDF.

The articles in the survey also describe how the GDFs are used as well as the experiences from using them. Visual programming in Alice, Scratch, and StarLogo TNG works well for introducing programming, learning programming concepts as well as object-oriented programming, and promoting CS. Many conclude that visual programming is a fun and engaging way of learning logic and sequences. Experiences from using Scratch show that visual programming can boost students' confidence in programming, which allows them to explore and improve their skills and knowledge significantly. Articles also show that mobile development platforms such as Android SDK or iOS SDK engage and motivate students through being able to play their own games on their own devices and share them with friends.

The use of graphic and game libraries or APIs is important to reduce the required effort and complexity to develop software that is fun to interact with. In most articles in the survey, the students are asked to create simple 2D games from ground up. Another approach is to use *game modding*, which means changing or modifying the existing code to change the behavior and looks of a game. Some articles have proved that game modding in Unreal, Warcraft, and Wu's Castle works well to introduce programming and programming concepts without the need to implement the whole game. A motivating factor for doing so is that the game being modified can be a highly rated commercial game with impressive graphics and game play. Several articles have emphasized the importance of using high-level APIs to accelerate the development enabling a stronger focus on learning other things than game development such as programming, software architecture, and AI. Finally, in studies from K-12, visual programming environments such as Scratch and Alice are most commonly used. There are also several studies where visual programming environments are used to introduce university students to programming with good results. The main benefit for the latter is a better understanding of programming concepts such as sequences and how different parts of a program interact.

2.3.3 Answer to RQ3: What Are the Experiences from Using Game Development in CS/SE Education?

This section summarizes the experiences found in the articles in the survey regarding the use of game development for teaching CS and SE.

The majority of articles report positive effects of using game development in teaching. Some articles do not share any experiences other than game development, which was a part of their course. These are typically courses where game development was used in one or two assignments and did not play a major role.

Most studies in the survey report that game development *improves student motivation and engagement*. Only one study reports about neutral or negative results (Rankin et al. 2008), but it is unclear whether the negative results were caused by improper usage of game development or the limited number of subjects in the study. Most articles report that game development makes programming fun as the students' results can be observed visually on the screen. Furthermore, students are more engaged and put more effort into projects when they do game development versus other type of software development. However, only few studies report increased learning in terms of better grades. A problem observed with introducing game development in CS and SE courses is the tendency that some students focus too much on the game and game development instead of focusing on the topic being taught.

The survey discovered several examples of how game development can be used to learn other topics such as parallel computing, outsourcing, software architecture, teamwork, AI, software testing, reverse engineering, logic, art, and literacy. It also showed that adding or modifying code in existing games is an effective and motivating approach for teaching AI, as the results of the AI can be observed visually in the game. This approach works with both games specially designed for teaching AI and commercial games that come with modification tools, such as Warcraft or Unreal Tournament. A novel approach to teach outsourcing described in one article is to have student groups from two different universities develop the same game, where parts of the game are outsourced to the students from the other university (Honig and Prasad 2007). Similarly, another article described how reverse engineering was taught by making the students change the executable files of a Tetris game (Mahoney and Gandhi 2012).

Finally, many articles in the survey reported that game development worked very well in recruiting students to study CS or SE, as well as improving enrolment of existing CS and SE courses. Especially many articles that described the use of game development at middle and high schools reported that the students got a more positive attitude to CS and SE, and they were more likely to chase a carrier in this field.

2.4 RECOMMENDATIONS FOR THE USE OF GDFs

In this section, we will give some recommendations for how to choose an appropriate GDF that will give the best result when teaching CS or SE. The recommendations divided into six main factors you should consider when introducing game development in a CS or SE course. The recommendations are based on the survey presented in this chapter as well as the work of Wu and Wang (2011).

Educational goal. The educational goal of the course will greatly affect the choice of GDF. For instance, if the course focuses on a complete development cycle, it should be possible to develop a game from scratch according to specified requirements and have tools available to specify the design and tools for testing. However, if the educational goal focuses only on some parts of the development cycle, such as software testing, AI, teamwork, software maintenance, outsourcing, or quality assurance, it is possible to use a game editor for an existing game such as *Unreal Tournament* or *Warcraft*.

Subject constraints. Most CS or SE subjects put constraints on what you should be able to do in the GDF. For example, if you teach a software architecture, it is very important for students to have the freedom to design and implement various design and architecture patterns in the framework chosen. Another example is that if your subject is AI, it is important that the framework or game being used allow specifying and implementing AI similar to what is being taught in the textbook. Often, additional articles must be used to link the subject to how it is used in games.

Programming experience. The programming experience of the students will highly affect the choice of GDF. Typically, young students without any programming experience should start with visual programming environments such as Scratch or Alice. For students with programming experience, one factor that should be considered when choosing a GDF is what programming languages the students know. What is most important here is whether the students only know procedural programming languages or also know object-oriented programming languages. Experiences from articles in the survey showed that, for example, it usually does not require too much work for students who know Java to learn C# or vice versa. The programming language used by the GDF should not be too far away from the students' programming background.

Staff expertise. One thing you have to consider when introducing game development into a CS or SE course is the course staff's knowledge and technical experience with a GDF. This is important both to plan the project to fit with the educational goals and to provide help to students getting stuck with technical problems. It is not necessary for the teacher to know everything about GDF in detail, but it is very useful to have at least one in the course staff that knows it fairly well. The minimum requirement is to be able to point the students to online resources where they can find help.

Usability of the GDF. We do not want the students to get stuck in technical problems during the project, as then they will not learn as much about the CS/SE topic. Thus, it is important that the GDF be easy to use and let the students be productive with relatively small amount of code. This means, in practice, that the course staff should, before introducing game development in a course, create some simple games in the GDF to get a feeling of how difficult it is to use. The GDF should provide high-level APIs, it should be well structured, and it should have a logical structure. In addition, it is important that the GDF be well supported through documentation, tutorials, example code, and a living development community. It is also a good thing if all resources are free for the students to use.

Technical environment. Technical considerations should also be taken into account when choosing a GDF. One very important consideration is the software and hardware requirements of the GDF. For example, if XNA is chosen, Microsoft Windows is required to run both the development platform and the resulting executables. This could be a challenge if many students have PCs running Mac OSX or Linux, or if the lab computers run other operating systems than Microsoft Windows. Hardware requirements are also important, as some GDFs can have some tough requirements in terms of CPU,

GPU, and memory. A problem could be that an existing computer lab does not have powerful enough PCs to run the GDF or the resulting games. Finally, it is important to consider licenses and cost of the GDF.

2.5 CONCLUSION

This chapter focused on describing how game development has been and can be used to teach and promote SE and CS. We shared our own experiences from introducing game development in a software architecture course. Further, we presented a literature survey with articles between 2004 and 2012 on game development in CS and SE. Finally, based on our own experiences and the survey, we gave some recommendations on how to choose a GDF to be used in a SE/CS course.

The goal of the chapter was to give answers to three research questions. The first research question was about finding the contexts and topics game development is used in CS/SE education (RQ1). We found that game development is being used to teach a variety of subjects, but the most common subject is programming and more specifically introduction to programming. Other major CS/SE topics are AI, software architecture, object-oriented design, and software testing. We also found that the majority of articles (81%) are studies from colleges or universities, whereas the remaining (19%) are from elementary, middle, and high schools. There is also a great difference in how and how much game development is used in various courses. Some courses simply use game development in a few short assignments, whereas others wrap the course around a large game development project.

The second research question was about what GDFs are being used for developing games in CS/SE courses (RQ2). The results of the literature study revealed use of a wide variety of tools and frameworks where the most frequent ones were own frameworks developed by the authors/researchers, Java, XNA, Android SDK, Alice, C++, GameMaker, Flash, and Scratch. In terms of programming languages, the three largest categories were visual programming frameworks (e.g., Alice, Scratch, etc.), C#, and Java. We foresee that the GDFs and programming languages used for this purpose will change significantly in the time to come. For example, Microsoft has stopped further development and support of XNA. At many universities, there has been a shift from Java programming courses to Python and HTML5/Javascript.

The third research question focused on experiences from using game development–based learning (RQ3). The main conclusion here is that the experiences are overall positive in terms of student motivation and engagement, and it works well for promoting CS/SE and recruiting students. However, there are too few studies that show significant improvement in terms of academic achievements (grades). More studies must be performed to study the educational effects of game development to teach other topics.

ACKNOWLEDGMENT

We thank Richard Taylor and Walt Scacchi at the Institute for Software Research, University of California, Irvine, California, for providing a stimulating research environment and for hosting a visiting researcher.

REFERENCES

Adipranata, R. (2010). Teaching object oriented programming course using cooperative learning method based on game design and visual object oriented environment. *Proceedings of the 2nd International Conference on Education Technology and Computer*, Shanghai, People's Republic of China, IEEE, June 22–24.

Al-Bow, M. et al. (2009). Using game creation for teaching computer programming to high school students and teachers. *ACM SIGCSE Bulletin* **41**(3): 104–108.

Alvarado, C. et al. (2012). Increasing women's participation in computing at Harvey Mudd College. *ACM Inroads* **3**(4): 55–64.

Ambrósio, A. P. L. and F. M. Costa (2010). Evaluating the impact of PBL and tablet PCs in an algorithms and computer programming course. *Proceedings of the 41st ACM Technical Symposium on Computer Science Education*, Milwaukee, WI, ACM, March 10–13.

Anewalt, K. (2008). Making CS0 fun: An active learning approach using toys, games and Alice. *Journal of Computing Sciences in Colleges* **23**(3): 98–105.

Angotti, R. et al. (2010). Game-themed instructional modules: A video case study. *Proceedings of the 5th International Conference on the Foundations of Digital Games*, New York, ACM, June 19–21.

Baker, A. et al. (2003). Problems and programmers: An educational software engineering card game. *Proceedings of the 25th International Conference on Software Engineering*, Portland, OR, IEEE Computer Society, May 3–10.

Barella, A. et al. (2009). JGOMAS: New approach to AI teaching. *IEEE Transaction on Education* **52**(2): 228–235.

Bierre, K. J. and A. M. Phelps (2004). The use of MUPPETS in an introductory java programming course. *Proceedings of the 5th Conference on Information Technology Education*, Salt Lake City, UT, ACM, October 28–30.

Bjørnson, F. O. et al. (2009). Improving the effectiveness of root cause analysis in post mortem analysis: A controlled experiment. *Information Software Technology* **51**(1): 150–161.

Carter, J. et al. (2011). Motivating all our students? *Proceedings of the 16th Annual Conference Reports on Innovation and Technology in Computer Science Education—Working Group Reports*, Darmstadt, Germany, ACM, June 27–29.

Chaffin, A. and T. Barnes (2010). Lessons from a course on serious games research and prototyping. *Proceedings of the 5th International Conference on the Foundations of Digital Games*, Monterey, CA, ACM, June 19–21.

Chang, W.-C. and Y.-M. Chou (2008). Introductory C programming language learning with game-based digital learning. *Proceedings of the 7th International Conference on Advances in Web-Based Learning*, Jinhua, People's Republic of China, Springer, August 20–22, pp. 221–231.

Chen, W.-K. and Y. C. Cheng (2007). Teaching object-oriented programming laboratory with computer game programming. *IEEE Transaction on Education* **50**(3): 197–203.

Chesebrough, R. A. and I. Turner (2010). Parallel computing: At the interface of high school and industry. *Proceedings of the 41st ACM Technical Symposium on Computer Science Education*, Milwaukee, WI, ACM, March 10–13.

Clements, P. and R. Kazman (2003). *Software Architecture in Practices*. Addison-Wesley Longman, Reading, MA.

Coleman, B. and M. Lang (2012). Collaboration across the curriculum: A disciplined approach to developing team skills. *Proceedings of the 43rd ACM Technical Symposium on Computer Science Education*, Raleigh, NC, ACM, pp. 277–282.

Coplien, J. O. (1998). Software design patterns: Common questions and answers. In Rising, L. (Ed.), *The Patterns Handbooks: Techniques, Strategies, and Applications*. Cambridge University Press, Cambridge, pp. 311–319.

Detmer, R. et al. (2010). Incorporating real-world projects in teaching computer science courses. *Proceedings of the 48th Annual Southeast Regional Conference*, Oxford, MS, ACM, April 15–17.

Distasio, J. and T. Way (2007). Inclusive computer science education using a ready-made computer game framework. *Proceedings of the 12th Annual SIGCSE Conference on Innovation and Technology in Computer Science Education*, Dundee, Scotland, ACM, June 23–27.

Eagle, M. and T. Barnes (2009). Experimental evaluation of an educational game for improved learning in introductory computing. *ACM SIGCSE Bulletin* **41**(1): 321–325.

El-Nasr, M. S. and B. K. Smith (2006). Learning through game modding. *Computer Entertainment* **4**(1): 7.

Elfes, A. (1990). Sonar-based real-world mapping and navigation. In Sukhatme, G. (Ed.), *Autonomous Robot Vehicles*. Springer-Verlag, New York, pp. 233–249.

Estey, A. et al. (2010). Investigating studio-based learning in a course on game design. *Proceedings of the 5th International Conference on the Foundations of Digital Games*, Monterey, CA, ACM, June 19–21.

Fesakis, G. and K. Serafeim (2009). Influence of the familiarization with scratch on future teachers' opinions and attitudes about programming and ICT in education. *ACM SIGCSE Bulletin* **41**(3): 258–262.

Foss, B. A. and T. I. Eikaas (2006). Game play in engineering education: Concept and experimental results. *The International Journal of Engineering Education* **22**(5): 1043–1052.

Garrido, A. et al. (2009). Using graphics: Motivating students in a C++ programming introductory course. *EAEEIE Annual Conference*, Valencia, Spain, IEEE, June 22–24.

Goldberg, D. S. et al. (2012). Engaging computer science in traditional education: The ECSITE project. *Proceedings of the 17th ACM Annual Conference on Innovation and Technology in Computer Science Education*, Haifa, Israel, ACM, July 3–5.

Goldweber, M. et al. (2013). A framework for enhancing the social good in computing education: A values approach. *ACM Inroads* **4**(1): 58–79.

Greenberg, I. et al. (2012). Creative coding and visual portfolios for CS1. *Proceedings of the 43rd ACM Technical Symposium on Computer Science Education*, Raleigh, NC, ACM, February 29–March 3.

Higgins, J. P. and S. Green (2008). *Front Matter*. John Wiley & Sons, New York.

Honig, W. L. and T. Prasad (2007). A classroom outsourcing experience for software engineering learning. *ACM SIGCSE Bulletin* **39**(3): 181–185.

Huang, C.-H. et al. (2008). Computer game programming course for art design students by using flash software. *International Conference on Cyberworlds*, Hangzhou, People's Republic of China, IEEE, September 22–24.

Hundhausen, C. et al. (2010). Does studio-based instruction work in CS 1? An empirical comparison with a traditional approach. *Proceedings of the 41st ACM Technical Symposium on Computer Science Education*, Milwaukee, WI, ACM, March 10–13.

Jenkins, J. et al. (2012). Perspectives on active learning and collaboration: JavaWIDE in the classroom. *Proceedings of the 43rd ACM Technical Symposium on Computer Science Education*, ACM.

Jiau, H. C. et al. (2009). Enhancing self-motivation in learning programming using game-based simulation and metrics. *IEEE Transactions on Education* **52**(4): 555–562.

Jun, H. (2010). Improving undergraduates' teamwork skills by adapting project-based learning methodology. *Proceedings of the 5th International Conference on Computer Science and Education*, Anhui, People's Republic of China, IEEE, August 24–27.

Kazman, R. et al. (1998). The architecture tradeoff analysis method. *Proceedings of the 4th International Conference on Engineering Complex Computer Systems*, Monterey, CA, IEEE.

Khan, K. S. et al. (2001). Undertaking systematic reviews of research on effectiveness: CRD's guidance for carrying out or commissioning reviews. NHS Centre for Reviews and Dissemination. Research Report, CRD Report, York, UK.

Kruchten, P. (1995). The 4+1 view model of architecture. *IEEE Software* **12**(6): 42–50.

Kurkovsky, S. (2009). Can mobile game development foster student interest in computer science? *Proceedings of the 1st International IEEE Consumer Electronics Society's Games Innovations Conference*, London, IEEE, August 25–28.

Lawrence, R. (2004). Teaching data structures using competitive games. *IEEE Transaction on Education* **47**(4): 459–466.

Lumia, R. et al. (1990). The NASREM robot control system and testbed. *International Journal of Robotics and Automation* **5**: 20–26.

Mahoney, W. and R. A. Gandhi (2012). Reverse engineering: Is it art? *ACM Inroads* **3**(1): 56–61.

Maier, M. W. et al. (2004). ANSI/IEEE 1471 and systems engineering. *Systems Engineering* **7**(3): 257–270.

McGovern, A. and J. Fager (2007). Creating significant learning experiences in introductory artificial intelligence. *Proceedings of the 38th SIGCSE Technical Symposium on Computer Science Education*, Covington, KY, ACM, March 7–11.

Natvig, L. et al. (2004). Age of computers: An innovative combination of history and computer game elements for teaching computer fundamentals. *Proceedings of the 2004 Frontiers in Education Conference*, Savannah, GA, October 20–23.

Navarro, E. O. and A. van der Hoek (2004). SimSE: An educational simulation game for teaching the Software engineering process. *Proceedings of the 9th Annual SIGCSE Conference on Innovation and Technology in Computer Science Education*, Leeds, ACM, June 28–30.

Nordio, M. et al. (2011). Teaching software engineering using globally distributed projects: The DOSE course. *Proceedings of the 2011 Community Building Workshop on Collaborative Teaching of Globally Distributed Software Development*, Honolulu, HI, ACM, May 21–28.

Owston, R. et al. (2009). Computer game development as a literacy activity *Computers & Education* **53**(3): 977–989.

Rankin, Y. et al. (2008). The impact of game design on students' interest in CS. *Proceedings of the 3rd International Conference on Game Development in Computer Science Education*, Miami, FL, ACM.

Rick, D. et al. (2012). Bringing contexts into the classroom: A design-based approach. *Proceedings of the 7th Workshop in Primary and Secondary Computing Education*, Hamburg, Germany, ACM, November 8–9.

Ritzhaupt, A. D. (2009). Creating a game development course with limited resources: An evaluation study. *ACM Transactions on Computing Education* **9**(1): 3.

Robertson, J. and C. Howells (2008). Computer game design: Opportunities for successful learning. *Computers & Education* **50**(2): 559–578.

Rodger, S. et al. (2012). Integrating computing into middle school disciplines through projects. *Proceedings of the 43rd ACM Technical Symposium on Computer Science Education*, Raleigh, NC, ACM, February 29–March 3.

Rollings, A. and D. Morris (2004). *Game Architecture and Design—A New Edition.* New Riders Publishing, Indianapolis, IN.

Rosas, R. et al. (2003). Beyond Nintendo: Design and assessment of educational video games for first and second grade students. *Computers & Education* **40**(1): 71–94.

Ryoo, J. et al. (2008). Teaching object-oriented software engineering through problem-based learning in the context of game design. *Proceedings of the 21st Conference on Software Engineering Education and Training*, Charleston, SC, IEEE Computer Society, April 14–17.

Schild, J. et al. (2010). ABC-Sprints: Adapting Scrum to academic game development courses. *Proceedings of the 5th International Conference on the Foundations of Digital Games*, Monterey, CA, ACM, June 19–21.

Seaborn, K. et al. (2012). Programming, PWNed: Using digital game development to enhance learners' competency and self-efficacy in a high school computing science course. *Proceedings of the 43rd ACM Technical Symposium on Computer Science Education*, Raleigh, NC, ACM, February 29–March 03.

Sharples, M. (2000). The design of personal mobile technologies for lifelong learning. *Computers & Education* **34**(3/4): 177–193.

Simmons, R. (1992). Concurrent planning and execution for autonomous robots. *IEEE Control Systems* **1**: 46–50.

Sindre, G. et al. (2009). Experimental validation of the learning effect for a pedagogical game on computer fundamentals. *IEEE Transaction on Education* **52**(1): 10–18.

Smith, J. et al. (2012). Using peer review to teach software testing. *Proceedings of the 9th Annual International Conference on International Computing Education Research*, Auckland, New Zealand ACM, September 10–12.

Stuurman, S. et al. (2012). A new method for sustainable development of open educational resources. *Proceedings of the 2nd Computer Science Education Research Conference*, Wroclaw, Poland, ACM, September 9–12.

Sullivan, A. and G. Smith (2011). Lessons in teaching game design. *Proceedings of the 6th International Conference on Foundations of Digital Games*, Bordeaux, France, ACM, June 28–July 01.

Sung, K. et al. (2011). Game-themed programming assignment modules: A pathway for gradual integration of gaming context into existing introductory programming courses. *IEEE Transactions on Education* **54**(3): 416–427.

Tan, P.-H. et al. (2009). Learning difficulties in programming courses: Undergraduates' perspective and perception. *International Conference on Computer Technology and Development*, IEEE.

Timm, I. J. et al. (2008). Teaching distributed artificial intelligence with RoboRally. In Bergmann, R., Lindemann, G., Kirn, S., Pěchouček, M. (Eds.), *Multiagent System Technologies*. Springer, Berlin, Germany, pp. 171–182.

Toal, D. et al. (2005). Subsumption architecture for the control of robots. *ACM SIGCSE Bulletin* **37**(3): 138–142.

van Delden, S. (2010). Industrial robotic game playing: An AI course. *Journal of Computing Sciences in Colleges* **25**(3): 134–142.

van Langeveld, M. C. and R. Kessler (2009). Two in the middle: Digital character production and machinima courses. *ACM SIGCSE Bulletin* **47**(1): 463–467.

Wang, A. I. (2009). An extensive evaluation of using a game project in a software architecture course. *IEEE Transactions on Computing Education* **11**(1): 1–28.

Wang, A. I. (2011). Extensive evaluation of using a game project in a software architecture course. *IEEE Transactions on Computing Education* **11**(1): 1–28.

Wang, A. I. and B. Wu (2009). An application of game development framework in higher education. Special Issue, *International Journal of Computer Games Technology* **2009**: 1–12.

Wang, A. I. and B. Wu (2011). Using game development to teach software architecture. *International Journal of Computer Games Technology* **2011**: 1–12.

Wang, K. et al. (2006). 3D game design with programming blocks in StarLogo TNG. *Proceedings of the 7th International Conference on Learning Sciences*, Bloomington, IN, International Society of the Learning Sciences, June 27–July 1.

Webb, H. C. and M. B. Rosson (2011). Exploring careers while learning Alice 3D: A summer camp for middle school girls. *Proceedings of the 42nd ACM Technical Symposium on Computer Science Education*, Bloomington, IN, ACM, June 27–July 1.

Weng, J.-F. et al. (2010). Teaching boolean logic through game rule tuning. *IEEE Transactions on Learning Technologies* 3(4): 319–328.

Werner, L. et al. (2009). Can middle-schoolers use storytelling Alice to make games?: Results of a pilot study. *Proceedings of the 4th International Conference on Foundations of Digital Games*, Port Canaveral, FL, ACM, April 26–30.

Williams, L. and T. Beaubouef (2012). Comparing learning approaches: Sample case studies. *Journal of Computing Sciences in Colleges* 27(5): 85–91.

Wu, B. and A. I. Wang (2011). Game development frameworks for SE education. *Proceedings of the International IEEE Games Innovation Conference*, Orange, CA, IEEE, November 2–3.

Wu, B. and A. I. Wang (2012). Comparison of learning software architecture by developing social applications versus games on the Android platform. *International Journal of Computer Games Technology* 2012: 5.

Wu, B. et al. (2009). XQUEST used in software architecture education. *International IEEE Consumer Electronics Society's Games Innovations Conference*, London, IEEE, August 25–28.

Wu, B. et al. (2010). Extending Google Android's application as an educational tool. *Proceedings of the 3rd IEEE International Conference on Digital Game and Intelligent Toy Enhanced Learning*, Kaosiung, Taiwan, IEEE, April 12–16.

Wynters, E. L. (2007). 3D video games: No programming required. *Journal of Computing Sciences in Colleges* 22(3): 105–111.

CHAPTER 3

Model-Driven Engineering of Serious Educational Games

Integrating Learning Objectives for Subject-Specific Topics and Transferable Skills

Kendra M.L. Cooper and Shaun Longstreet

CONTENTS

3.1	Introduction	60
3.2	Holistic Approach to SEGs	66
	3.2.1 External Entities	67
	3.2.2 Traditional Game Elements	67
	3.2.3 Educational Game Elements	69
3.3	Overview of the SimSYS Approach	71
	3.3.1 Informal Model	71
	3.3.1.1 Storyboard	71
	3.3.1.2 SimSYS Storyboard	73
	3.3.2 SimSYS Use Case Model	75
	3.3.2.1 UML Use Case	75
	3.3.2.2 SimSYS Use Case	76
	3.3.3 Formal Model	78
	3.3.3.1 XML	78
	3.3.3.2 SimSYS XML Game Script	79

3.4 Conclusions and Future Work 83

References 84

Appendix 3A: Semiformal Model—Tabular, Tailored Use Case
for Challenge 1 87

Abstract: Educational infrastructure faces significant challenges, including the need to rapidly, widely, and cost-effectively introduce new or revised course material; encourage the broad participation of students; and address changing student motivations and attitudes. The course material needs to address learning objectives, which span standardized subject-specific content and transferable skills, such as collaboration, critical thinking, creative thinking, problem solving, reasoning abilities, learning to learn, and decision making that span diverse domains. Serious educational games have significant pedagogical potential as they provide immersive, engaging, and fun environments for students. To improve their development, our research project SimSYS provides a model-driven engineering-based approach that uniquely integrates elements of traditional entertainment game design, pedagogical content, and software engineering methodologies. Our approach has three main steps: (1) create an informal model of the game (captured like a storyboard with textual descriptions of the learning objectives and game play in addition to user interface concepts, e.g., graphics and audio); (2) transform the informal model into a semiformal, tailored Unified Modeling Language use case model (visual and tabular, template-based specifications); and (3) transform the semiformal model into formal, executable models (e.g., extensible markup language [XML], which can be loaded and played in the game engine). Our approach can be applied in an agile, iterative development process, for example, by describing a part of the game informally, semiformally, and formally (executable), allowing earlier assessment and feedback on a running (partial) game. A key feature of our approach is the thorough integration of learning objectives, for both topic-specific subject matter and transferable skills.

Keywords: Serious educational game engineering, model-driven engineering, learning objectives, transferable skills

3.1 INTRODUCTION

Educational infrastructure from elementary to higher education to corporate training faces significant challenges with increasingly limited resources. Course materials need to address concrete learning objectives, which span standardized subject-specific content (e.g., STEM, humanities, management) and transferable skills, such as collaboration, critical thinking, creative thinking, problem solving, reasoning abilities, learning to learn, and decision making that span diverse domains. Inserting games into a curriculum can create a highly motivating learning environment. We contend that educational games have significant pedagogical potential and they have distinct advantages over other forms of e-learning such as learning management systems (LMS), simulations, and so-called edutainment. At the same time, significant challenges have hampered efforts to introduce and distribute games in the K-18 curricula. We address some of those challenges in the development of a new model-driven game project, SimSYS.

Broadly established corporate and open-source LMSs such as Blackboard (http://www.blackboard.com), Desire2Learn (http://www.desire2learn. com), and Sakai (https://sakaiproject.org) rely on traditional forms of pedagogy. That is, an institutionally based LMS is highly content centered and acts as an online focal point for gathering information, discussion, and assessment. Students mostly engage faculty and peers in an asynchronous fashion; they rely heavily on a publishing model for acquiring knowledge, with input on mastery coming from traditional assessments such as quizzes and exams. Students remain highly dependent on instructor- and text-centered pedagogy, have fewer opportunities for feedback, and will experience a generalized, nonindividually oriented learning environment. LMSs are more like repositories for information and assessment, and even with built-in release conditions, they do not offer individualized learning experiences beyond content selection and cannot adapt to students' needs. They are heavily read–write-based instructional tools; it would be a stretch of the imagination to describe them as interactive activities.

Simulations have been used in educational contexts for some time now (Horn and Cleaves 1980; Riis 1995; Anderson and Morrice 2000; Chen and Samroengraja 2000; Mustafee and Katsaliaki 2010). Simulations can provide a personalized learning experience and encourage students to practice lower-level skills in a safe environment with rapid, if not immediate, feedback on their abilities. Simulations are limited, however, in that they typically present users with a consistent mode of activities in which only variables change; neither the goals nor the mode of interaction alters significantly (Crookall and Saunders 1989). The player must learn how to use the simulation and may transfer that knowledge into real-world activities. Simulations do require higher levels of thinking because users must weigh variables and options in order to succeed (Dantas et al. 2005;

Walker and Shelton 2008; Westera et al. 2008; Nadolski et al. 2010). In the end, a simulation is primarily task oriented and repetitive; it is not a game in that it lacks typical game trappings as described below.

In addition to the LMS and simulation, two other recent variations of e-learning are currently in play in education circles. *Edutainment* is typically a rote exercise situated in an entertainment setting, for example, a math exercise on a tablet PC that requires the player to add and subtract when a game character levels up. Little or no learning occurs in edutainment, only the practice of previously acquired knowledge and skills. The concept of gamification has muddied the waters of e-learning. The term *gamification* can be described as the process of adopting game technology, thinking, mechanics, and game design methods outside of the gaming industry to solve problems and engage users (Deterding et al. 2011). Whereas gamification incorporates elements of games (Brathwaite and Schreiber 2008; Deterding et al. 2011), we have determined that serious educational game development, not gamification, is the more productive path for effective education. Studies have already indicated the effectiveness of game-based learning (Prensky 2001; Gee 2003), whereas there are significant questions concerning the impact of gamification (Deterding et al. 2011).

Refocusing now on educational computer games, let us clarify our understanding of games and gaming. There are different approaches to defining a game, and we follow traditional definitions that describe games as stated rule systems motivated by player competition or adversity toward particular goals or outcomes (Dempsey et al. 2002; Salen and Zimmerman 2004; Juul 2005). Consequently, unlike simulations and edutainment, inserting games into a curriculum can create a highly motivating learning environment; it draws on students' sense of fantasy and amusement; it is self-directed, appealing to an individual student's curiosity; and it is a continuous challenge wherein any existing tasks or knowledge that appears incomplete, inconsistent, or incorrect motivates a student to foster deeper levels of learning. It is necessary, however, to insure that the game goals are in alignment with desired learning outcomes. And in that necessity lies the challenge for developing serious educational games (SEGs): creating a sophisticated pedagogically motivated experience using game design in which a player learns desired learning outcomes while playing (Malone 1980). At the same time, game development is costly and difficult to scale, and specific games are difficult to transfer contextually. These factors have typically limited the rollout and subsequent research on the impact of gaming in education.

In spite of the development challenges, SEGs have significant potential because they can provide immersive, engaging, and fun environments that require deep thinking and complex problem solving within a construct of overcoming obstacles and challenges (Gee 2003; Hämäläinen 2008; Walker and Shelton 2008; Sanchez and Olivares 2011). They create interactive student-centered environments rather than a passive content-centered classroom environment. This allows students to generate a personalized learning experience, progressively incorporating new knowledge and scaffolding it into what they already know. The possible variability within this interactive environment permits students to work on lower-level tasks repeatedly as they develop broader analytical skills and progress to complete the game objectives. Because each student is able to engage course-based material at his or her own pace, underprepared or at-risk students can focus on needed skills at their convenience. Moreover, feedback is frequent and immediate, thereby reinforcing mastery of fundamental skills that is required for advancing further into the game.

So, if there are so many potential benefits to adopting games into curricula, then where do we find these games? As with other software applications, we can consider acquiring them off the shelf (e.g., Sanford 2006), modifying an existing game (Lopes and Bidarra 2011; Scacchi 2011), or developing new games. The problem with the first option is that off-the-shelf games are purposed with entertainment in mind and a curricula needs to develop around the game rather than develop through the game. Modifying an existing game requires specialized software development knowledge, and the game itself still retains a limited functional scope. Games are complex applications; developing new ones has been time consuming and expensive and has required substantial expertise from diverse stakeholders: game developers, software developers, educators, and players. Established game development approaches are document centric. Two kinds of documents are often used to specify games: preproduction game design document (GDD) and production game software requirements specification (SRS) (Rollings and Adams 2003; Oxland 2004; Gregory 2009; Adams 2010). Although systematic, the traditional approaches have some limitations with respect to creating SEGs. They do not focus on developing executable versions of the game early on; feedback on a running game may take many months. The documents are developed by different stakeholders (game designers, game software developers), likely captured using different notations. For example, storyboard and comic-style representations are well suited

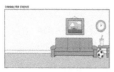   

FIGURE 3.1   Storyboard—Partial example for choosing the character.

for capturing the flow of the game and the desired user interface (UI) concepts (graphics) (Truong et al. 2006; Williams and Alspaugh 2008), but need to be transformed into specifications for the game developers (Figure 3.1) (Cooper and Longstreet 2012b). The relationships (traceability) between one document and another document are difficult to establish and maintain. With a document-centric approach, it is also difficult to maintain the consistency of the GDD and SRS, which can lead to costly delays in the project. These approaches do not explicitly support the creation of SEGs, which have specific learning objectives and assessment criteria.

The software engineering community continues to move away from document-centric development approaches. MDE is now an established approach for systematically developing complex applications (Kent 2002). Models of the application are created, analyzed (validated/verified), and subsequently transformed from the requirements level down to the code level of abstraction; one goal is to (automatically) transform the models. Engineering standards to support MDE have been broadly adopted, including the Object Management Group's model-driven architecture (OMG 2003), Unified Process (OMG 2008), and Unified Modeling Language (UML) (OMG 2009). UML 2.0 is a well-known notation that provides graphical notations with semiformal syntax and semantics, and an associated language, the Object Constraint Language, for expressing logic constraints. MDE has been applied across diverse domains; however, little is available on its application to support the rapid, cost-effective development of SEGs.

To improve the development of SEGs, our research project, SimSYS, is under way. SimSYS is an MDE-based approach that uniquely integrates elements of traditional game design, pedagogical content, and software engineering methodologies. Our approach has three main steps: (1) create an informal model of the SEG (captured like a storyboard with textual descriptions of the learning objectives and game play in addition to UI concepts, e.g., graphics and audio); transform the informal model into a semiformal, tailored UML use case model (visual and tabular, template-based specifications); transform the semiformal model into formal, executable models (statechart for comprehensive simulation and XML, which can be loaded and played in the game engine). Our MDE-based approach can be applied in an agile, iterative development process, for example, by describing a part of the game informally, semiformally, and formally (executable), allowing earlier assessment and feedback on a running (partial) game. A key feature of our approach is the thorough integration of learning objectives, for both topic-specific subject matter and transferable skills.

In a previous work, we presented the underlying meta-model for the approach (Longstreet and Cooper 2012), in addition to preliminary work on the MDE-based approach (Cooper and Longstreet 2012a, 2012b; Cooper et al. 2014). The meta-model facilitates the development of high-quality, engaging educational games because it explicitly ties knowledge requirements, transferable skills, and course outcomes to game production. The key features of our meta-model are the modularization of domain-specific bodies of knowledge (BOKs), a learning taxonomy (e.g., Bloom's), and skill-based challenges. This supports the wide adoption across curricula, as domain-specific knowledge can be *plugged-in* across multiple disciplines (e.g., STEM, humanities). In addition, our model situates learning opportunities in a plotline wherein the student player advances by succeeding against time, nonplayer adversaries, and his or her own best scores. Knowledge-based challenges framed by a learning taxonomy develop the transferable skills required by accreditation standards that also provide feedback to both the player and the faculty member. Situating assessment challenges in an immersive game environment makes them more engaging and imaginative than typical online tests or assignments.

Here, we present the model refinements within the context of the overall three-step, iterative approach. The approach is illustrated with part of an example test game. Currently, our transformations are done manually; we plan to automate the transformations as future work and provide an intelligent, semiautomated wizard to assist in the creation of SEGs. Related work is available indicating that the automated transformation from use cases to formal models is feasible (Riebisch and Hübner 2004); prototypes are under way for the game generation wizard. The goal is to significantly reduce the effort needed to define the games and support their comprehensive verification with simulation tools.

To the best of our knowledge, SimSYS is the first MDE-based approach for SEGs. Previous work on UML-based game specifications (e.g., Hausmann et al. 2001) has focused on tailoring statecharts (Harel 1987); they offer a rigorous, state machine-based foundation, but may be more difficult for some stakeholders to use. Game designers with experience working with storyboards, for example, may find a tabular use case specification format easy to learn and use. Storyboards are often presented as a sequence of cells in a tabular format. Tabular specifications are well established in requirements engineering (Pollack et al. 1971; Heitmeyer et al. 1996). They are considered straightforward to define, understand, and maintain.

The remainder of this chapter is structured as follows: Section 3.2 presents an outline of the semantic building blocks that serves as a meta-model for SimSYS development. Section 3.3 presents an overview of the SimSYS MDE-based approach, including the informal model, semiformal model, and formal models; a test game example is discussed for illustration. Section 3.4 conclusions and recommendations for future work.

3.2 HOLISTIC APPROACH TO SEGs

As noted above, aligning game design with pedagogical goals in mind poses a challenge for creating SEGs. Likewise, scalability, economics, and contextual flexibility prove to be a consistent difficulty. To address this, we outline a holistic view to gaming and learning by outlining a semantic construct that defines the elemental building blocks with rules to govern their interplay (Figure 3.2). These blocks and the rules that affect them provide a structure upon which similar categories of game play components may be designed across a greater variety of contexts. The result can provide myriad opportunities of player experiences within a pedagogically sound learning environment. Our initial meta-model approach establishes that educational games are immersive, entertaining environments that embed specific learning objectives into challenges that require proficiency of particular skills as classified by a learning taxonomy.

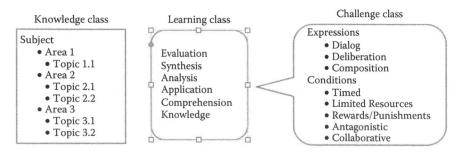

FIGURE 3.2 Educational game elements.

3.2.1 External Entities

Our meta-model considers two primary external entities. First, the game engages student players who function as the game protagonist. An introduction to the game requires the player to choose his or her character as part of an orientation to the game environment and the game play fundamentals. Depending on the parameters of the game set by the instructor, the student player may have some input as to his or her character's abilities (e.g., strength or agility). Otherwise, he or she will be able to adjust specific physical characteristics and the name of the player avatar. The benefit of customizing the player avatar is the unique investment the player has while inside the game world. Afterward, the player must navigate a series of game challenges that, if completed successfully, will allow his or her to defeat computer-played nonplayer character (NPC) rivals and progress into the next faculty-designed challenge. The specific challenges within the game are designed to reinforce and demonstrate content knowledge, application, analysis, and evaluation. As a game modeled with real-world parameters, the challenges will develop transferable skills required by programs and/or international accreditation agencies while providing continual, immediate feedback to the student player.

The second external entity is the instructor and/or game developer. Instructors/developers establish the game parameters: by toggling contexts, characters, and challenges, they create a learning environment for the student through the use of proposed templates and draw from an established asset repository. Templates support the modularization of game specifications; they are an established best practice in SE/systems engineering processes. Game designers can instantiate the templates using a WYSIWYG UI. Although the student player receives feedback during game play, the instructor will also receive feedback on the student player's or players' progress and abilities. This can allow the instructor to more accurately adjust future class session and/or continuing game content. At the same time, aggregate player information can inform assessment and accreditation reports and address progress toward program learning outcomes.

3.2.2 Traditional Game Elements

The external entities interface with the SimSYS game and their interaction functions through traditional video game components. These game components draw upon reusable base forms and functional processes; for the instructor developer, the components are toggled as part of the curriculum/game development process. Subsequently, the player engages the game that has been set out by the instructor. We contend that separating the functional game components from the rapidly changeable educational elements is key to developing flexible, scalable, and adaptable educational games. In SimSYS, the various game components, traditional and educational, are categorized into functionally determined classes. The primary entry point into the game for the player entity is the character that he or she takes on when entering the game. The character class is the set of actors within the game; every game must include the protagonist (student player), but then can contain a variety of NPCs. For example, a secondary NPC likely to be ubiquitous is the antagonist, who provides personified adversity for the player in a more interactive manner. Each NPC has a profile and a set of variable attributes consisting of name and title, function type (e.g., Protagonist, Antagonist, Director, Constructor, Interlocutor), role (e.g., employer, client, colleague, friend, lab partner), relevant technical skills (i.e., degrees, talents), years of experience (i.e., strength or effectiveness), communication skill (i.e., intelligence), leadership skill (i.e., charisma), and teamwork skill (i.e., dexterity). In addition, NPCs can have pertinent demographic information for encouraging students' thought about studying and working in a diverse social environment (e.g., gender/ ethnicity/nationality). NPCs may be assigned a frequency of presence to the student player to encourage or limit the level of assistance/challenge that the NPC offers. Finally, there are two kinds of character behavior: autonomous or allonomous.

The Context class establishes the simulation environment for the player/protagonist. It provides a grammar for the simulation environment and game play. The Context class contains the elements that create an immersive world within which students can interface. It includes the scenario (e.g., an office, a hospital), the game situation (e.g., a mission briefing or a confrontation), a place within the game's story arc and transitions and goals (e.g., moving from junior to senior staff, graduating from college), and provides the framework for the challenges in the game (e.g., final exam, a company project, or a roadblock). The interplay between the player/protagonist within the plot context and the NPCs is designed to help students better understand the course content from multiple perspectives, as well as reinforcing the effects of good and bad decision making.

The last class within the traditional game elements is Mechanics. The Mechanics class provides the fundamental, low-level game functions and coordinates reusable assets such as character interactions, music, and graphics. It also supports maintaining the state of the game, including the players' progress (where they are in the game) and the track of their assessment (how well they are doing in the game, e.g., points). This class supports the Context class and the Challenge class.

3.2.3 Educational Game Elements

To facilitate the pedagogical base for rapid development of simulation games across curricula and training programs, we have separated the game functionality (i.e., the raw simulation components) from the knowledge content and student assessment via specific modalities of game challenges. This allows faculty and trainer designers to input and switch out content quickly from course to course and, depending on student progress, from class to class. That is, instructor designers could toggle a laboratory or a crime scene environment for the game Context, and then input chemistry- or forensic-specific content in the game challenges that can vary from course section to course section.

Practically every discipline or subject matter consists of a knowledge and skills base that determines competency. This is the case for fourth-grade reading, for human resources' compliance training, and for software engineering. We structure the current SimSYS Knowledge class in such a way that users can identify, prioritize, and select information that can be invoked for game scenarios and assessment. Along similar lines as the software engineering education knowledge (Abran et al. 2004), content information in SimSYS is divided into subdisciplinary areas, with each area divided into smaller units and topics. Although not all levels of the Knowledge class are necessary for every game, it does provide flexibility for greater variety and scalability.

To align game challenges with different types of mastery over the BOK, the student player's knowledge in SimSYS is categorized through a learning taxonomy. This allows for knowledge and skills assessment at different levels and through varied forms of assessment. The Learning class represents the skills and abilities reflected in the game learning objectives. In developing SimSYS, we use Bloom's taxonomy as the types of skills that student players must demonstrate a level of competency in the educational game challenges (Anderson and Krathwohl 2001). For each knowledge base topic, one or several of Bloom taxonomy levels can be assigned, indicating what skill level graduates should possess. The six skills we draw from Bloom's taxonomy are knowledge (remembering learned material), comprehension (understanding information and the meaning of course content), application (ability to use the learned material in new and concrete situations), synthesis and analysis (seeing the connections and components of larger systems), and evaluation (being able to assess the value of varied and variable information within specific contexts and requirements). Different challenges are designed to pull from different levels of thought. For example, if content retention is the desired type of learning that needs assessment, then the instructor can toggle a Dialog challenge asking students to demonstrate knowing a term's definition in a conversation with an inquisitive NPC. Likewise, more complex challenges would require demonstrating higher skill sets within the simulation game, thereby providing opportunities for increased knowledge and skills building.

The Challenge class holds different formative educational activities that are tied to specific, faculty-defined learning outcomes. As it is the linchpin of the educational simulation game, we developed additional modalities onto the Challenge class to allow for a wider range of possible learning opportunities. Challenges represent traditional, formative educational opportunities. Challenges are populated by NPCs who function in a variety of roles to communicate, assist, or complicate the challenge for the student protagonist. The challenges are situated in a plotline wherein the student is seeking to advance. It is this narrative context, and possible competition against player and nonplayer adversaries, that makes the challenge fun and imaginative rather than a text-based multiple-choice test or written assignment.

To enable different levels of learning and difficulty, the Challenge class is divided into two subcategories: Expression and Conditions. There are three Expression forms by which the game's assessment takes place: Dialog, Deliberation, and Composition. There are five Conditions forms that affect limitations and motivations for student players in their engaging with the Challenges: Timed, Limited Resources, Rewards/ Punishment, Competition and Collaboration with the NPC Antagonist character. In the dialog Challenge, an Interlocutor NPC asks the student player a line of questions, which require content knowledge at first but embedded follow-up questions require both understanding and appropriate applications of that knowledge. This encourages a Socratic approach to learning in the game and encourages student players to demonstrate their mastery of course content in a more engaged manner. Primarily, the Dialog Challenge appeals to lower levels of a learning taxonomy such as Bloom's (i.e., knowledge, understanding, application). For example, an Interlocutor NPC in the role of a Staff Sargent can ask the student player to identify a particular cultural custom; then, through answering a series of follow-up questions, the student can further demonstrate his or her understanding of that custom by identifying appropriate contexts for its practice (application) in particular populations.

3.3 OVERVIEW OF THE SIMSYS APPROACH

The SimSYS MDE approach has three main steps (Figure 3.3) and uses tailored versions of well-established approaches. The first step is to create an informal, high-level model of the SEG. The narrative captures the game like a storyboard with textual descriptions of the learning objectives and game play in addition to UI concepts (e.g., graphics, audio).

The second step is to transform the informal model into a semiformal, tailored UML use case model (visual and tabular, template-based specifications). The overall game is organized into Acts, Scenes, Screens, and Challenges; each of these has a tabular template to assist in the game development. Tabular, template-based approaches for specifying systems are well established (Pollack et al. 1971; Heitmeyer et al. 1996); tabular representations are considered straightforward to develop, review, and maintain; they allow the modularization of a specification into subtables to manage complexity. As this semiformal model is developed and reviewed, errors in the original narrative can be identified and corrected.

The third step is to transform the semiformal model into formal, executable models (e.g., statechart, XML). The statechart can undergo comprehensive simulation/animation to verify the model's behavior; errors can be identified and corrected in both the statechart model and the semiformal model as needed. The XML is the game specification, which can be loaded, played, and tested using the SimSYS Game Play Engine. Our MDE-based approach can be applied in an agile, iterative development process, for example, by describing a part of the game informally, semiformally, and formally (executable), allowing earlier assessment and feedback on a preliminary version of the game.

The three models are described in more detail below. For each one, the original and tailored versions of the approaches are presented.

3.3.1 Informal Model

3.3.1.1 Storyboard

Storyboards are an established, informal approach used in diverse creative endeavors (e.g., animation, cartoons, films, games, instructional design) to effectively capture the flow of events over time using a combination of

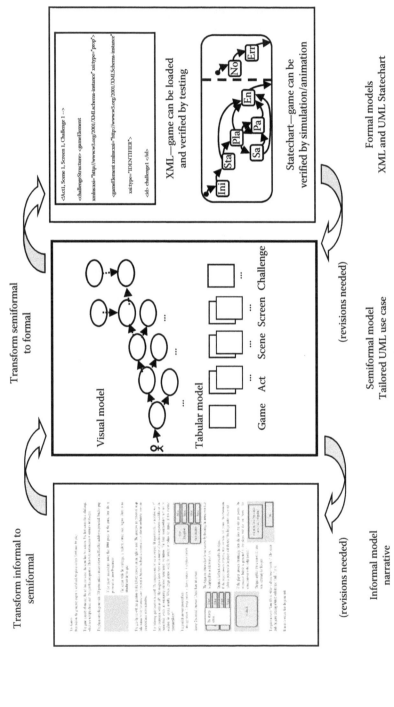

FIGURE 3.3   Overview of models in the SimSYS approach (informal, semiformal, formal models).

graphics and text (Hart 1999; Tumminello 2004; Truong et al. 2006). They are a planning, or previsualization, tool used to present, discuss, and revise the concept before costly development work has been done. Storyboards present a sequence of panels, or cells, which include graphics and text to explain what is happening. They have been selected for use in this work on SEGs for the following reasons:

- Storyboards have been adopted in game development, making them a familiar approach to many stakeholders.

- Storyboards are straightforward to create, understand, and revise by stakeholders with diverse backgrounds. This is an important consideration for creating SEGs, which involves game developers, software developers, and educators.

- Storyboards are versatile, as they can be applied at a high level of abstraction (presenting the overall concept of a game) or at a more detailed step-by-step description (presenting the details of part of a game).

3.3.1.2 SimSYS Storyboard

The SimSYS storyboard is an informal model, which provides a narrative with preliminary graphics, audio, characters, and learning objectives/standards (Figure 3.4). This is a straightforward, familiar way to begin the SEG development. The informal model is organized into a title, an overview that describes the structure of the game at a high level (number of acts, scenes, screens, challenges), the learning objectives (both topic specific and transferable skills), initial conditions for the game such as number of points a player starts with, backdrop for the scenes, and rules that need to be applied as the game is played. After this, the game play is described.

In the simple example Test Game 4 SE Design, there is one Act; it has one Scene with two Screens; the first Screen has a challenge in it. The layout of the Challenge is presented (a collection of standard layouts is available to reuse); the Challenge is a simple multiple choice quiz—there is no timer or NPC competing in the quiz. The question and possible answer options are captured; the player can see a hint for each answer; the reward for a correct and an incorrect answer is described in addition to the feedback provided to the player. In this model, the details are not necessarily complete—for example, the narrative indicates that a hint should be available for each

Title: Test Game 4 SE Design

The game consists of one act; the act has one scene; the scene has two screens. The first screen has a challenge, which is a multiple choice quiz. The quiz has one question; it is a dialog question requiring critical thinking, problem solving, and analytical skills in addition to SWEBOK Software Design topics (general, process, context). The Bloom's taxonomy categories are knowledge and application. There is no introduction or summary for this quiz. The second screen provides a summary of the player's progress in the game.

The player starts the game with 1000 points and is a student intern; the BlueSky backdrop is presented (BlueSky.png).

If the player accumulates more than 1000 points in the game, then she is promoted to Junior Programmer.

The screen with the challenge, a multiple choice quiz, begins. There is no introduction for this quiz.

The quiz layout with the question on the left and answers on the right is used. The questions are presented in an information bubble; the answers are presented as buttons; feedback is presented in an information bubble; hints are presented in an information box.

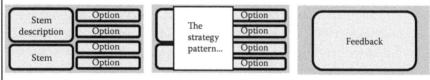

The following description is presented: The designers need to use a complex AI algorithm that is available as a third-party component with an API. The designers know that there are a number of possible components available on the marketplace, which are undergoing extensive performance evaluations. The final recommendation will not be available for several months.

The following question is asked: Which design pattern would be suitable to reduce the impact of this eventual recommendation?

The possible options (answers) presented are as follows:
1. strategy pattern   2. bridge pattern   3. factory pattern   4. singleton pattern

Answer 2 is correct. Answers 1, 3, and 4 are not correct.

The player can obtain a hint for each answer by hovering the mouse over it; it is displayed in an information box.

Question feedback is provided to the player.

If the player answers correctly, then she wins 500 points. An information bubble is presented to the player with the text "The bridge pattern is correct!"

If the player answers incorrectly, then she does not win any points. An information bubble is presented to the player with the text "Sorry—the correct answer is the bridge pattern."

The quiz and the first screen end; there is no summary for this quiz.

In the second screen, the game presents "Your title is <title> and you have <points>!" The player ends the game by clicking a button with the text "End..." on it.

If an error occurs, then the game ends.

FIGURE 3.4   Informal model of the example Test Game.

answer option, but it is not defined at this point. The narrative continues, describing the second screen, which wraps up the game with a summary of their title (they may have been promoted by answering the question correctly) and their point total. Sample images of the game are presented to help communicate the look and feel of the UI. For our Test Game, we are using a cartoonlike style to keep the look lighthearted, fun, and engaging.

3.3.2 SimSYS Use Case Model

3.3.2.1 UML Use Case

The UML is a standardized, general-purpose, visual modeling language (OMG 2009). It provides a rich collection of 13 diagrams for modeling software artifacts; three extension mechanisms are defined to support tailoring the diagrams. The static views of the system are modeled with structure diagrams (class, composite structure, component, deployment, object, and package diagrams). The dynamic views of the system are modeled with behavior diagrams (use case, activity, statechart, communication, interaction overview, sequence, and timing diagrams). The extension mechanisms are stereotypes, tagged values, and constraints. Stereotypes extend the vocabulary of the UML by creating new model elements that are derived from existing ones. Stereotypes are represented using guillemet, for example, <<Act>>. Tagged values extend the properties of a UML building block to create new information in its specification. Constraints specify properties that are always true for the element. The UML diagrams have been tailored to support diverse development needs, including platforms, modeling paradigms, and domains (e.g., health care, finance, aerospace).

A variety of UML diagrams may be used to represent the software requirements, including the use case diagram. A UML use case diagram visually represents (1) the people or external systems that interact with the system under development with Actors and (2) the functional capabilities of the system with use cases. Actors are represented using stick figures, and use cases are represented using ovals. The relationship that describes which actor interacts with each use case is represented with a directed arrow. For example (see Figure 3.5), a Player is an actor who can request a variety of capabilities in the system, such as starting, playing, pausing, resuming, and saving a game. To improve the modularization and reuse in the use case model, use cases can interact with other use cases. Two additional associations are defined to support this: *uses* and *extends*. The *uses* association provides the ability for one use case to explicitly call another use case to provide the needed behavior. The *extends* association also provides the ability for a use case to provide additional functionality to another. However, the insertion of the functionality is defined by the extending use case; the use case being modified has no knowledge of the extension.

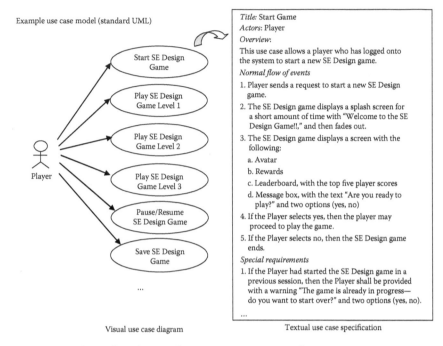

Example use case model (standard UML)

Player

Start SE Design Game

Play SE Design Game Level 1

Play SE Design Game Level 2

Play SE Design Game Level 3

Pause/Resume SE Design Game

Save SE Design Game

...

Visual use case diagram

Title: Start Game

Actors: Player

Overview:

This use case allows a player who has logged onto the system to start a new SE Design game.

Normal flow of events

1. Player sends a request to start a new SE Design game.

2. The SE Design game displays a splash screen for a short amount of time with "Welcome to the SE Design Game!!," and then fades out.

3. The SE Design game displays a screen with the following:

   a. Avatar

   b. Rewards

   c. Leaderboard, with the top five player scores

   d. Message box, with the text "Are you ready to play?" and two options (yes, no)

4. If the Player selects yes, then the player may proceed to play the game.

5. If the Player selects no, then the SE Design game ends.

Special requirements

1. If the Player had started the SE Design game in a previous session, then the Player shall be provided with a warning "The game is already in progress—do you want to start over?" and two options (yes, no).

...

Textual use case specification

FIGURE 3.5   Visual and textual UML use case example.

The visual model provides a high-level overview of the capabilities and actors in the system. However, it lacks a detailed description needed by developers to proceed with the analysis and design of the system. Detailed descriptions for a use typically include the title, actors, overview, normal flow of events, alternate flow of events, and special (nonfunctional) requirements (Figure 3.5). The flow of events describe the interactions between the Actors and the system as externally visible, black box behavior. For example, the Player makes a request to pause a game; the system responds by displaying a message, indicating that it has successfully been paused.

3.3.2.2 SimSYS Use Case

The informal narrative is iteratively refined into a tailored, semiformal use case model (visual model and supporting tabular specifications). An UML use case diagram provides a visual overview of the structure of an example game (Figure 3.6), organizing the game into Acts, Scenes, Screens, and Challenges. The built-in association <<includes>> is used to

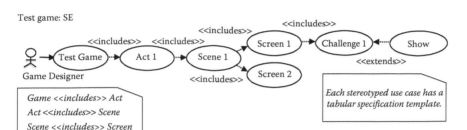

FIGURE 3.6   A tailored UML use case diagram for Test Game 4.

describe the relationships among these use cases. The built-in association <<extends>> is used to describe use cases with asynchronous capabilities such as a player (unpredictably) requesting to show a hint, show a character's profile, or show a character's rewards. There is a simple mapping from the informal narrative to the visual model: each act in the narrative is an act in the visual model; each scene in the narrative is a scene in the visual model; and so on.

Each of the tailored use cases (game, act, scene, screen, challenge) has a tabular specification template. We found that defining a template for each level of abstraction in the game provided a clear, easy-to-understand specification, as opposed to defining one general-purpose template that could be tailored for different levels (perhaps by leaving some part blank or marking them not applicable). The templates defined to support the game specification are available elsewhere (SimSYS 2012). The tabular templates integrate elements from a SEG meta-model (Longstreet and Cooper 2012) and storyboard features (game play, graphics, audio) (Truong et al. 2006). The meta-model uniquely integrates concepts from the game (e.g., game plot, characters, mechanics) and education (e.g., learning objectives, assessment, course content) domains. The tabular specifications have been manually created; a semiautomated, intelligent wizard to create games and output formal models is future work (Figure 3.7).

The informal narrative is mapped to the Game, Act, Scene, Screen, and Challenge templates (SimSYS 2012). The game, act and scene templates are relatively simple—they provide the structure and sequencing to organize the screens. The majority of the game play is defined in the Screens and Challenges. See Appendix 3A for a Challenge represented as a tabular, semiformal model.

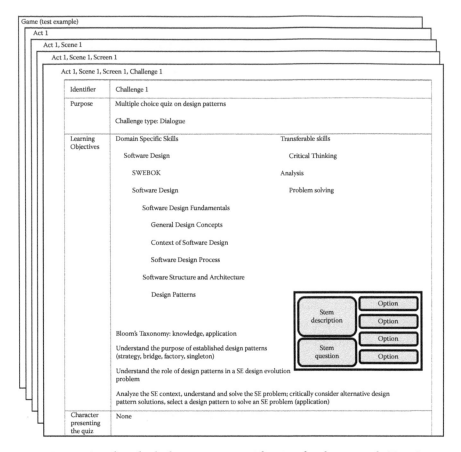

FIGURE 3.7   A tailored tabular use case specification for the example Test Game.

3.3.3 Formal Model

3.3.3.1 XML

XML is a formal, textual, document markup language originally designed to easily distribute information across the World Wide Web (WWWC 2006). XML has been selected for use in this work for the following reasons:

- *XML is formal and concise.* The specification for XML includes a formal grammar specification using Extended Backus_Naur Form notation. The grammar gives a comprehensive syntax for XML and provides a means for all XML documents to be checked for well formedness. A well-formed XML document allows a parser that conforms to the XML grammar specification to parse and manipulate data from the document without error.

- *XML documents are human legible.* Because markup text in an XML document can be customized, the XML document may be written with descriptive names that allow humans to easily understand the type of data that is stored. Comments may also be used to provide further description within the document without impacting the syntax of the document. The feature is important because the XML documents may also serve as a record of the transformation to verify successful model transformation.

- *Writing programs to process XML documents is straightforward.* XML documents are text-based documents that can be parsed to extract data and manipulation as necessary. Many programming languages provide standard libraries for data manipulation in the XML documents.

- *XML supports a wide variety of applications.* XML is a widespread language now being used in multiple applications in multiple industries.

3.3.3.2 SimSYS XML Game Script

The tabular, semiformal notation is transformed into a single XML file that can be loaded into the SimSYS Game Play Engine. Part of the XML file is illustrated in Table 3.1; the XML schema definition for the game is defined. The transformation is done one part at a time, using tags to organize the content. For example, the Challenge's one question is related to subject-specific topics in SE Design and transferable skills described in the tabular specification (What kind of knowledge is in the Challenge?); these

TABLE 3.1   XML Partial Representation of the Test Game Challenge

```
1.1 …
<!- Act 1, Scene 1, Screen 1, Challenge 1- >
<challengeStructure>
    <gameElement xmlns:xsi = "http://www.w3.org/2001/
    XMLSchema-instance" xsi:type = "prop">
    <gameElement xmlns:xsi = "http://www.w3.org/2001/
    XMLSchema-instance" xsi:type = "IDENTIFIER">
    <id> challenge1 </id>
    <challengeItemList>
    <item>
```

(Continued)

TABLE 3.1 (*Continued*)   XML Partial Representation of the Test Game Challenge

```
<! What kind of knowledge is in the challenge?- >
<domainKnowledgeList>
     <domainKnowledge>software engineering</
     domainKnowledge>
     <area>Software Design</area>
     <topic_list>
     <topic>General_Design_Concepts<\topic>
     <topic>Context_of_Software_Design<\topic>
     <topic>Software_Design_Process<\topic>
     <topic>Software_Design_Re-use<\topic>
     </topic_list>
<\domainKnowledgeList>
<transferableKnowledgeList>
     <transferableKnowledge>analysis
     </transferableKnowledge>
     <transferableKnowledge>critical_thinking
     </transferableKnowledge>
     <transferableKnowledge>problem_solving
     </transferableKnowledge>
<\transferableKnowledgeList>
<! How is the knowledge being assessed?- >
     <expression>dialog</expression>
     <learningTaxonomyList>
          <learningTaxonomy>knowledge</learningTaxonomy>
          <learningTaxonomy>application
          </learningTaxonomy>
     </learningTaxonomyList>
<! Challenge item- >
<! The challenge item has a stem, with zero or one
text (description or vignette), zero or more images,
and a question.- >
<!- stem description- >
<stemDescription>
     <type>
          <typeName>InformationBox</typeName>
          <event>
               <eventName>NONE</eventName>
               <animation>FADEIN</animation>
               <time>QUICK</time>
          </event>
          <color>YELLOW</color>
          <location>UUR</location>
```

(*Continued*)

TABLE 3.1 (*Continued*)   XML Partial Representation of the Test Game Challenge

```
            <size>MEDIUM</size>
        <text>The designers need to use a complex AI
            algorithm that is available as a 3rd party
            component with an API. The designers know
            there are a number of possible components
            available on the marketplace, which are
            undergoing extensive performance
            evaluations. The final recommendation will
            not be available for several months.
        </text>
    </type>
    <!- stem question- >
    <stemQuestion>
        <type>
            <typeName>InformationBox</typeName>
            <event>
                <eventName>NONE</eventName>
                <animation>FADEIN</animation>
                <time>QUICK</time>
            </event>
            <color>YELLOW</color>
            <location>UUR</location>
            <size>MEDIUM</size>
            <text> Which design pattern would be suitable
                to reduce the impact of this eventual
                recommendation?</text>
        </type>
    </stemQuestion>
    <!- options (answers)- >
    <! Each option has text, hint, evaluation, reward, and
    feedback.
    <stemOptionList>
        <stemOption>
            <type>
                <typeName>Button</typeName>
            <event>
                eventName>NONE</eventName>
                <animation>FADEIN</animation>
                <time>QUICK</time>
            </event>
            <event>
                <eventName>Click</eventName>
                <animation>FADEOUT</animation>
                <next> FeedbackScreen1 </next>
            </event>
```

(*Continued*)

TABLE 3.1 (*Continued*)   XML Partial Representation of the Test Game Challenge

```
        <!   -->
        <name> Option1 </name>
        <location> UUL </location>
        <color> Yellow </color>
        <text> Strategy Pattern </text>
        <! Hint -- >
        <type>
            <typeName> InformationBox</typeName>
            <name> Hint1 </name>
            <eventName> HOVER</eventName>
            <location> UUL </location>
            <color> Yellow </color>
            <text>The Strategy pattern defines a family
            of algorithms, encapsulates each one, and
            makes them interchangeable; algorithms are
            selected at runtime. It is a behavioral
            pattern. <\text>
        <\type>
        <! Evaluation -- >
        <evaluation> Incorrect </evaluation>
        <!—Reward ->
        <reward>NONE<\reward>
        <type>
            <! Feedback   -- >
            <typeName> MessageBox </typeName>
            <location> UC </location>
            <color> Yellow </color>
            <text>: Sorry - the correct answer is the
                    bridge pattern<\text>
        </type>
        </stemOption>
            ...
    <\stemOptionList>
    <\item>
    ...
<\challengeItemList>
    ...
...
```

are represented in XML using two kinds of tags to define lists of topics (`<domainKnowledgeList>`, `<transferableKnowledgeList>`). The next tags define the assessment approach for the question, How is the knowledge being assessed? The question with four answer options—evaluation, hints, rewards, and feedback—follow in the XML file. Although the file is quite long, it is straightforward to read; the manual mapping from the semiformal tabular model to the XML is time consuming, but not too difficult.

3.4 CONCLUSIONS AND FUTURE WORK

The SimSYS approach to engineering SEGs is an iterative, three-step approach that is model based and integrates learning objectives from the earliest stages in the game development. The approach begins with an informal narrative, like a storyboard, which is subsequently transformed into a tailored semiformal UML use case model (with visual and tabular specifications) and finally into formal models. Our first formal model uses XML; the XML is the game specification that can be loaded and tested in the SimSYS Game Play Engine. In applying the three-step approach to engineering a collection of test games, we have found it to be straightforward, but labor intensive. In particular, the formal XML model required a significant amount of time to create; manually testing the games was also time consuming.

An Intelligent Automated Game Generation module is currently under investigation to alleviate the effort in populating the informal narrative and semiformal models (template instantiation) and automatically generate the XML models. We also plan to explore the transformation of the semiformal model into a statechart representation that can be loaded, animated, or simulated with the existing commercial tool support (e.g. IBM 2012), providing a complementary verification approach.

We recognize that the validation of the approach is limited to our preliminary prototyping work (symbolic test games, software engineering test games). Additional validation is needed, both by continuing our own project and by external educational game researchers and educators to explore issues such as the scalability of the approach to larger games and collections of related games.

REFERENCES

Abran, A., Moore, J.W., and Bourque, P. (2004). *Guide to the Software Engineering Body of Knowledge (SWEBOK): 2004 Version*. IEEE Computer Society, Los Alamitos, CA. Appendix D.

Adams, E. (2010). *Fundamentals of Game Design*. 2nd edition. New Riders Publishing, Berkeley, CA.

Anderson, Jr., E.G. and Morrice, D.J. (2000). Simulation game for teaching service-oriented supply chain management: Does information sharing help managers with service capacity decisions? *Production and Operations Management* 9: 40–55.

Anderson, L. W., Krathwohl, D. R., et al. (Eds.) (2001). *A Taxonomy for Learning, Teaching, and Assessing: A Revision of Bloom's Taxonomy of Educational Objectives*. Allyn & Bacon (Pearson Education Group). Boston, MA.

Brathwaite, B. and Schreiber, I. (2008). *Challenges for Game Designers*. Charles River Media, Boston, MA.

Chen, F. and Samroengraja, R. (2000). The stationary beer game. *Production and Operations Management* 9: 19–30.

Cooper, K. and Longstreet, C.L. (2012a). Towards model-driven game engineering for serious educational games: Tailored use cases for game requirements. *Proceedings of the IEEE 17th International Conference on Computer Games*, Louisville, KY, July 30–August 1, pp. 208–212.

Cooper, K. and Longstreet, C.L. (2012b). Towards model-driven game engineering in SimSYS: Requirements for the Agile software development process game. Technical report, co-published UTDCS-06-12. The University of Texas at Dallas, Richardson, TX; MU-CTL-01-12 Marquette University, Milwaukee, WI, March.

Cooper, K., Nasr, E., and Longstreet, C.L. (2014). Towards model-driven requirements engineering for serious educational games: Informal, semi-formal, and formal models. *Proceedings of the 20th International Working Conference on Requirements Engineering: Foundation for Software Quality*, Essen, Germany, April 7–10, pp. 17–22.

Crookall, D. and Saunders, D. (Eds.) (1989). Toward an integration of communication and simulation. In *Communication and Simulation from Two Fields to One*. Multilingual Matters, Clevedon.

Dantas, A.R., Barros, M.O., and Werner, C. (2005). Simulations models applied to game-based training for software project managers. *Process Simulation and Modeling Workshop*, St. Louis, MO, May 14–15, pp. 110–116.

Dempsey, V.J., Haynes, L.L., Lucassen, B.A., and Casey, M.S. (2002). Forty simple computer games and what they mean for educators. *Simulation and Gaming* 33(2):157–168.

Deterding, S., Dixon, D., Khaled, R., and Nacke, L. (2011). From game design elements to gamefulness: Defining "gamification." *Proceedings of the 15th International Academic Mindtrek Conference*, Tampere, Finland, September 28–30, pp. 9–15.

Gee, J.P. (2003). *What Video Games Have to Teach Us about Learning and Literacy?* Macmillan, New York.

Gregory, J. (2009). *Game Engine Architecture.* A.K. Peters, Natick, MA.

Hämäläinen, R. (2008). Designing and evaluating collaboration in a virtual game environment for vocational learning. *Computers & Education* **50**(1): 98–109.

Harel, D. (1987). Statecharts: A visual formalism for complex systems. *Science of Computer Programming* **8**(13): 231–274.

Hart, J. (1999). *The Art of the Storyboard: Storyboarding for Film, TV, and Animation.* Focal Press, New York.

Hausmann, J.H., Heckel, R., and Sauer, S. (2001). *Towards Dynamic Meta Modeling of UML Extensions: An Extensible Semantics for UML Sequence Diagrams.* University of Berlin, Germany, Society Press, pp. 80–87.

Heitmeyer, C.L., Jeffords, R., and Labaw, B. (1996). Automated consistency checking of requirements specifications. *ACM Transactions on Software Engineering and Methodology* **5**(3): 231–261.

Horn, R.E. and Cleaves, A. (1980). *The Guide to Simulation/Games for Education and Training.* Sage Publications, Newbury Park, CA.

IBM (2012). IBM Rational Rhapsody for Java, Version 8.0. Available at: http://www-142.ibm.com.

Juul, J. (2005). *Half-Real: Video Games between Real Rules and Fictional Worlds.* MIT Press, Cambridge, MA.

Kent, S. (2002). Model driven engineering. *Proceedings of the 3rd International Conference on Integrated Formal Methods,* Turku, Finland, May 15–17, pp. 286–298.

Longstreet, C.S. and Cooper, K. (2012). A meta-model for developing simulation games in higher education and professional development training. *Proceedings of the IEEE 17th International Conference on Computer Games,* Louisville, KY, July 30–August 1, pp. 39–44.

Lopes, R. and Bidarra, R. (2011). Adaptivity challenges in games and simulations: A survey. *IEEE Transactions on Computational Intelligence and AI in Games,* **3**(2): 85–99.

Malone, T. (1980). What makes things fun to learn? Heuristics for designing instructional computer games. *Proceedings of the 3rd ACM SIG SMALL Symposium Small Systems,* Palo Alto, CA, September 18–19.

Mustafee, N. and Katsaliaki, K. (2010). The blood supply game. In Johansson, B., Jain, S., Montoya-Torres, J., Hugan, J., and Yücesan, E. (Eds.), *Proceedings of the 2010 Winter Simulation Conference,* Baltimore, MD, December 5–8, pp. 327–338.

Nadolski, R.J., Hummel, H.G.K., van den Brink, H.J., Hoefakker, R.E., Slootmaker, A., Wu, B., and Bakken, S.K., (2010). Experiences from implementing a face-to-face educational game for iPhone/iPod Touch. *Proceedings of the 2nd International IEEE Consumer Electronics Society's Games Innovation Conference,* Hong Kong, People's Republic of China, December 21–23.

Object Management Group (2003). OMG model driven architecture (MDA) Guide, Version 1.0.1, March. Available at: http://www.omg.org.

Object Management Group (2008). OMG Software & Systems Process Engineering Metamodel specification (SPEM), Version 2.0. Available at: http://www.omg.org.

Object Management Group (2009). OMG Unified Modelling Language, Version 2.2. Available at: www.omg.org.

Oxland, M. (2004). *Gameplay and Design*. Addison-Wesley, New York.

Pollack, S.L., Hicks, H.T., and Harrison, W.J. (1971). *Decision Tables: Theory and Practice*. Wiley, New York.

Prensky, M. (2001). *Digital Game Based Learning*. McGraw-Hill, New York.

Riebisch, M. and Hübner, M. (2004). Refinement and formalization of semi-formal use case descriptions. *Proceedings of the 2nd Workshop on Model-Based Development of Computer Based Systems: Appropriateness, Consistency and Integration of Models*, Brno, Czech Republic, May 26–27.

Riis, J.O. (1995). *Simulation Games and Learning in Production Management*. International Federation for Information Processing. Springer, Berlin, Germany.

Rollings, A. and Adams, E. (2003). *Game Architecture and Design: A New Edition*. New Riders Publishing, Berkeley, CA.

Salen, K. and Zimmerman, E. (2004). *Rules of Play: Game Design Fundamentals*. MIT Press, Cambridge, MA.

Sánchez, J. and R. Olivares, (2011). Problem solving and collaboration using mobile serious games, *Computers & Education* **57**(3): 1943–1952.

Sanford, R. (2006). Teaching with games: COTS games in the classroom. Innovating e-learning: Transforming Learning Experiences online conference. Available at: http://www.online-conference.net/jisc/content/Sandford%20-%20teaching%20with%20games.pdf.

Scacchi, W. (2011). Modding as a basis for developing game systems. *Proceedings of the 1st International Workshop on Games and Software Engineering*, Waikiki, Honolulu, HI, May 21–28, pp. 5–8.

SimSYS (2012). SimSYS homepage. Available at: www.utdallas.edu/~kcooper.

Truong, K., Hayes, G., and Abowd, G. (2006). Storyboarding: An empirical determination of best practices and effective guidelines. *Proceedings of the 6th Conference on Designing Interactive Systems*, University Park, PA, June 26–28, pp. 12–21.

Walker, A. and Shelton, B.E. (2008). Problem-based educational games: connections, prescriptions, and assessment. *Journal of Interactive Learning Research*, **19**(4): 663–684.

Wang, A., and van der Hoek, A. (2004) SimSE: an educational simulation game for teaching the Software engineering process. *Proceedings of the 9th Annual SIGCSE conference on Innovation and Technology in Computer Science Education*, Leeds, UK, June 28–30.

Williams, A. and Alspaugh, T., (2008), Articulating Software Requirements Comic Book Style. *Proceedings of the 3rd International Workshop on Multimedia and Enjoyable Requirements Engineering—Beyond Mere Descriptions and with More Fun and Games*, Barcelona, Spain, September 9.

World Wide World Consortium (2006), Extensible Markup Language (XML) 1.0 (fourth edition), World Wide World Consortium, August 2006. Available at: http://www.w3.org/TR/xml/.

APPENDIX 3A: SEMIFORMAL MODEL—TABULAR, TAILORED USE CASE FOR CHALLENGE 1

Act 1, Scene 1, Screen 1, and Challenge 1

Identifier	Challenge 1
Purpose	Multiple choice quiz on design patterns Challenge type: Dialogue

Learning objectives	Domain specific	Transferable
	Software design	Critical thinking
	SWEBOK	Analysis
	Software design	Problem solving

Software design fundamentals
General design concepts
Context of software design
Software design process
Software design principles
Software structure and architecture
Design patterns
Understand the purpose of established design patterns (strategy, bridge, factory, singleton)
Understand the role of design patterns in an SE design evolution problem
Analyze the SE context, understand, and solve the SE problem; critically consider alternative design pattern solutions and select a design pattern to use

Character presenting the quiz	None
Competing characters	None

Quiz style	Layout (overall organization)
	Multiple choice
	Question (stem description, stem question) on the left
	Answer options on the right (two or more)
	Generic interaction props
	Question: information bubbles
	Answer: button
	Hint: information box
	Feedback: information bubble

Reward scheme	Correct answer: add 500 points
	Incorrect answer: no change to points

(Continued)

Declarations and initialization

Quiz interaction props	*Stem*	*Options*	*Hints*
	Stem Description Information Bubble 1	Answer Option Button 1	Hint Information Box 1
	Text: The designers need to use a complex AI algorithm that is available as a 3rd party component with an API. The designers know there are a number of possible components available on the marketplace, which are undergoing extensive performance evaluations. The final recommendation will not be available for several months.	Text: Strategy pattern Hint: Hint Information Box 1 Evaluation: incorrect Player Feedback: Feedback Information Bubble 4	Text: The Strategy pattern defines a family of algorithms, encapsulates each one, and makes them interchangeable; algorithms are selected at runtime. It is a behavioral pattern.
		Answer Option Button 2 Text: Bridge pattern Hint: Hint Information Box 2 Evaluation: correct Player Feedback: Feedback Information Bubble 3	Hint Information Box 2 Text: The Bridge pattern decouples an interface and its implementation. The implementation can be modified without changing the interface. It is a structural pattern.
	Stem Question Information Bubble 2 Text: Which design pattern would be suitable to reduce the impact of this eventual recommendation?	Answer Option Button 3 Text: Factory pattern Hint Information Box 3 Evaluation: incorrect Player Feedback: Feedback Information Bubble 4	Hint Information Box 3 Text: The Factory pattern defines an interface for creating an object, but lets the classes that implement the interface decide which class to instantiate. It is a creational pattern.
	Player Feedback: Feedback Information Bubble 3 Text: The bridge pattern is correct!	Answer Option Button 4 Text: Singleton pattern Hint Information Box 4 Evaluation: incorrect Player Feedback: Feedback Information Bubble 4	
	Feedback Information Bubble 4 Text: Sorry—the correct answer is the bridge pattern.		Hint Information Box 4 Text: The Singleton pattern that restricts the instantiation of a class to only one object. It is a creational pattern.
Timers	None		

(*Continued*)

Game Play Interactions (normal flow of events)	Note: Challenge 1 (a multiple choice quiz) is presented.

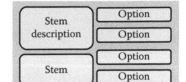

Start Challenge 1
Play Challenge 1
Present question and answers
FADE IN stem description, stem question, and answers as a QUICK EFFECT

Player displays hint
If the player moves the mouse over an answer option, display the hint.

If the player moves the mouse away from an answer, remove the hint from the display.

Players' answers
FADE OUT stem description, stem question, and answers as a QUICK EFFECT

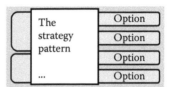

Evaluate answers
Answer option 1: no change
Answer option 2: add 500 points for the player
Answer option 3: no change
Answer option 4: no change

Present player feedback
If answer option is 1, 2, 3, or 4, then display the feedback for a MODERATE amount of time.
End Challenge 1

Note: At the end of the challenge, the game needs to remove the visual setting from the display.

Alternate flow of events — If an error occurs, then end the game.

CHAPTER 4

A Gameful Approach to Teaching Software Design and Software Testing*

Swapneel Sheth, Jonathan Bell, and Gail Kaiser

CONTENTS

4.1	Introduction	92
4.2	Background and Motivation	93
	4.2.1 Student Software Testing	93
	4.2.2 HALO Software Engineering	94
	4.2.3 Software Design	95
4.3	Gameful Testing Using HALO	95
	4.3.1 HALO Plug-In for Eclipse	95
	4.3.2 COMS 1007—Object-Oriented Programming and Design with Java	96
	4.3.3 A Case Study with HALO	97
	4.3.3.1 An Assignment on Java Networking: Getting and Analyzing Data from the Internet—The CIA World Factbook	97

---

* This chapter is based on an earlier work "Secret Ninja testing with HALO software engineering," in *Proceedings of the 4th International Workshop on Social Software Engineering*, 2011. Copyright ACM, 2011. http://doi.acm.org/10.1145/2024645.2024657; A competitive-collaborative approach for introducing software engineering in a CS2 class, in *26th IEEE Conference on Software Engineering Education and Training*, 2013. Copyright IEEE, 2013. http://dx.doi.org/10.1109/CSEET.2013.6595235.

4.3.3.2   HALO Quests   98
4.3.3.3   Student-Created HALO Quests   99
4.4   Better Software Design via a Battleship Tournament   101
4.5   Feedback and Retrospectives   105
    4.5.1   Student Feedback   105
    4.5.2   Thoughts on CS Education a Year Later   107
        4.5.2.1   Reflections on HALO   107
        4.5.2.2   Reflections on Tournaments   108
4.6   Related Work   108
4.7   Conclusion   110
Acknowledgments   110
References   111

4.1 INTRODUCTION

Introductory computer science courses traditionally focus on exposing students to basic programming and computer science theory, leaving little or no time to teach students about software testing [1,2,3]. A great deal of students' mental model when they start learning programming is that "if it compiles and runs without crashing, it must work fine." Thus, exposure to testing, even at a very basic level, can be very beneficial to the students [4,5]. In the short term, they will do better on their assignments as testing before submission might help them discover bugs in their implementation that they had not realized. In the long term, they will appreciate the importance of testing as part of the software development life cycle.

However, testing can be tedious and boring, especially for students who just want their programs to work. Although there have been a number of approaches to bring testing to students early in the curriculum [3,4,5], there have been significant setbacks due to low student engagement and interest in testing [1]. Past efforts to teach students the introductory testing practices have focused on formal testing practices, including approaches using test-driven development [1,4].

Kiniry and Zimmerman [6] propose a different approach to teaching another topic that students are often uninterested in—formal methods for verification. Their approach, which they call *secret ninja formal methods*, aims to teach students formal methods without their realizing it (in a sneaky way). We combine this *secret ninja* methodology with a social environment and apply it to testing in order to expose students to testing while avoiding any negative preconceptions about it.

We propose a social approach to expose students to software testing using our game-like environment Highly Addictive, sociaLly Optimized (HALO) software engineering [7]. HALO uses massively multiplayer online role-playing game (MMORPG) motifs to create an engaging and collaborative development environment. It can make the software development process and, in particular, the testing process more fun and social by using themes from popular computer games such as *World of Warcraft* [8]. By hiding testing behind a short story and a series of quests, HALO shields students from discovering that they are learning testing practices. We feel that the engaging and social nature of HALO will make it easier to expose students to software testing at an early stage. We believe that this approach can encourage a solid foundation of testing habits, leading to future willingness to test in both coursework and industry.

In addition to testing, we also want to inculcate good software design principles in early CS classes. We used a competitive tournament for this purpose—participation in the tournament for the students would be contingent upon their following good software design principles for their assignment. We describe our experiences on using these approaches in a CS2 class taught by the first author at Columbia University.

4.2 BACKGROUND AND MOTIVATION

4.2.1 Student Software Testing

We have anecdotally observed many occasions in which students do not sufficiently test their assignments prior to submission and conducted a brief study to support our observations. We looked at a sampling of student performance in the second-level computer science course at Columbia University, COMS 1007: Object Oriented Programming and Design in Java during the summer of 2008. This course focuses on honing design and problem-solving skills, building upon students' existing base of Java programming knowledge. The assignments are not typically intended to be difficult to get to "work"—the intention is to encourage students to use proper coding practices.

With its design-oriented nature, we believe that this course presents an ideal opportunity to demonstrate students' testing habits. Our assumption is that in this class, students who were missing (or had incorrect) functionality did so by accident (and did not test for it) rather than due to technical inability to implement the assignment. We reviewed the aggregate performance of the class (15 students) across four assignments to gauge the opportunities for better testing.

We found that 33% of the students had at least one "major" functionality flaw (defined as omitting a major requirement from the assignment) and over 85% of all students had multiple "minor" functionality flaws (defined as omitting individual parts of requirements from assignments) in at least one assignment. We believe that this data shows that students were not testing appropriately and suggests that student performance could increase from a greater focus on testing. Similar student testing habits have also been observed at other institutions [9].

4.2.2 HALO Software Engineering

HALO software engineering represents a new and social approach to software engineering. Using various engaging and addictive properties of collaborative computer games such as *World of Warcraft* [7], HALO's goal is to make all aspects of software engineering more fun, increasing developer productivity and satisfaction. It represents software engineering tasks as *quests* and uses a storyline to bind multiple quests together—users must complete quests in order to advance the plot. Quests can be either individual, requiring a developer to work alone, or group, requiring a developer to form a team and work collaboratively toward their objective.

This approach follows a growing trend to "gamify" everyday life (i.e., bring gamelike qualities to it) and has been popularized by alternate reality game proponents such as Jane McGonigal [10]. These engaging qualities can be found in even the simplest games, from chess to *Tetris*, and result in deep levels of player immersion [10]. Gamification has also been studied in education, where teachers use the engaging properties of games to help students focus [11].

We leverage the inherently competitive–collaborative nature of software engineering in HALO by providing developers with social rewards. These social rewards harness operant conditioning—a model that rewards players for good behavior and encourages repeat behavior. Operant conditioning is a technique commonly harnessed in games to retain players [12,13]. Multiuser games typically use peer recognition as the highest reward for successful players [13].

Simple social rewards in HALO can include titles—prefixes or suffixes for players' names—and levels, both of which showcase players' successes in the game world. For instance, a developer who successfully closes over 500 bugs may receive the suffix *The Bugslayer*. For completing quests, players also receive experience points that accumulate, causing them to *level up* in recognition of their ongoing work. HALO is also designed to create an immersive environment that helps developers to achieve a flow state, a technique that has been found to lead to increased engagement and addiction [14]. Although typically viewed as negative behavior, controlled addiction can be beneficial, when the behavior is productive, as in the case of software testing addiction. These methods try to motivate players similar to what is suggested in Reference [15].

4.2.3 Software Design

In our experience, students in early computer science classes do not understand or appreciate software design. We believe that this is largely because all the early programming they have done focuses on "getting it working." Further, typical early CS assignments are a few hundred lines of Java code. Finally, most introductory CS courses at Columbia University (and other universities [16]) typically have only individual assignments and allow no collaboration on the assignments. When programs become larger and when you have to work in large teams, software design becomes a lot more critical.

Our goal was to inculcate good software design principles via a competitive tournament where participation would be contingent based on the students' code adhering to good design principles.

4.3 GAMEFUL TESTING USING HALO

As we have found that students do not test as thoroughly as they ought to, we use HALO to make software testing more enjoyable and fun. For example, students are given a number of "quests" that they need to complete. These quests are used to disguise standard software testing techniques such as white and black box testing, unit testing, and boundary value analysis. Upon completing these quests, the students get social rewards in the form of achievements, titles, and experience points. They can see how they are doing compared to other students in the class. Although the students think that they are competing just for points and achievements, the primary benefit of such a system is that the students' code gets tested a lot better than it normally would have. Our current prototype implementation of HALO is a plug-in for Eclipse and a screenshot is shown in Figure 4.1.

4.3.1 HALO Plug-In for Eclipse

We used HALO in a class taught at Columbia University: COMS 1007— Object-Oriented Programming and Design with Java. The rest of this section describes some background about the class, how HALO was used, and the results of our case study.

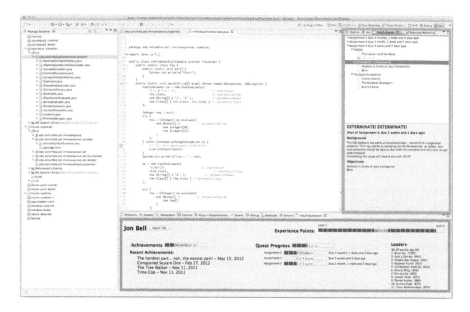

FIGURE 4.1   The HALO eclipse plug-in: The bottom part shows the dashboard, which keeps track of the achievements, experience points, and leaderboards; the top right part shows the quest list and progress.

4.3.2 COMS 1007—Object-Oriented Programming and Design with Java

COMS 1007—Object-Oriented Programming and Design with Java was the second course in the track for CS majors and minors at Columbia University. The class was also required for majors in several other engineering disciplines, including electrical engineering and industrial engineering, and was used by other students to satisfy their general science or computer science requirement. The first author taught this course in Spring (January–May) 2012.* The course goals were as follows: A rigorous treatment of object-oriented concepts using Java as an example language and Development of sound programming and design skills, problem solving and modeling of real world problems from science, engineering, and economics using the object-oriented paradigm [17]. The prerequisite for the course was familiarity with programming and Java (demonstrated through a successful completion of

---

* The introductory sequence of courses has undergone a change and COMS 1007 has become an honors version of the CS1 course since Fall 2012.

the CS1 course at Columbia or another university, or passing marks on the AP Computer Science Exam).

In Spring 2012, the class enrolment was 129, which consisted largely of freshmen and sophomores (first- and second-year undergraduates, respectively). The list of topics covered was object-oriented design, design patterns, interfaces, graphics programming, inheritance and abstract classes, networking, and multithreading and synchronization. There were five roughly biweekly assignments, which contained both theory and programming, one midterm exam, and one final exam.

As explained above, HALO uses gamelike elements and motifs from popular games such as *World of Warcraft* [8] to make the whole software engineering process and, in particular, the software testing process more engaging and social. HALO is not a game; it leverages game mechanics and applies them to the software development process. We now describe how we used HALO in our class.

4.3.3 A Case Study with HALO

In this class, we used HALO for three assignments. In the first two cases, HALO was not a required part of the assignment; students could optionally use it if they wanted to. For the last case, students could earn extra credit (10 points for the assignment, accounting for 0.8% of the overall course grade) by completing the HALO quests.

The final course assignment allowed students to design their own projects, making it difficult for us to predefine HALO quests, because each project was different. Instead, students were offered extra credit in exchange for creating HALO quests for their projects, thus emphasizing the *learning by example* pedagogy. Out of the 124 students who submitted Assignment 5, 77 students (62.1%) attempted the extra credit, and 71 out of these 77 students (92.21%) got a perfect score for the HALO quests that they had created.

4.3.3.1 An Assignment on Java Networking: Getting and Analyzing Data from the Internet—The CIA World Factbook

We now describe an assignment that was given to the class and the HALO quests that were created for it. The rest of the assignments and the quests are described in our technical report [18].

The Central Intelligence Agency (CIA) has an excellent collection of detailed information about each country in the world, called the CIA *World Factbook*. For this assignment, students had to write a program in Java to analyze data from the CIA *World Factbook* website, interacting directly with the website. The student programs had to interactively answer questions such as the following:

1. List countries in *South America* that are prone to *earthquakes*.

2. Find the country with the lowest elevation point in *Europe*.

3. List all countries in the *southeastern* hemisphere.

4. List all countries in *Asia* with more than *10* political parties.

5. Find all countries that have the color *blue* in their flag.

6. Find the top *five* countries with the highest electricity consumption per capita (electricity consumption as a percentage of population).

7. Find countries that are entirely landlocked by a single country.

   For the italicized parts in the above list, the code had to be able to deal with any similar input (e.g., from a user). This should not be hard coded.

4.3.3.2 HALO Quests
We now describe the HALO quests that we used for the above assignment.

1. *TARDIS*—To interact with the CIA *World Factbook*, it would be nice to have a TARDIS. No, not like in the show, but a Java program that can transfer and read data from Internet sites. Completing this quest will reward you with 30 experience points (XP). This quest has two tasks:

   a. *New Earth*—This will probably be your first program that talks to the Internet. Although this is not as complex as creating a new Earth, you should test out the basic functionality to make sure it works. Can your program read one page correctly? Can it read multiple pages? Can it read all of them?

   b. *The Unicorn and the Wasp*—Just like Agatha Christie, you should be able to sift through all the information and find the important things. Are you able to filter information from the web page to get only the relevant data?

2. *EXTERMINATE! EXTERMINATE!*—The CIA Factbook has some unstructured data—not all of it is organized properly. This may not be as annoying (or life threatening) as Daleks, but your programs should

be able to deal with this correctly and not crash (or get exterminated). Completing this quest will reward you with 30 XP and unlock Achievement: Torchwood. This quest has two tasks:

a. *Partners in Crime or Your Companion*—You can get help for parsing through the HTML stuff—you could do it yourself, you could use regular expressions, or you could use an external HTML parsing library. Regardless of who your partner in crime is, are you sure that it is working as expected and not accidentally removing or keeping information that you would or would not need, respectively?

b. *Blink*—Your program does not need to be afraid of the Angels and can blink, that is, take longer than a few seconds to run and get all the information. However, this should not be too long, say 1 hour. Does your program run in a reasonable amount of time?

3. *The Sonic Screwdriver*—This is a useful tool used by the Doctor to make life a little bit easier. Does your code make it easy for you to answer the required questions? Completing this quest will reward you with 40 XP. This quest has three tasks:

a. *Human Nature*—It might be human nature to hard code certain pieces of information in your code. However, your code needs to be generic enough to substitute the italicized parts of the questions. Is this possible?

b. *The Sontaran Stratagem*—For some of the questions, you do not need a clever strategy (or algorithm). However, for some of the latter questions, you do. Do you have a good code strategy to deal with these?

c. *Amy's Choice*—You have a choice of two wild card questions. Did you come up with an interesting question and answer it?

4.3.3.3 Student-Created HALO Quests

We now describe one of the HALO quests that some students created for their own project. This highlights that students understood the basics of software testing, which was the goal with HALO. We include a short description of the project (quoted from student assignment submissions) along with the quests, because students could define their own project.

4.3.3.3.1 Drawsome Golf   Drawsome Golf is a multiplayer miniature golf simulator where users draw their own holes. After the hole is drawn, users take turns putting the ball toward the hole, avoiding the obstacles in their path. The person who can get into the hole in the lowest amount of strokes is the winner. There are four tasks to complete for the quest for Drawsome Golf:

1. Perfectly Framed (Task): Is the panel for the hole situated on the frame? Is there any discrepancy between where you click and what shows up on the screen? Is the information bar causing problems?

2. Win, Lose, or Draw (Task): Are you able to draw lines and water? Are you able to place the hole and the tee box? Can you add multiple lines and multiple ponds? Could you add a new type of line?

3. Like a Rolling Stone (Task): Does the ball move where it is supposed to? Do you have a good formula for realistic motion of the ball?

4. When We Collide (Task): Does the ball handle collisions correctly? Is the behavior correct when the ball hits a line, a wall, the hole, or a water hazard?

4.3.3.3.2 Matrix Code Encoder/Decoder   The user will select a text file that he or she would like to encode or decode and will select the alphabet and numerical key for use. Encoded messages can be sent to a designated user using the networking principles we have learned in class.

1. I'll Handel It: Are your classes passing each other the correct information? Make sure there is no overlap between the calculations performed by one class and those of another. Are variables updated correctly to reflect user input?

2. Liszt Iterators: During the matrix multiplication process, it is necessary to keep track of several iterators simultaneously. Is each of these iterators incrementing and/or resetting at appropriate moments? Does each one accomplish a specific task?

3. What are you Haydn? Encapsulation is key! Encapsulation makes it much easier to understand code and to make changes later on. Have you broken tasks into subtasks, each united by a mini-goal? How can you break up the encoding and decoding methods? Can you break the GUI into bite-sized pieces?

4.4 BETTER SOFTWARE DESIGN VIA A BATTLESHIP TOURNAMENT

The second assignment for the class focused on design principles and, in particular, using interfaces in Java. For the assignment, which constituted 8% of the overall course grade, the students had to implement a battleship game. Battleship is a two-player board game where each player has a 10 × 10 grid to place five ships of different lengths at the start of the game. Each player's grid is not visible to the other player, and the player needs to guess the location of the other player's ships. Thus, by alternating turns, each player calls out "shots," which are grid locations for the other player. If a ship is present at that location, the player says "hit"; else it is a "miss." The game ends when one of the players has hit all the parts of all the opponent's ships.

The students needed to implement this game in Java with an emphasis on good design and none on the graphical aspects; the students could create any sort of user interface they wanted—a simple command line–based user interface would suffice as far as the assignment was concerned. To emphasize good design, we provided the students with three interfaces as a starting-off point for the assignment. The three interfaces, Game, Location, and Player, are shown in Listings 1.1, 1.2, and 1.3.

To reinforce the notion of "programming to an interface, not to an implementation" [19], there was a tournament after the assignment submission deadline. For the tournament, the teaching staff would provide implementations of the Game and Location interfaces and use each student's Player implementation. (In particular, the students were told to provide two implementations of the Player—a human player who is interactive and can ask the user for input and a computer player that can play automatically; this latter player would be used for the tournament.) As long as the students' code respected the interfaces, they would be able to take part in the tournament.

The tournament logistics were as follows. First, all student players played 1000 games against a simple AI written by the teaching staff. From these results, we seeded a single-elimination bracket for the student players to compete directly. Thus, players with good strategies would progress through the rounds and defeat players with weaker strategies. As an added extra incentive, there were extra credit points awarded to students based on how well they performed in the tournament.

Even though the extra credit was not a lot (accounting for only 0.8% of the total course grade), the combination of the extra credit and the competitive aspect made almost the entire class participate in the tournament.

116 out of 129 students (89.92%) of the class elected to take part in the tournament, and of those that wanted to be in the tournament, 107 (92.24%) had implementations that functioned well enough (e.g., did not crash) and competed in the tournament.

Listing 1.1: The Game Interface

```
1 /**
2  * The game interface - this will control the
   Battleship game.
3  * It will keep track of 2 versions of the "board"
   - one for each player.
4  * It will let players take turns.
5  * It will announce hits, misses, and ships sunk
   (by calling the appropriate methods in the Player
   interface/class).
6  * @author swapneel
7  *
8  */
9 public interface Game {
10
11        int SIZE = 10;
12
13        int CARRIER = 5;
14        int BATTLESHIP = 4;
15        int SUBMARINE = 3;
16        int CRUISER = 3;
17        int DESTROYER = 2;
18
19        /**
20         * This method will initialize the game.
21         * At the end of this method, the board has
            been set up and the game can be started
22         * @param p1 Player 1
23         * @param p2 Player 2
24         */
25        void initialize(Player p1, Player p2);
26
27        /**
28         * This is the start point of playing the game.
29         * The game will alternate between the players
            letting them take shots at the other team.
```

```
30          * @return Player who won
31          */
32          Player playGame();
33}
```

Listing 1.2: The Location Interface

```
1  /**
2   * The Location interface to specify how x and y
     coordinates are represented.
3   * This can be used to represent the location of a
     ship or a shot.
4   * If the location is a shot, the isShipHorizontal()
     method can return an arbitrary value.
5   * @author swapneel
6   *
7   */
8  public interface Location {
9
10          /**
11          * Gets the x coordinate
12          * @return the x coordinate
13          */
14          int getX ();
15
16          /**
17          * Gets the y coordinate
18          * @return the y coordinate
19          */
20          int getY ();
21
22          /**
23          * This method will indicate whether the ship
               is horizontal or vertical.
24          * Can return an arbitrary value if the location
               is used to indicate a shot (and not a ship)
25          * @return true if ship is horizontal, false
               otherwise
26          */
27          boolean isShipHorizontal ();
28
29}
```

Listing 1.3: The Player Interface

```
1 /**
2  * The Player interface
3  * Each player will get to choose where to place the 5
   ships and how to take turns shooting at enemy ships
4  * @author swapneel
5  *
6  */
7 public interface Player {
8
9         /**
10         * This method will place a ship on the grid.
11         * This method should guarantee correctness of
           location (no overlaps, no ships over the edge
           of the board, etc.)
12         * @param size the size of the ship to place
13         * @param retry if an earlier call to this method
           returned an invalid position, this method will
           be called again with retry set to true.
14         * @return The Location of the ship
15         */
16        Location placeShip (int size, boolean retry);
17
18        /**
19         * This method will get the new target to aim
   for
20         * @return The Location of the target
21         */
22        Location getTarget ();
23
24        /**
25         * This method will notify the Player of the
           result of the previous shot
26         * @param hit true, if it was a hit; false
           otherwise
27         * @param sunk true, if a ship is sunk; false
           otherwise
28         */
29        void setResult (boolean hit, boolean sunk);
30
31}
```

4.5 FEEDBACK AND RETROSPECTIVES

In this section, we describe the feedback about the course structure given by the students and our thoughts and retrospectives on using gameful approaches for CS education.

4.5.1 Student Feedback

The student feedback comes from various sources such as midterm and end of semester surveys, public reviews of the class, and e-mail sent to the first author.

HALO received mixed reviews—many students found that it was very useful; other students found that it was not beneficial. Figure 4.2 shows the students' reasons on why HALO was beneficial. Figure 4.3 shows why students thought that it was not beneficial. The main take-away for us with HALO was the following: because it was either completely optional or only for extra credit, typically only students who are doing really well in the class will use it. Students who are having a hard time in the class will not want to do something that is optional. In an analogous manner, students will only do the extra credit if they have managed to complete the assignment early enough and sufficiently well. Thus, HALO quests needed to be more oriented toward the students

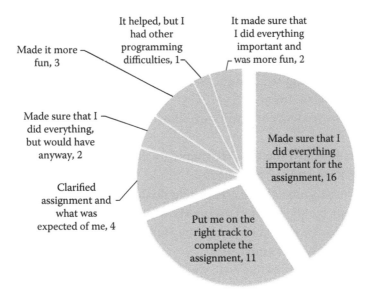

FIGURE 4.2   Reasons why HALO helped students ($n = 39$).

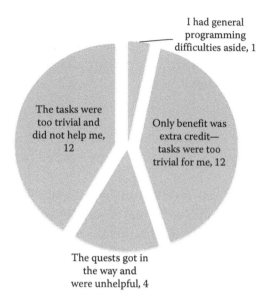

FIGURE 4.3   Reasons why HALO was not beneficial to students ($n = 29$).

doing well in the assignment. However, HALO quests need to entice the struggling students as they might benefit the most by being able to complete the basic tasks of the assignment. Ideally, we would like to have some adaptability or dynamic nature of the quests where the difficulty of the quests will self-adjust based on what the students would find it most useful for. For example, students who are struggling with the assignment might want quests for very basic things, whereas students who are doing well might want quests for the more challenging aspects of the assignment.

Some of the student comments are shown below:

- I really liked the class tournaments. If only there was a way to make them like mandatory.
- The assignments are completely doable, and he helps us with them by giving us Halo quests which provide a checklist of things one should be doing (they're themed, so the last one was Doctor Who themed!).
- I think it's awesome that you're sneaking your taste in music into the HALO quests. The Coldplay references are hilarious. PLEASE make every HALO quest music-themed. It keeps me awake and happy as I do my homework.

4.5.2 Thoughts on CS Education a Year Later

Our experience with using gameful elements in a classroom has been largely positive. The first author taught COMS 1007 again, which is now an honors CS1 class, in spring 2013. For that semester, we made a few changes based on our experiences from the previous year. We now describe our decisions and rationale behind these changes.

4.5.2.1 Reflections on HALO

First, we decided not to use HALO in the class. Our decision was largely based on two aspects: resource constraints and research challenges.

4.5.2.1.1 Constraints   The second author developed the HALO eclipse plug-in and helped students set it up during the first iteration of COMS 1007. For use in future semesters, the plug-in would need to be updated and maintained. Creating student accounts and having them install and use the plug-in is straightforward albeit very time consuming, especially for a class with over 100 students. Note that the students in our classes are typically freshmen and sophomores with very little experience with Java and Eclipse. One option would be to get an extra TA, if possible, for future courses if we want to use HALO.

4.5.2.1.2 Assignment and Quest Design   A big advantage with HALO is that there are no constraints with assignment creation and design. However, there are a few implications as far as quest design is concerned. First, creating good and fun quests takes a significant amount of time. In our experience, quest creation took about 30% of the time that it takes to create an assignment. In other words, creating quests for three to four assignments is about the same time as creating an entire new assignment. This needs to be factored in with the other time constraints that an instructor might have. Second, quest creation is much easier and faster if the same person creates both the assignment and the quests for it. In our case, there were a few assignments that were designed or conceived by TAs, and unfortunately, they could not create the quests themselves as they had not taken a software engineering or software testing class yet. This meant that quest creation had to be done by the first author, and hence needed much more time.

4.5.2.1.3 Adaptive Quests   As the student feedback shows, we need HALO quests that can target *both*, struggling students and students who are doing well. One option would be to create specific sets of quests for the different target demographics. This is not an ideal option however; we would need to spend much time on quest creation. Further, unless this particular assignment has been used in previous classes, it might be hard to know *a priori* what parts of it will be easy and what parts will be difficult, thereby making it challenging to design appropriate quests. In our experience, instructor and student opinions on the ease or difficulty of assignments do not always converge. The better option would be to have some way of automatically "scaling" the difficulty of quests, but we are not completely sure of what this entails and much more research is required on this topic.

4.5.2.2 Reflections on Tournaments

Second, we continued using the tournament structure for encouraging students to use good design. The tournament required significant resources as well. Because we had over 100 students who would participate in the tournament, the second author wrote a generic framework that would take all the student code and create and run the tournament as described above. Automating the entire process certainly was essential as it helped save a lot of time and the code could be reused for future tournaments. In spite of being able to reuse this for the Spring 2013 semester, a significant amount of additional time and effort was still needed. The first reason was to create the game framework and tournament AI for the students to compete against. We could not reuse this as we changed the assignment to use Othello instead of Battleship. The second reason was actually running the tournament—we ran 1000 games for each student in the first round. The official timeout policy was 1 minute per game, that is, if the game took longer than 1 minute to complete, the player would be disqualified. Using a very conservative estimate that each game takes 1 second to run, we would still need roughly 28 CPU hours to run just the first round for 100 students. Typically, we try to release homework grades 1 week after homework is due. If a tournament is to be run, these numbers need to factor into time and resource allocation constraints for the class, instructor, and TAs.

4.6 RELATED WORK

There has been ongoing work in studying how best to teach students testing. Jones [3,5] proposed integrating software testing across all computer science courses and suggested splitting different components of testing across different courses, teaching aspects incrementally so as not to overwhelm students all at once with testing. Edwards [4] proposed a *test first* software engineering curriculum, applying test-driven development to all programming assignments, requiring students to submit complete test cases with each of their assignments. Our approach is similar to these in that we also propose early and broad exposure to testing.

Goldwasser proposed a highly social, competitive means to integrate software testing where students provided test cases that were used in each other's code [20]. Elbaum et al. [1] presented Bug Hunt—a tool to teach software testing in a self-paced, web-driven environment. With Bug Hunt, students progress through a set of predefined lessons, creating test cases for sample code. Both of these approaches introduce testing directly into the curriculum; with HALO, we aim to introduce testing surreptitiously.

Kiniry and Zimmerman [6] proposed teaching formal verification through *secret ninja formal methods*—an approach that avoids students' apprehension to use complex mathematics by hiding it from them. The secret ninja approach differs from those mentioned earlier in that it exposes students to new areas without them realizing it. They implemented this technique at multiple institutions, receiving positive student responses (based on qualitative evaluations). We adapted their *secret ninja* method for HALO.

Much work has also been done to create games to teach software engineering concepts. Horning and Wortman [21] created Software Hut, turning the course project itself into a game, played out by all of the students together. SimSE and card game were games created to teach students software engineering through a game environment [22,23]. Eagle and Barnes [24] introduced a game to help students learn basic programming techniques: basic loops, arrays, and nested for loops. However, none of these games focused specifically on testing practices. There has been research into teaching aspects such as global software development [25] in a classroom, but these do not focus on software testing.

TankBrains [26] is a collaborative and competitive game used in a CS course where students competed to develop better AIs. Bug Wars [27] is a classroom exercise where students seed bugs in code, swap examples, and compete to find the most bugs (in each other's code). Although TankBrains and Bug Wars are specific programming activities, we present a general approach to teaching introductory computer science that is both cooperative and competitive.

There have been several approaches toward integrating games into CS curricula. One of the earliest such attempts was Software Hut, where the authors formulated their project-based software engineering course as a game [21]. Groups competed to be the most "profitable"—where performance was tracked by "program engineering dollars" (a fictional currency). This technique is similar to ours in that we both tracked student performance with points and added in other game concepts, such as quests and achievements. KommGame is an interface that encapsulates many collaborative software development activities such as creating documentation or reporting and resolving bugs and tracks each student with karma points [28]. This social and collaborative environment represented real-world open-source development environments.

SimSE [23] and *Problems and Programmers* [22] are two simulation-oriented games that give students a "real-world" software engineering experience. Somewhat similar, *Wu's Castle* [24] is a game to teach students basic programming constructs such as loops. These three projects are games, whereas we have built a game layer on top of the regular course environment.

4.7 CONCLUSION

In this chapter, we described how we incorporated gameful elements for teaching software testing and software design in a CS2 class. Students learnt software testing using a social learning environment. We described our HALO prototype, an assignment, and the accompanying quests for HALO to enhance teaching of software testing in a CS2 class. Students learnt software design via a competitive tournament, and we described details of our assignment and on how the tournament was run. The feedback from the students for both these aspects was largely positive.

We believe that our approach will make testing and design more engaging and fun for students, leading to better systems. We also feel that this will inculcate good software engineering habits at an early stage.

ACKNOWLEDGMENTS

We thank Joey J. Lee of Teachers College's Games Research Lab and Jessica Hammer of Carnegie Mellon University's Human-Computer Interaction Institute, for their assistance with the pedagogical aspects of this work. We thank all the students who participated in the COMS 1007 class. We thank the teaching assistants, Lakshya Bhagat, Amrita Mazumdar, Paul Palen, Laura Willson, and Don Yu, for helping with the class.

The authors are members of the Programming Systems Laboratory (PSL) at Columbia University. PSL is funded in part by NSF CCF-1302269, NSF CCF-1161079, NSF CNS-0905246, and NIH U54 CA121852.

REFERENCES

1. Sebastian Elbaum, Suzette Person, Jon Dokulil, and Matt Jorde. Bug hunt: Making early software testing lessons engaging and affordable. *Proceedings of the 29th International Conference on Software Engineering*, pp. 688–697, IEEE Computer Society, Washington, DC, 2007.

2. Ursula Jackson, Bill Z. Manaris, and Renée A. McCauley. Strategies for effective integration of software engineering concepts and techniques into the undergraduate computer science curriculum. *Proceedings of the 28th SIGCSE Technical Symposium on Computer Science Education*, pp. 360–364, ACM, New York, 1997.

3. Edward L. Jones. Integrating testing into the curriculum arsenic in small doses. *SIGCSE Bulletin*, 33:337–341, 2001.

4. Stephen H. Edwards. Rethinking computer science education from a test-first perspective. *Companion of the 18th Annual ACM SIGPLAN Conference on Object-Oriented Programming, Systems, Languages, and Applications*, pp. 148–155, ACM, New York, 2003.

5. Edward L. Jones. An experiential approach to incorporating software testing into the computer science curriculum. In *Proceedings of the 31st Annual Frontiers in Education Conference*, vol. 2, pp. F3D-7–F3D-11, IEEE Computer Society, Washington, DC, 2001.

6. Joseph R. Kiniry and Daniel M. Zimmerman. Secret ninja formal methods. *Proceedings of the 15th International Symposium on Formal Methods*, pp. 214–228, Springer-Verlag, Berlin, Germany, 2008.

7. Swapneel Sheth, Jonathan Bell, and Gail Kaiser. HALO (Highly Addictive, sociaLly Optimized) software engineering. *Proceedings of the 1st International Workshop on Games and Software Engineering*, pp. 29–32, ACM, New York, 2011.

8. Blizzard Entertainment. *World of Warcraft*. http://us.battle.net/wow/en.

9. David Ginat, Owen Astrachan, Daniel D. Garcia, and Mark Guzdial. "But it looks right!": The bugs students don't see. *Proceedings of the 35th SIGCSE Technical Symposium on Computer Science Education*, pp. 284–285, ACM, New York, 2004.

10. Jane McGonigal. *Reality Is Broken: Why Games Make Us Better and How They Can Change the World*. Penguin Press, New York, 2011.

11. Joey J. Lee and Jessica Hammer. Gamification in education: What, how, why bother? *Academic Exchange Quarterly*, 15(2):2, 2011.

12. John P. Charlton and Ian D.W. Danforth. Distinguishing addiction and high engagement in the context of online game playing. *Computers in Human Behavior*, 23(3):1531–1548, 2007.

13. Patricia Wallace. *The Psychology of the Internet*. Cambridge University Press, New York, 2001.

14. SungBok Park and Ha Hwang. Understanding online game addiction: Connection between presence and flow. In *Human-Computer Interaction. Interacting in Various Application Domains, Lecture Notes in Computer Science*, vol. 5613, pp. 378–386, Springer, Berlin, Germany, 2009.

15. Tracy Hall, Helen Sharp, Sarah Beecham, Nathan Baddoo, and Hugh Robinson. What do we know about developer motivation? *IEEE Software*, 25(4):92–94, 2008.

16. Laurie Williams and Lucas Layman. Lab partners: If they're good enough for the natural sciences, why aren't they good enough for us? *Proceedings of the 20th Conference on Software Engineering Education & Training*, pp. 72–82, 2007.

17. Columbia Engineering—The Fu Foundation School of Engineering and Applied Science. Bulletin 2011–2012. http://bulletin.engineering.columbia.edu/files/seasbulletin/2011Bulletin.pdf, 2011.

18. Swapneel Sheth, Jonathan Bell, and Gail Kaiser. A gameful approach to teaching software design and software testing—Assignments and quests. Technical Report cucs-030-13, Department of Computer Science, Columbia University, New York, 2013. http://mice.cs.columbia.edu/getTechreport.php?techreportID=1557.

19. Erich Gamma, Richard Helm, Ralph Johnson, and John Vlissides. *Design Patterns: Elements of Reusable Object-Oriented Design*, Addison-Wesley, 1995.

20. Michael H. Goldwasser. A gimmick to integrate software testing throughout the curriculum. *SIGCSE Bulletin*, 34:271–275, 2002.

21. James (Jim) Horning and David B. Wortman. Software hut: A computer program engineering project in the form of a game. *IEEE Transactions on Software Engineering*, 3(4):325–330, 1977.

22. Alex Baker, Emily Oh Navarro, and André van der Hoek. An experimental card game for teaching software engineering processes. *Journal of Systems and Software*, 75(1/2):3–16, 2005.

23. Emily Oh Navarro and André van der Hoek. SimSE: An educational simulation game for teaching the software engineering process. *Proceedings of the 9th Annual SIGCSE Conference on Innovation and Technology in CS Education*, Leeds, UK, p. 233, 2004.

24. Michael Eagle and Tiffany Barnes. Experimental evaluation of an educational game for improved learning in introductory computing. *SIGCSE Bulletin*, 41:321–325, 2009.

25. Ita Richardson, Sarah Moore, Daniel Paulish, Valentine Casey, and Dolores Zage. Globalizing software development in the local classroom. *Proceedings of the 20th Conference on Software Engineering Education Training*, pp. 64–71, July 2007.

26. Kevin Bierre, Phil Ventura, Andrew Phelps, and Christopher Egert. Motivating OOP by blowing things up: An exercise in cooperation and competition in an introductory Java programming course. In *Proceedings of the 37th SIGCSE Technical Symposium on Computer Science Education*, pp. 354–358, 2006.

27. Renee Bryce. Bug Wars: A competitive exercise to find bugs in code. *Journal of Computing Sciences in Colleges*, 27(2):43–50, 2011.

28. Terhi Kilamo, Imed Hammouda, and Mohamed Amine Chatti. Teaching collaborative software development: A case study. *Proceedings of the 2012 International Conference on Software Engineering*, pp. 1165–1174, 2012.

CHAPTER 5

Educational Software Engineering

Where Software Engineering, Education, and Gaming Meet

Tao Xie, Nikolai Tillmann,
Jonathan de Halleux, and Judith Bishop

CONTENTS

5.1	Introduction	114
5.2	Background: Online Programming Exercise Systems	115
	5.2.1 CodingBat	115
	5.2.2 CloudCoder	117
	5.2.3 Practice-It	117
	5.2.4 CodeLab	118
	5.2.5 Codecademy	118
	5.2.6 BetterProgrammers	119
	5.2.7 Discussion	119
5.3	Pex4Fun: Gamification of an Online Programming Exercise System	120
	5.3.1 Software Engineering Technologies Underlying Pex4Fun	121
	5.3.2 Gaming in Pex4Fun	122
	5.3.3 Social Dynamics in Pex4Fun	123
	5.3.3.1 Ranking of Players and Coding Duels	123
	5.3.3.2 Live Feeds	123
	5.3.4 Educational Usage of Pex4Fun	125
	5.3.5 Code Hunt	126

5.4   Discussion   128
5.5   Conclusion   129
Acknowledgment   130
References   130

5.1 INTRODUCTION

Among various subfields of software engineering, software engineering education [1] has been an important one, focusing on educational topics for software engineering (e.g., how to better teach and train software engineering skills). In general, research work on software engineering education does not appear in research tracks of major software engineering conferences but appears in their education tracks or conferences with focus on software engineering education. For example, the International Conference on Software Engineering (ICSE; http://www.icse-conferences.org) generally has a track on software engineering education. The ACM SIGPLAN Conference on Object-Oriented Programming, Systems, Languages, and Applications has also recently included a colocated Educator's Symposium (http://www.splashcon.org/history). The Conference on Software Engineering Education and Training (http://conferences.computer.org/cseet) has focused on software engineering education and training since 1987. Indeed, research work on software engineering education sometimes also appears in meetings on computer science education, such as the SIGCSE Technical Symposium (http://www.sigcse.org/events/symposia) and the Annual Conference on Innovation and Technology in Computer Science Education (http://www.sigcse.org/events/iticse).

In this chapter, we define and advocate the subfield of educational software engineering (i.e., software engineering for education) within the domain of software engineering research. This subfield develops software engineering technologies (e.g., software testing and analysis [2], software analytics [3,4]) for general educational tasks, going beyond educational tasks for software engineering. For example, general educational tasks can even be on teaching math [5–7]. As an analogy, data mining for software engineering [8] (also called mining software repositories [9]) leverages data mining technologies (which typically come from the data mining community) to address tasks in software engineering, whereas educational software engineering leverages software engineering technologies (which comes usually from the software engineering community) to address tasks in education. In addition, in the solution space, gaming technologies often play an important role together with software engineering technologies.

We expect that researchers in educational software engineering would be among the key players in the education domain and in the coming age of massively open online courses (MOOCs) [10,11], which have recently gained high popularity among various universities and even in global societies. Educational software engineering can and will contribute significant solutions to address various critical challenges in education, especially MOOCs, such as automatic grading [12,13], intelligent tutoring [14], problem generation [5–7], and plagiarism detection [15,16].

To provide a concrete example of educational software engineering, in this chapter,* we first lay out the background on online programming exercise systems by describing a number of existing representative systems. As a concrete example of gamificating an online programming exercise system, we illustrate Pex for Fun [13] (Pex4Fun, for short), which leverages software engineering and gaming technologies to address educational tasks on teaching and learning programming and software engineering skills. In particular, our illustration of Pex4Fun focuses on its underlying software engineering technologies (Section 5.3.1), its gaming (Section 5.3.2), social dynamics (Section 5.3.3), and educational usage (Section 5.3.4), which are the four common aspects of a typical project on educational software engineering. We also describe Code Hunt (Section 5.3.5), which is a recent gaming platform evolved from Pex4Fun.

5.2 BACKGROUND: ONLINE PROGRAMMING EXERCISE SYSTEMS

5.2.1 CodingBat

CodingBat (http://codingbat.com/), created by Nick Parlante, is an online platform for providing a set of programming exercises in Java and Python. Note that some of the exercises in CodingBat are equipped with hint text and/or the solution code. We next use an example (http://codingbat.com/prob/p146974) to illustrate how a student can solve an exercise problem in CodingBat. In this example, the web page for the exercise problem includes a short natural language problem statement: "Given an array of scores, return true if each score is equal or greater than the one before.

---

* This chapter significantly extends a previous short article [31] presented in the *3rd International Workshop on Games and Software Engineering* (2013). This new extension in this chapter primarily includes surveying-related online programming exercise systems (Section 5.2); restructuring and enriching the description of Pex4Fun as an example for gamificating an online programming exercise system, adding the description of Code Hunt (Section 5.3.5), a recent gaming platform evolved from Pex4Fun; and discussing additional more recent related work.

The array will be length 2 or more." In addition, the web page also includes a table for showing a small number of sample expected input/output pairs:

```
scoresIncreasing({1, 3, 4}) → true
scoresIncreasing({1, 3, 2}) → false
scoresIncreasing({1, 1, 4}) → true
```

Then the code editor in the middle of the web page includes an empty method body for `public boolean scoresIncreasing(int[] scores)` (note that when a problem creator creates a problem, the method, such as `scoresIncreasing` in the problem, should return a value). A student who tries to solve the problem is expected to fill in code in the empty method body to solve the given programming problem. After the student fills in code and clicks the Go button, CodingBat displays compilation issues, if any, that are encountered when the code is compiled; otherwise, CodingBat runs a predefined set of test cases (prepared by the problem creator) against the code and reports these test cases being labeled as failing test cases or passing test cases. Note that these test cases are reported in the form of the preceding example expected input/output pairs. Based on the feedback (i.e., the reported test cases and their failing/passing statuses), the student can further attempt to improve his or her code to make all test cases as passing test cases.

Because the predefined set of test cases is visible to the student, the student can "fool" CodingBat by writing code that includes a conditional statement for each reported test case so that the conditional in the conditional statement checks whether the method arguments are the same as the input in a reported test case and then the true branch of the conditional statement simply returns the expected output in the reported test case. Apparently, the code written in this way to overfit the reported test cases is not the correct code for the exercise problem. However, CodingBat would still report All Correct because all the predefined test cases are indeed passing test cases.

CodingBat allows the student to view the progress graph for a problem, showing the problem-solving history (e.g., the percentage of passing test cases and percentage of failing test cases) for each version of the code written and submitted by the student for the problem over time. The student can also view graphs from some random users just for fun. A student can earn *code badges* by solving problems across all of the fundamental sections (which include very common code patterns that often come up at coding, such as problems related to strings, arrays, and logic). For example, a student earns a five-star badge when the student solves three problems in each fundamental section. The student can share his or her account with a "teacher" account, from which the associated teacher can view the problem-solving statistics of the student along with the code written by the student for each problem. However, the teacher is not advised to use CodingBat as a grading platform of exams or homework assignments, but is advised to leverage CodingBat as a practice platform for students.

5.2.2 CloudCoder

CloudCoder [17] (http://cloudcoder.org/) and *CodeWrite* [18] (http://code-write.cs.auckland.ac.nz/) are two systems closely related to CodingBat. CloudCoder is an open-source web-based programming exercise system with exercises in C/C++, Java, Python, and Ruby. CloudCoder provides similar mechanisms as CodingBat's for students to solve problems based on the testing results against a predefined set of test cases. However, CodeWrite allows a student to construct an exercise problem along with the test cases for the problem so that other peer students can solve the exercise problem (in the same way as solving an exercise problem in CodingBat or CloudCoder). Note that in CodingBat or CloudCoder, only teachers or platform providers (not students) are supposed to construct exercises.

5.2.3 Practice-It

Practice-It (http://practiceit.cs.washington.edu/) is an online platform for students to practice solving Java programming problems. Many of the problems were drawn from the University of Washington's introductory programming courses. A student can select a problem from the list of problems organized by chapter topics of a programming textbook or section topics of the University of Washington's introductory programming courses. Once granted permission by the platform administrators, users of the platform can also create and upload a problem. If the problem creator defines some constraints for the problem, Practice-It first checks the student's code against such constraints and reports constraint violation errors such as the following: Error: Your solution doesn't meet one or more constraints required by this problem. Your solution must use a static method. (must appear 2 times in your solution). If the student's code does not compile, Practice-It reports repairing hints based on the compilation errors. After the student's code compiles, Practice-It runs a predefined set of test cases (prepared by the problem creator) against the student's code. Then Practice-It reports a table that includes testing information for each test case: the test input, expected output, actual output (produced by the student's code), and result (pass or fail). When the expected output is different from the actual output, the result is fail; the different outcomes of the actual output and the expected output are also reported.

5.2.4 CodeLab

CodeLab (http://www.turingscraft.com/), providing paid access of full exercises to students, is a web-based programming exercise system with exercises in Python, Java, C++, C, JavaScript, C#, VB, and SQL. CodeLab provides short exercises, each of which typically focuses on a programming concept or language construct. Different from other related systems, CodeLab does not report any explicit test cases (i.e., input/output pairs) to a student after the student submits code for a given exercise problem. Instead, CodeLab informs the student whether his or her submitted code is correct (the correctness judgment of the code seems to be based on running a predefined set of test cases, without considering code elegance or efficiency). If incorrect, CodeLab additionally informs the student of repairing hints such as likely locations of faulty code portions and hint sentences, for example, "You almost certainly should be using: /." These repairing hints seem to be identified based on syntactic comparison of the submitted code and the solution code. CodeLab provides no feedback to the student in terms of specific correct (or incorrect) input/output behaviors of the submitted code. CodeLab organizes exercises in a sequence related to a programming concept or language construct (typically 3–10 exercises in a sequence). The exercises included in a sequence are of gradually increasing sophistication. The teacher of a class is suggested to allocate 5%–10% of a student's class grade to be correct completion of the CodeLab exercises. Besides leveraging the existing exercises in CodeLab, a teacher can create additional exercises in CodeLab for his or her class to use.

5.2.5 Codecademy

Codecademy (http://www.codecademy.com/) is an online interactive platform that offers free programming classes in Python, PHP, jQuery, JavaScript, Ruby, HTML, and CSS. In a browser, on the left-hand side, a student is provided short texts that illustrate a programming knowledge point and instructions for the student to carry out a related programming exercise in the online code editor displayed in the middle of the browser.

The instructions also include a hint portion that can be viewable only after the student clicks "Stuck? Get a hint." After the student finishes writing code in the code editor following the instructions and then clicks the button "Save and Submit Code," Codecademy assesses the written code against the instructions (based on checking the outputs of the code against the predefined outputs of the exercise); if the code is incorrect, Codecademy provides a simple hint sentence to the student, such as Did you include two console.log()s in your code? (This hint is based on syntactic differences of the student's code and the solution code.)

Note that, as opposed to programming exercise systems (such as CodingBat) in which code written by students needs to be in the form of a method with non-void return, CodeLab and Codecademy allow code written by students to be just one or multiple lines of code.

5.2.6 BetterProgrammers

BetterProgrammers (http://www.betterprogrammer.com/) is an online platform for Java programmers to solve a sequence of programming tasks with increasing complexities. Instead of focusing on training, the platform focuses on assessing and certifying programmers so that companies can leverage such certification information in interviewing and hiring programmer candidates. The top 50 programmers ranked by the platform are posted on the front page of the platform website. The platform does not provide a rich code editor but just requests programmers to copy the code skeleton embedded with the task description as code comments (from the simple code editor in the platform) to the programmers' favorite Java IDE, finish the programming task, copy the completed code for the task back to the simple code editor in the platform, and submit the completed code. It is unclear how BetterProgrammers checks the correctness of the submitted code. For each programming task, the recommended time and maximum time for task completion are listed along with the elapsed task time in real time.

5.2.7 Discussion

Software engineering technologies underlying the existing online programming exercise systems [19] are typically simple. For example, a simple testing technique (i.e., running a predefined set of test cases against the code submitted by a student to check the code's correctness) is commonly used in these existing systems. Some systems such as Practice-It and CodeLab seem to use lightweight static program analysis to check the code submitted by students against some predefined constraints or against the correct solution code to give the students repairing hints. Gamification does not play an explicit role in designing these existing systems. Some systems provide some social dynamics: a user can view progress graphs from some random users (CodingBat), a user can earn code badges (CodingBat), a user can construct exercise problems for other users to solve (CodeWrite), and users are ranked (BetterProgrammers). All these systems place heavy emphasis on their educational value.

5.3 PEX4FUN: GAMIFICATION OF AN ONLINE PROGRAMMING EXERCISE SYSTEM

In this section, we present Pex4Fun [13] (http://www.pexforfun.com/), an example of gamificating an online programming exercise system based on software engineering technologies. In particular, Pex4Fun is an interactive gaming-based teaching and learning platform for .NET programming languages such as C#, Visual Basic, and F#. Figure 5.1 shows a screen snapshot of the user interface of the Pex4Fun website, which includes an example coding duel to be solved by a player. It is a browser-based teaching and learning environment [20] with target users as teachers, students, and

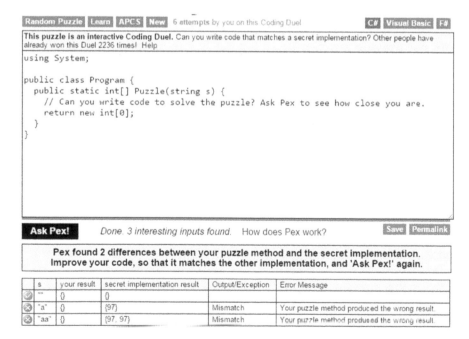

FIGURE 5.1 The user interface of the Pex4Fun website.

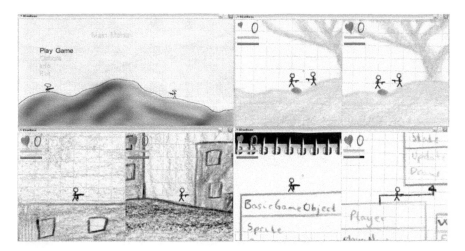

FIGURE 2.1   Screenshots from the *BlueRose* XNA game.

FIGURE 5.4   The main page of the Code Hunt website.

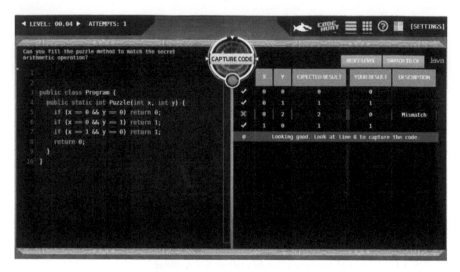

FIGURE 5.6   An example coding duel in Code Hunt.

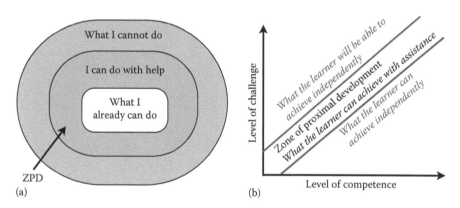

FIGURE 6.1   (a,b) Zone of proximal development can be expanded and changes over time.

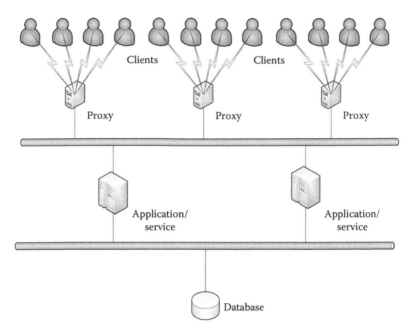

FIGURE 7.1   A tiered architecture.

FIGURE 7.3   Multiplayer jigsaw puzzle with 25 pieces.

FIGURE 8.1 Typical iTron game.

(a)

(b)

FIGURE 8.4 (a) Point-and-shoot interface for the iTESS shotgun weapon and (b) screen display during a shotgun shot animation.

FIGURE 9.1 The AGAD game shows a search question (3), then lets you search for the answer with Google (1). You work through the questions (2) scoring points as you unlock and solve additional questions.

FIGURE 9.2   The movement of the eye on the display is shown by a connected graph. The numbers indicate which fixation, or pause, it represents and the size of the circle represents the duration of the eye fixation at that point. The number 1 is near the bottom right, where the player clicked the button on the previous page.

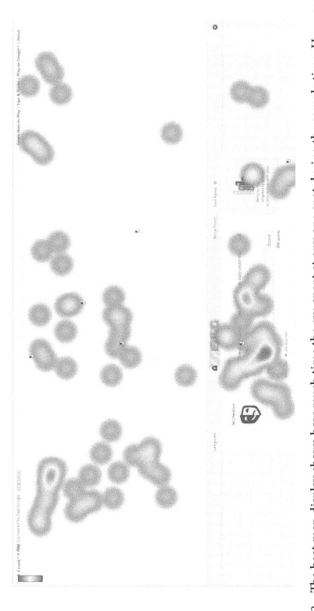

FIGURE 9.3   The heat map display shows how much time the eye spent at any one spot during the sample time. Here we can see the player spent most of the time reading the question (next to the theatrical mask glyph at the bottom and near the top at the search query).

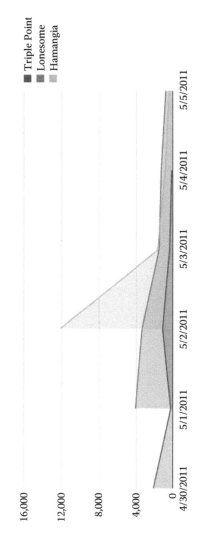

FIGURE 9.4 Tracking data on questions by day. The graph shows player volume for 6 days for three different questions ("Triple Point," "Lonesome," and "Hamangia"). "Triple Point" was introduced on 4/30/2011, yet players kept backing up to that question 4 days later.

even software practitioners. In particular, in a coding duel game, a major game type in Pex4Fun, a student needs to write the code to implement the functionalities of a secret specification (in the form of sample solution code not visible to the student). Based on an automated test generation tool, Pex4Fun finds any discrepancies in behavior between the student's code and the secret specification. Such discrepancies are given as feedback to the student to guide how to fix the student's code to match the behavior of the secret specification.

We next illustrate Pex4Fun by focusing on its underlying software engineering technologies (Section 5.3.1), its gaming (Section 5.3.2), social dynamics (Section 5.3.3), and educational usage (Section 5.3.4), which are the four common aspects of a typical project on educational software engineering. Finally, we describe Code Hunt (Section 5.3.5), which is a recent gaming platform evolved from Pex4Fun.

5.3.1 Software Engineering Technologies Underlying Pex4Fun

Behind the scenes on the server in the cloud, the Pex4Fun website leverages dynamic symbolic execution (DSE) [21] implemented by Pex [22,23], in order to (1) determine whether the code submitted by a student is correct, (2) check the code's correctness and game progress of the player, and (3) compute customized feedback [24]. Pex is an automatic white box test generation tool for .NET. It has been integrated into Microsoft Visual Studio as an add-in. Besides being used in the industry, Pex was also used in classroom teaching at different universities [25].

In particular, DSE [21] is a variation of symbolic execution [26,27] and leverages run-time information from concrete executions. DSE is often conducted in iterations to systematically increase code coverage such as block or branch coverage. In each iteration, DSE executes the program under test with a test input, which can be a default or randomly generated input in the first iteration or an input generated in one of the previous iterations. During the execution of the program under test, DSE performs symbolic execution in parallel to collecting symbolic constraints on program inputs obtained from predicates in branch statements along the execution. Then DSE flips a branching node in the executed path to construct a new path that shares the prefix to the node with the executed path, but then deviates and takes a different branch. Finally, DSE relies on a constraint solver to compute a satisfying assignment (if possible), which forms a new test input whose execution will follow the flipped path.

5.3.2 Gaming in Pex4Fun

The core type of Pex4Fun games is a *coding duel* where the player has to solve a particular programming problem. A coding duel created by a game creator (who could be any user of Pex4Fun) consists of two methods with the same method signature and return type.* One of these two methods is the secret (golden) implementation, which is not visible to the player. The other is the player implementation, which is visible to the player and can be an empty implementation or a faulty implementation of the secret implementation. The player implementation can include optional comments to give the player some hints in order to reduce the difficulty level of gaming.

After a player selects a coding duel game to play, the player's winning goal is to modify the player implementation (visible to the player, shown in the upper part of Figure 5.1) to make its behavior (in terms of the method inputs and results) to be the same as the secret implementation (not visible to the player). Apparently, without any feedback or help, the player has no way to guess how the secret implementation would behave. The player can get some feedback by clicking the button Ask Pex! (shown in the middle-left part of Figure 5.1) to request the following two types of feedback: (1) under what sample method input(s), the player implementation and the secret implementation have the same method result and (2) under what sample method input(s), the player implementation and the secret implementation have different method results. An example feedback is shown in the table near the bottom of Figure 5.1. In the table, the first line prefixed indicates the first type of feedback, and the second and third lines indicate the second type of feedback.

As described in Section 5.3.1, Pex4Fun leverages the underlying test generation engine called Pex [22,23] to generate such feedback and determine whether the player wins the game: the player wins the game if the test generation engine cannot generate any method input to cause the player implementation and the secret implementation to have different method results.

The design of coding duel games and the gaming platform follows a number of design principles [13]. For example, the games need to be interactive, and the interactions need to be iterative and involve multiple rounds. The feedback given to the player should be adaptive and personalized

---

* The method signature of a coding duel must have at least one input parameter. The return type of a coding duel must not be void.

to the modifications made by the player on the player implementation. The games should have a clear winning criterion. There should be no or few opportunities for the player to cheat the games (e.g., by adding very complicated code portions in the player implementation to pose difficulties for the underlying test generation engine).

5.3.3 Social Dynamics in Pex4Fun

To add more fun to Pex4Fun, we have developed a number of features related to social dynamics, making games in Pex4Fun a type of social games. For example, Pex4Fun allows a player to learn what coding duels other people were already able to win (or not). For a given coding duel opened by a player, the description text box above the working area shows some statistics such as the following: Can you write code that matches a secret implementation? Other people have already won this Duel 322 times! (see Figure 5.1).

5.3.3.1 Ranking of Players and Coding Duels

Initially, when only a relatively small number of coding duels were provided by us in Pex4Fun, we provided a mechanism of earning medals to encourage users to play coding duels. After signing in, a user could earn virtual medals for winning coding duels. The user got the first medal for winning any five of the coding duels that were built into Pex4Fun. The user got the second medal for winning another 20 of the built-in coding duels.

Furthermore, a user can click the Community link on the Pex4Fun main page to see how the user's coding duel skills compare with other users. In the community area (http://www.pexforfun.com/Community. aspx), there are two ranked lists of all users (one based on the number of points earned by a user and the other one based on the number of coding duels won by a user), as well as coding duels that other users have published. Figure 5.2 shows the ranked list of all users based on their earned points. A user can earn points by winning a coding duel, rating a coding duel that the user won, registering in a course, creating a coding duel that somebody else attempts to win, creating a coding duel that somebody else wins, and so on. Note that a user can rate any coding duel that the user wins as Fun, Boring, or Fishy. All ratings are shared with the community.

5.3.3.2 Live Feeds

A player can click the Live Feed link on the Pex4Fun main page to see what coding duels other players are winning (or not) right now (http://www.pexforfun.com/Livefeed.aspx). Maybe someone else is trying to win

Pex for fun - Community

Join the **Pex for fun** Community! Sign in with your Windows Live™ ID. Choose your **Pex for fun** nickname, opt in to show your nickname in the high score lists and to publish self-created Coding Duels. Visit our MSDN Forums for Pex, and like Pex on Facebook.

High Score List

> By Points

Who has most points:

1. MaF (951)
2. meisl (854)
3. StevePa (685)
4. Kai (600)
5. Mohammed (514)
6. TheRama (463)
7. DarrenW (404)
8. tony (403)
9. Mike S (388)

FIGURE 5.2   User ranking in Pex4Fun.

1,633,069 clicked 'Ask Pex!'

User174824 won C# - «Shade_of_Gray»

5 minutes ago

User174824 tried to win C# - «Shade_of_Gray»

5 minutes ago

User174824 tried to win C# - «Shade_of_Gray»

5 minutes ago

User174823 tried to win C# - «Shade_of_Gray»

7 minutes ago

User174823 tried to win C# - «Shade_of_Gray»

9 minutes ago

FIGURE 5.3   Example screenshot of the Live Feed.

a coding duel that the player has created or the player is also trying to win. Figure 5.3 shows an example screen snapshot of the live feed.

Social dynamics in Pex4Fun share similar motivations as other recent gamification examples in software engineering. For example, Stack Overflow badges (http://stackoverflow.com/badges) have been used to provide incentives for Stack Overflow users to ask or answer questions there. Through asking or answering questions, a user earns reputation points. For example, 10 reputation points are given to a user when his or her answer to a question receives an "up" vote. In addition, a user can earn three ranks of badge: bronze, silver, and gold badges. Bronze badges are given to users who often help teach other users on how to use the system. Silver badges are given to users who post very insightful questions and answers, and show dedication to moderate and improve the Stack Overflow contents. Gold badges are given to users who demonstrate outstanding dedication or achievement. Such badges earned by a user appear on the user's profile and in the user's user card. Along a similar spirit, early 2012, Microsoft added a new plug-in to the Microsoft Visual Studio to allow software developers to unlock achievements (http://channel9.msdn.com/achievements/visualstudio), receive badges, and increase their ranking on a leaderboard based on the program code that they have written.

5.3.4 Educational Usage of Pex4Fun

The game type of coding duels within Pex4Fun is flexible enough to allow game creators to create various games to target a range of skills such as skills of programming, program understanding, induction, debugging, problem solving, testing, and specification writing, with different difficulty levels of gaming. In addition, Pex4Fun is an open platform: anyone around the world can create coding duels for others to play besides playing the existing coding duels themselves. Teachers can create virtual classrooms in the form of courses by customizing the existing learning materials and games or creating new materials and games. Teachers can also enjoy the benefits of automated grading of exercises assigned to students. Pex4Fun has provided a number of open virtual courses that include learning materials along with games used to reinforce students' learning (http://www.pexforfun.com/Page.aspx#learn/courses).

Pex4Fun was adopted as a major platform for assignments in a graduate software engineering course. A coding duel contest was held at a major software engineering conference (2011) for engaging conference attendees to solve coding duels in a dynamic social contest. Pex4Fun has been gaining high popularity in the community: Because it was released to the public in June 2010, the number of clicks of the Ask Pex! button (indicating the attempts made by users to solve games at Pex4Fun) has reached over 1.5 million (1,540,970) as of July 21, 2014.

Various Pex4Fun users posted their comments on the Internet to express their enthusiasm and interest (even addiction) to Pex4Fun. Here we included some examples:

PEX4fun could become a better FizzBuzz than FizzBuzz.

it really got me *excited*. The part that got me most is about spreading interest in/teaching CS: I do think that it's REALLY great for teaching—learning!

Frankly this is my favorite game. I used to love the first person shooters and the satisfaction of blowing away a whole team of Noobies playing Rainbow Six, but this is far more fun.

Teaching, learning—isn't this really the same, in the end? In fact, for me personally, it's really about leveraging curiosity, be it mine or someone else's—at best both! And PexForFun (+ all the stuff behind) is a great, promising platform for this: you got riddles, you got competition, you get feedback that makes you think ahead...

I'm afraid I'll have to constrain myself to spend just an hour or so a day on this really exciting stuff, as I'm really stuffed with work.

PexForFun improves greatly over projecteuler w.r.t. how proposed solutions are verified; in fact what it adds is that you don't just get a 'nope' but something more articulate, something you can build on. That's what I think is really great and exciting—let's push it even further now!

5.3.5 Code Hunt

Code Hunt [28,29] is a recent gaming platform evolved from Pex4Fun. Code Hunt includes more gaming aspects to offer more engaging experiences to the player. Figure 5.4 shows the main page of the Code Hunt website. The gaming platform also has sounds and a leaderboard to keep the player engaged.

With coding duels as the game type, Code Hunt organizes games in a series of worlds, sectors, and levels, which become increasingly challenging. Figure 5.5 shows the example list of sectors available for the player to choose from. In each level, a coding duel game is played by the player, who has to discover a secret code fragment and write code (in Java or C#) for it. Figure 5.6 shows an example coding duel for the player to play, with the player's code shown on the left-hand side of the figure. After the player clicks the Capture Code button (shown near the middle-top part of the figure, with the same effect of clicking the Ask Pex! button in Pex4Fun),

FIGURE 5.4   **(See color insert.)** The main page of the Code Hunt website.

FIGURE 5.5   Example sectors in Code Hunt.

the underlying Pex tool gives customized progress feedback to the player via the generated test cases, as displayed in the table on the right-hand side of Figure 5.6. In addition, Code Hunt might hint a user to focus on a particular line of code, as shown in the last line of the table on the right-hand side of the figure. When the player's code achieves the same result as the secret implementation, Code Hunt flashes Captured Code and provides a score to the player based on how good the code was. Other improvements

FIGURE 5.6   (**See color insert.**) An example coding duel in Code Hunt.

for Code Hunt beyond Pex4Fun are that Code Hunt offers Java as a supported language (via a source code translator) and it runs on Microsoft Azure, making it scalable to a large number of simultaneous users.

5.4 DISCUSSION

Educational software engineering is closely related to the field of educational games [30] (i.e., games for education), with example conferences such as the Games+Learning+Society Conference (http://www.gameslearning-society.org/conference) and example initiatives such as the MacArthur Digital Media and Learning initiative (http://www.macfound.org/programs/learning). The field of educational games typically focuses on gaming technologies for supporting educational purposes, whereas educational software engineering typically focuses on software engineering technologies for supporting educational purposes. In the context of Pex4Fun and Code Hunt, the field of educational games would focus more on the aspect of gaming (Section 5.3) whereas the field of educational software engineering would focus more on the aspect of software engineering technologies (Section 5.3.1). Note that educational software engineering deals with not only educational games but also other educational tools not being games.

In addition, it is reasonable to consider that software engineering for developing educational games or generally educational tools (such as software quality assurance for educational game software) would be part of educational software engineering. In other words, educational software engineering is not limited to software engineering technologies as infrastructure support for educational tools (as exemplified by Pex4Fun and Code Hunt) and can also include software engineering tools or processes to assist the development of educational tools.

We advocate educational software engineering to be within software engineering research and to contribute to software engineering research in three example ways:

1. First, when targeting at educational tasks, researchers may be able to leverage or develop software engineering technologies (to be effective for such tasks), which generally may not be effective or mature enough to deal with tasks related to software industry. An example case would be developing program synthesis technologies for educational tasks [5–7]. Another example case would be developing test generation technologies for Pex4Fun and Code Hunt, because secret implementations created for coding duels tend to be simpler than real-world code implementations.

2. Second, targeting at educational tasks may pose unique requirements for software engineering technologies. For example, test generation for software engineering tasks such as achieving code coverage aims at generating and reporting test inputs that can achieve new code coverage. However, test generation for Pex4Fun and Code Hunt aims at generating and reporting test inputs that can serve as feedback to achieve effective learning purposes.

3. Some educational tasks (such as intelligent tutoring [14] and problem generation [5–7]) call for creation of new software engineering technologies, which may not exist in traditional software engineering (because there are no counterparts in the software engineering domain for such tasks in the education domain).

5.5 CONCLUSION

In this chapter, we have defined and advocated educational software engineering as an emerging subfield of software engineering. Educational software engineering develops software engineering technologies for general educational tasks. In this subfield, gaming technologies often play an important role together with software engineering technologies. We have presented Pex4Fun (along with Code Hunt), one of our recent examples on leveraging software engineering and gaming technologies for teaching and learning programming and software engineering skills. Pex4Fun and Code Hunt can also be used in the context of MOOCs to address issues such as automatic grading.

ACKNOWLEDGMENT

We thank the reviewers for their valuable feedback. Tao Xie's work is supported in part by a Microsoft Research Award, NSF grants CCF-1349666, CNS-1434582, CCF-1434596, CCF-1434590, and CNS-1439481, and the NSF of China, number 61228203.

REFERENCES

1. Mary Shaw. Software engineering education: A roadmap. In *Proceedings of FOSE*, pp. 371–380, Limerick, Ireland, 2000.
2. Mary Jean Harrold. Testing: A roadmap. In *Proceedings of FOSE*, pp. 61–72, Limerick, Ireland, 2000.
3. Dongmei Zhang, Yingnong Dang, Jian-Guang Lou, Shi Han, Haidong Zhang, and Tao Xie. Software analytics as a learning case in practice: Approaches and experiences. In *Proceedings of MALETS*, pp. 55–58, Lawrence, KS, 2011.
4. Dongmei Zhang, Shi Han, Yingnong Dang, Jian-Guang Lou, Haidong Zhang, and Tao Xie. Software analytics in practice. Special Issue, *IEEE Software*, 5(30):30–37, 2013.
5. Erik Andersen, Sumit Gulwani, and Zoran Popovic. A trace-based framework for analyzing and synthesizing educational progressions. In *Proceedings of CHI*, pp. 773–782, Paris, France, 2013.
6. Sumit Gulwani, Vijay Korthikanti, and Ashish Tiwari. Synthesizing geometry constructions. In *Proceedings of PLDI*, pp. 50–61, San Jose, CA, 2011.
7. Rohit Singh, Sumit Gulwani, and Sriram Rajamani. Automatically generating algebra problems. In *Proceedings of AAAI*, Toronto, ON, 2012.
8. Tao Xie, Suresh Thummalapenta, David Lo, and Chao Liu. Data mining for software engineering. *IEEE Computer*, 42(8):35–42, 2009.
9. Ahmed E. Hassan. The road ahead for mining software repositories. In *Proceedings of FoSM*, pp. 48–57, Beijing, China, 2008.
10. Armando Fox and David Patterson. Crossing the software education chasm. *Communications of the ACM*, 55(5):44–49, 2012.
11. Ken Masters. A brief guide to understanding MOOCs. *The Internet Journal of Medical Education*, 1, 2011. https://ispub.com/IJME/1/2/10995. doi:10.5580/1f21.
12. Rishabh Singh, Sumit Gulwani, and Armando Solar-Lezama. Automated feedback generation for introductory programming assignments. In *Proceedings of PLDI*, pp. 15–26, Seattle, WA, 2013.
13. Nikolai Tillmann, Jonathan De Halleux, Tao Xie, Sumit Gulwani, and Judith Bishop. Teaching and learning programming and software engineering via interactive gaming. In *Proceedings of ICSE, Software Engineering Education (SEE)*, pp. 1117–1126, San Francisco, CA, 2013.

14. Tom Murray. Authoring intelligent tutoring systems: An analysis of the state of the art. *International Journal of Artificial Intelligence in Education*, 1(10):98–129, 1999.
15. Chao Liu, Chen Chen, Jiawei Han, and Philip S. Yu. GPLAG: Detection of software plagiarism by program dependence graph analysis. In *Proceedings of KDD*, pp. 872–881, Philadelphia, PA, 2006.
16. Saul Schleimer, Daniel S. Wilkerson, and Alex Aiken. Winnowing: Local algorithms for document fingerprinting. In *Proceedings of SIGMOD*, pp. 76–85, San Diego, CA, 2003.
17. Andrei Papancea, Jaime Spacco, and David Hovemeyer. An open platform for managing short programming exercises. In *Proceedings of ICER*, pp. 47–52, San Diego, CA,2013.
18. Paul Denny, Andrew Luxton-Reilly, Ewan Tempero, and Jacob Hendrickx. CodeWrite: Supporting student-driven practice of Java. In *Proceedings of SIGCSE*, pp. 471–476, Dallas, TX, 2011.
19. Qianxiang Wang, Wenxin Li, and Tao Xie. Educational programming systems for learning at scale. In *Proceedings of Learning at Scale*, pp. 177–178, Atlanta, GA, 2014.
20. Judith Bishop, Jonathan de Halleux, Nikolai Tillmann, Nigel Horspool, Don Syme, and Tao Xie. Browser-based software for technology transfer. In *Proceedings of SAICSIT, Industry Oriented Paper*, pp. 338–340, Cape Town, South Africa, 2011.
21. Patrice Godefroid, Nils Klarlund, and Koushik Sen. DART: Directed automated random testing. In *Proceedings of PLDI*, pp. 213–223, Chicago, IL, 2005.
22. Nikolai Tillmann and Jonathan de Halleux. Pex—White box test generation for .NET. In *Proceedings of TAP*, pp. 134–153, Prato, Italy, 2008.
23. Tao Xie, Nikolai Tillmann, Peli de Halleux, and Wolfram Schulte. Fitness-guided path exploration in dynamic symbolic execution. In *Proceedings of DSN*, pp. 359–368, Lisbon, Portugal, 2009.
24. Kunal Taneja and Tao Xie. DiffGen: Automated regression unit-test generation. In *Proceedings of ASE*, pp. 407–410, L'Aquila, Italy, 2008.
25. Tao Xie, Jonathan de Halleux, Nikolai Tillmann, and Wolfram Schulte. Teaching and training developer-testing techniques and tool support. In *Proceedings of SPLASH, Educators' and Trainers' Symposium*, pp. 175–182, Reno/Tahoe, NV, 2010.
26. Lori A. Clarke. A system to generate test data and symbolically execute programs. *IEEE Transactions on Software Engineering*, 2(3):215–222, 1976.
27. James C. King. Symbolic execution and program testing. *Communications of the ACM*, 19(7):385–394, 1976.
28. Nikolai Tillmann, Judith Bishop, Nigel Horspool, Daniel Perelman, and Tao Xie. Code Hunt—Searching for secret code for fun. In *Proceedings of SBST*, Hyderabad, India, 2014.
29. Nikolai Tillmann, Jonathan de Halleux, Tao Xie, and Judith Bishop. Code Hunt: Gamifying teaching and learning of computer science at scale. In *Proceedings of Learning at Scale*, pp. 221–222, Atlanta, GA, 2014.

30. James Paul Gee. *What Video Games Have to Teach Us about Learning and Literacy?* Palgrave Macmillan, New York, 2007.
31. Tao Xie, Nikolai Tillmann, and Jonathan de Halleux. Educational software engineering: Where software engineering, education, and gaming meet. In *Proceedings of GAS*, pp. 36–39, San Francisco, CA, 2013.

CHAPTER 6

Adaptive Serious Games

Barbara Reichart, Damir Ismailović,
Dennis Pagano, and Bernd Brügge

CONTENTS

6.1	Introduction	134
6.2	Background	135
6.3	Basis for Exploratory Studies: Development of Four Serious Games	136
6.4	An Exploratory Study: How to Characterize Players in Serious Games?	138
	6.4.1 Study Design	139
	6.4.2 Results	140
	6.4.3 Conclusion	143
6.5	An Exploratory Study: How to Provide Help in Serious Games?	143
	6.5.1 Study Design	143
	6.5.2 Results	144
	6.5.3 Conclusion	145
6.6	Threats to Validity	146
6.7	Toward a Definition of Adaptivity	146
6.8	Outlook	148
6.9	Summary and Conclusion	148
References		149

Abstract: Learning is associated with a lot of effort and perseverance. In learning theories, motivation can be observed as a key factor for successful learning. Serious games can increase motivation because they involve use of a variety of elements, such as visual environments, storylines, challenges, and interactions with nonplayer characters. This makes serious games ideal learning environments as the learning experience becomes so intrinsically satisfying and rewarding that external pressures or rewards for learning are of secondary importance. Even though games have such motivational power, several studies have shown that there are no known forms of education as effective as a professional human tutor, because tutors select learning content based on the learners' skills, thus adapting to the learner every step along the way. This chapter explores the interaction between human tutors and learners in seriousgame development with the focus on social development theory. It presents results that show how human tutors observe players in executing learning tasks and interacting with the game environment in serious games. Based on the results of these studies, we provide a definition of adaptivity for serious games.

6.1 INTRODUCTION

Serious games can engage the learner in a way most traditional teaching methods cannot. They provide a platform where the two points, motivation and interactive learning, can be perfectly put together.

This chapter describes studies that explore the effects of human tutors in serious games. Observations by developing serious games showed that without help, children require more time to learn how to play the game than adults, although both groups could reach the same time with help [1]. Learning theories such as Vygotsky's social development theory [2], Piaget's stages of cognitive development [3], and Erikson's developmental stages [4] explain this phenomenon based on the social context of learners during the learning process.

The reason why learning progresses faster with human tutors than with other tools is the higher *adaptivity* to the learner. The problem is that serious games of the current state of the art do not adapt to the learner [5–8]. Consequently, a major goal in modern serious-game development and research is to make the game adapt to the learner and provide intelligent actions in order to achieve higher individuality [1,9].

Although one could argue that techniques to realize adaptivity have already been developed for e-learning systems, the *intelligent tutoring systems* (*ITSs*) usually foster very different activities than those seen in a game. The aim of this chapter is therefore, to explore the ways of adaptivity that are specific to serious games and to build a foundation for software frameworks for adaptivity in serious games.

The contribution of this chapter is twofold. First, we provide two studies that explore the role of human tutors in serious games. Second, based on the results and conclusions of these exploratory studies, we provide a definition for adaptivity for serious games, which considers different aspects of the role of human tutors in serious games.

6.2 BACKGROUND

Learning theories attempt to explain how learners learn. Although behaviorism focuses on input and output of the learner [10,11], constructivism considers the role of human tutors more intricately. This is why we will focus on constructivistic research throughout this chapter. In constructivistic theories, learners are believed to learn by constructing knowledge and by interacting with other humans. Learning is seen as an active and constructive process. Learners actively construct or create their own representations of reality. When new information is linked to prior knowledge, subjective mental representations are created. "Constructivist stance maintains that learning is a process of constructing meaning; it is how people make sense of their experience" [12, p. 261].

Constructivism suggests that learning is not a passive, but an active and social process [13]. The only way knowledge can be gained is through construction by the learner. Each individual representation of knowledge is subjective and is based on knowledge schemata where learning is a social, cultural, and linguistic process. Therefore, teaching should be based on experiences.

One of the most important and influential theories of the social aspects of learning is provided by Vygotsky [2]. Vygotsky defines the maximum level for the challenge of one specific content or topic for each individual as the upper limit of the zone of proximal development (ZPD) [14]. The lower limit of the ZPD is the minimum level that can be learned by each individual without help. "ZPD is the distance between the actual developmental level as determined by independent problem solving and the level of potential development as determined through problem solving under adult guidance, or in collaboration with more capable peers" [2, p. 131] (Figure 6.1).

In this theory, the *more knowledged other* (*MKO*) is someone or something that has a better understanding of a specific topic (task, process, or concept) than the learner and that has a social interaction with the learner. The MKO can be a teacher, a coach, an older adult, a peer, or even a computer or a serious game.

Building on these theories the *knowledge space theory* (*KST*) has been developed. Although originally intended for the assessment of knowledge, it was later adapted to support adaptivity in the ITS [15]. In KST,

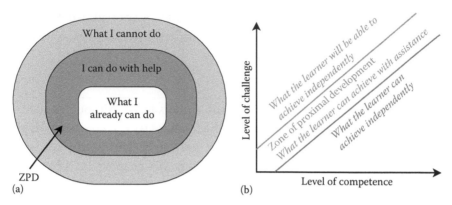

FIGURE 6.1 **(See color insert.)** (a,b) Zone of proximal development can be expanded and changes over time.

knowledge over a specific topic is not given by a single score, but instead it also provides information about the specific strengths and weaknesses of a student within the field. This is done by splitting the content into several smaller learning goals. The connection between those different goals is then given in the form of prerequisite relationships. For example, looking at learning how to divide numbers, the division by a digit, can be seen as a prerequisite for learning about division by numbers bigger than 10. This knowledge allows the ITS to select lessons based on the learners' skills.

6.3 BASIS FOR EXPLORATORY STUDIES: DEVELOPMENT OF FOUR SERIOUS GAMES

In order to research the role of tutors on learning and how their competencies could be transferred into serious games, we conducted two studies. In the first study, we wanted to find out which observations tutors used to assess the learners' skills. The second study then uses the results of this assessment to adapt to the learner.

Both studies required a very high control over the game elements including, but not limited to, the content, the difficulty level, and the game speed. Unfortunately, existing serious games do not give us this level of control. Therefore, we needed to develop our own serious games.

We developed four small serious games with focus on elementary school mathematics. Their goal is to teach skills ranging from writing (Figure 6.2a) and reading numbers (Figure 6.2b), simple addition

(a)

(b)

FIGURE 6.2 (a) Writing numbers with the guidance of a flashlight. (b) Practice counting quickly to safe bugs. (*Continued*)

(Figure 6.2c) and subtraction, to classifying geometric figures by form and color (Figure 6.2d). These contents were directly selected from the official curriculum of German elementary schools.

During the development process of the games, experts from different fields were involved. This was necessary, so that important aspects from the technical, psychological, and pedagogical side would not be overlooked.

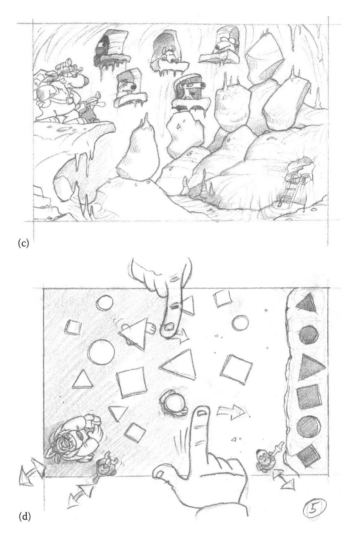

FIGURE 6.2 (*Continued*)   (c) Central screen for "Emil and Pauline in the cave," where the kids can track their progress and select which game they want to play. (d) Practice geometry and generalization. All shapes that fullfil a specific criterion follow the finger of the kid. The task of the kid is to figure out the commonality (e.g., shape, color, size).

6.4 AN EXPLORATORY STUDY: HOW TO CHARACTERIZE PLAYERS IN SERIOUS GAMES?

As we already argued, there are no known forms of education as effective as a professional human tutor [7,8]. The reason is based on the fact that in the current state of the art, no computer system is as good at adapting to users as humans [5,6].

According to the social development theory, tutors observe learners and try to provide help when necessary. Using their observations, tutors can analyze the learner and decide at what point help is necessary. Help is then provided through direct interaction with the student. The ZPD defines the difference of the learning outcome between children learning with a personal tutor and without a tutor [14].

Applying this theory to serious games requires finding out what exactly tutors can observe when watching and learning with the learner using a serious game. Additionally, we need to understand how the observed information is used by the tutors to characterize learners.

When a human tutor observes and consequently provides help to the learner, he or she can identify the learner's skills. In order to transfer this method to serious games, we need to find out how tutors carry out this task in a serious game. Therefore, we focus on answering the following question: What can be observed when a learner plays a serious game and how can this information be used to characterize the individual learner?

6.4.1 Study Design

To answer this research question, we applied qualitative research methods by interviewing experts and by observing children while playing.

We developed a serious game in an iterative process with experts (pedagogues, psychologists, professional game developers, serious-game researchers, students, and players). During the development process, we carried out informal, conversational interviews with all participants during each iteration. The constructed game provided us with a real example to the given question and supported experts to reflect on their answers. Additionally, we used this serious game to observe children while playing in order to be able to provide more data for the experts. Finally, we carried out retrospective interviews with experts based on this project. We repeated the process in four serious games. An overview of the steps followed in the study is given in Figure 6.3. We iterated the steps described in the figure for each serious game independently.

The goal of this study is to provide a detailed description of data that can be observed in a concrete serious game for children with one specific topic and a detailed description of how experts characterize the child in the given example.

The difference between the design of this study and the study proposed by Vygotsky in the theory described previously is as follows: in the serious games proposed here, there is no direct interaction with the learner. This is done based on the fact that in the current state of the art of mobile technology, no computer system can observe and react in as much nuance

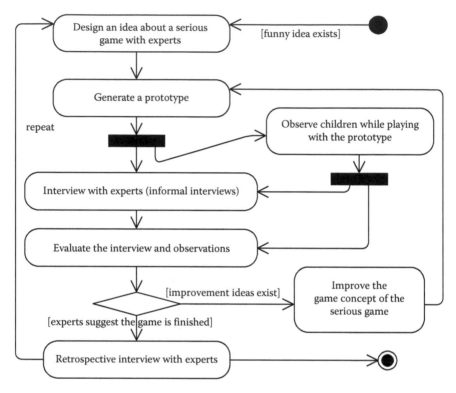

FIGURE 6.3   Iterative development process for serious games.

as a human. Therefore, we reduced the interaction between the child and the tutor to a level more similar to that possible between the computer and the child. When we conducted this study, we hoped that the observation of the learner in a serious game (without directly interrupting the serious game) is meaningful enough to characterize the learner.

Participants of the project were researchers from the Technische Universitat München, student and senior developers, and two professional serious-game development companies from Munich. The two companies provided a professional game designer, a professional story author, and two professional graphic designers. Additionally, we worked together with an experienced child psychologist.

6.4.2 Results

Interviews with experts during the development process helped us to identify the game elements and learning content that are related to adaptivity as presented in Table 6.1. When we conducted the study, we assumed

TABLE 6.1 Game Elements and Learning Content Identified in the Study

Serious games	SG1	SG2	SG3	SG4
Learning goals	C, W, R	C, R	A, S	A
Game elements	3	7	9	4
Skills for learning content	3	2	4	4
Skills for nonlearning content	1	2	1	1

A, addition; C, count; R, recognize numbers; S, subtraction; W, write numbers.

that the tutor characterizes the learner by recognizing his or her skills. Therefore, we let the experts identify all skills necessary for the content of each serious game. As a result of the research question "what can be observed?" we identified different game elements, learning goals, and skills in the game as presented in Table 6.1.

According to the social development theory, a tutor makes decisions by observing skills and relations between different skills. The answer to the question "How can this information be used to characterize the skills of the individual learner?" is based on the KST in this work [16]. KST is a mathematical model for the description of learning content and thus provides a mathematical model for characterizing learners based on their skills [17]. In comparison with other assessment methods, it provides not only a single value that is supposed to represent the skills of the learner but also provides a more detailed analysis of the learner regarding different elements of a skill. Furthermore, it also already provides a representation of the dependencies between different elements, thus providing a great basis for adaptivity. Therefore, we use the concept of KST as described in reference [18] to design the model for the content of adaptive serious games as presented in Figure 6.4.

Using this model, we can define skills and relations between skills. In attempting to answer the question of "How do tutors characterize the learner in these games?" we found the following results: First, a pedagogue and different psychologists argued that they need to recognize an assessment situation, where they need to see if the learner is able to solve

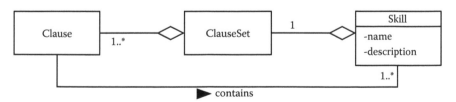

FIGURE 6.4 Model for content in adaptive serious games. Content can be presented as a set of clauses, which in turn consist of skills.

TABLE 6.2 Domain-Specific Tasks Identified in the Study

Task Sets	SG1	SG2	SG3	SG4
1	W 1,2,3	C	A with $c < 10$	A with $c < 10$
2	W 4,5,7	R	A with $c \leq 20$	A with $c \leq 15$[a]
3	W,C^{-9}		A, S: $a \pm b = c$[b]	A with $c \leq 20$[a]
4				A with $c \leq 20$

A, addition; C, count; R, recognize numbers; S, subtraction; W, write numbers.

A: $a + b = c$.

[a] Addition $a_1 + a_2 + \ldots + a_n = c$ with $c \leq 15$ and in some situations $\forall a_i, a_j, a_k$ with $i < j < k$. If $c = 10$, then $(a_i + \ldots + a_j) < 10 \wedge a_k < 10$, and if $c > 10$, then $(a_i + \ldots + a_j) \geq 10 \vee a_k \geq 10$.

[b] $c \leq \pm 20$ and $a > 9$ or $b > 9$.

a specific task. Therefore, the tutor needs to know the possible tasks and to be able to solve them. Additionally, the tasks need to be associated with skills that would group the tasks in specific sets. After several iterations, we found different reasonable task sets groupings as shown in Table 6.2. This grouping needs to reflect the skills identified in Table 6.1. The difference in the amount of skills and task sets SG3 is based on the grouping of the tasks related to addition and subtraction.

To answer the research question, we first rephrase it as follows: "How can a tutor use the observed information to recognize and rate a skill of a learner?"

Based on the given observations and data in Tables 6.1 and 6.2, we found that a tutor would observe the correct and incorrect solutions of the tasks. Based on the amount of correct and incorrect solutions, the tutor is able to rate a skill related to the given task set. Additionally, we found that the correct and incorrect execution of the tasks is not always a binary decision. In some of the games, the incorrect execution of the task was related to the difficulty of the game elements. Therefore, the tutors were observing the intention of the learner while trying to solve the task.

We observed a situation where the learner is trying to throw a stone in the game to the left side, and the correct solution was also on the left side. When a learner was not able to throw the stone fast enough to reach the goal, the tutor would recognize the right intention and count this as correct, even if the execution was unsuccessful.

We can conclude that the assessment situation produces a result that can be correct but unsuccessful. However, an incorrect result can be successful by coincidence. Figure 6.5 shows the resulting model for the assessment situations.

FIGURE 6.5 Assessment situations can produce results. While sometimes the answer given by the child might be correct, it does not necessarily mean it actually knows the correct answer.

6.4.3 Conclusion

We found that when observing the players, the human tutor observes the correct and incorrect execution of the tasks in the game as well as the motorical execution. We additionally found that tutors rate the skills of learners in a fuzzy way as illustrated in Figure 6.5.

Based on this study, we conclude that for games that require knowledge as well as hand–eye coordination and timing, there exists a strong link between the player's motorical skills and the skills related to learning content determined by tutors.

Additionally, we observed that changes in game elements are well suited to change the difficulty of the game. A change of learning content is not necessary in all cases. This is especially true for skills, where quick retrieval is crucial. Therefore, changing the difficulty and topic of the learning content to early even could hinder effective learning in the long term.

6.5 AN EXPLORATORY STUDY: HOW TO PROVIDE HELP IN SERIOUS GAMES?

The next step when trying to simulate the tutor in a serious game is to define what needs to be changed in a serious game in order to make it adaptable. The research question that needs to be answered is as follows: "which changes need to be applied to a serious game (while playing) in order to change the difficulty of the tasks based on the model in Figure 6.4?"

The goal of this study is to find the possibilities for changes in learning content and game elements. Additionally, we need to find the relation between the skills for learning content and the motorical skills.

6.5.1 Study Design

To answer this question, we used the serious games we designed in order to explore possible changes in the game together with experts. We interviewed experts and observed children and redesigned the game according to the results. An overview of the steps of the study is given in Figure 6.6.

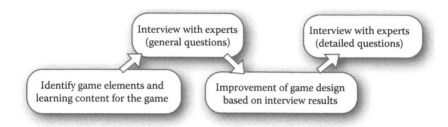

FIGURE 6.6   Steps in serious games development.

In the previous study, we identified game elements and learning content in the game. In this study, we focused on finding out what experts would do to apply help. We interviewed them and presented them some recordings of children playing the game. Our intention was to find a way to increase the difficulty of the serious game so that the player would remain in the ZPD. We used the data (recordings and game specifications) and discussed the following question with experts in informal interviews: What can be changed in the given game to make the game more difficult/easier?

We then made improvements to each serious game based on the answers to this question. Finally, we executed a second interview by asking more detailed and specific questions:

- What can be changed in the given learning content to make the game more difficult/easy?

- What can be changed in the given game elements to make the game more difficult/easy?

- If this game had four difficulty levels, how should they be designed in this game?

Our assumption was that the changes in the game would include both adaptivity of the game environment and adaptivity of learning content.

6.5.2 Results

In the first interviews, we discussed the four serious games with experts. As we wanted to find out whether the experts would distinguish between game elements and content when they wanted to provide help, we explicitly asked abstract questions where we did not make the distinction.

TABLE 6.3   Adaptable Properties in the Serious Games

Serious games	SG1	SG2	SG3	SG4
Number of adaptable properties	2	4	4	1
Number of adaptable properties related to learning content	2	2	2	0

We collected a wide range of suggestions. For example, some experts suggested increasing the tolerance of the writing recognition in one of the serious games reducing frustration for beginners. In one game, players had to shoot a mud ball at a target. Many experts already considered a solution as correctly given even when the child missed the target as long as it shot in the correct direction. This made clear that a similar approach might also be helpful for the algorithm. After the collection process, we made changes to the serious games accordingly.

In the next step, we focused on finding different levels of difficulty that experts considered reasonable. The study provided a detailed description of data that can be changed in each of the developed serious games in order to provide different levels of difficulty.

Additionally, we found that changes to some game elements affect specific skills. For example, in one game, the goal was to practice counting. Several bugs crawl along the screen. The goal is to free as many bugs with the correct number of dots on their backs as possible. In this game, the difficulty could hugely be varied by changing the color, speed, or look of the bugs. We call these game elements *adaptable properties*. Changes to those adaptable properties can be used to make the same task more difficult for experienced players to keep the game exciting and increase the practice effect. The amount of such adaptable properties is summarized in Table 6.3.

6.5.3 Conclusion

After we agreed with experts on different levels of difficulty for each game, we found game elements that can be adapted (called *adaptable elements*) in order to change the difficulty for the learner. We found a link between adaptable properties and skills necessary for learning content.

Some of the adaptable properties (such as the speed of a game element) directly affected some skills necessary for math (such as counting).

We can conclude that the connection between adaptable properties and learning content makes the development of the game more difficult because the changes take place on the side of the game elements.

Each time something needs to be changed, and new game elements are developed; they need to implement interfaces and apply design principles required in order to make them adaptable.

6.6 THREATS TO VALIDITY

The discussion of validity is based on the *qualitative validity* criteria described in reference [19].

We spent sufficient time (2 years) on developing the four serious games. During these two years, we observed and iteratively interviewed participants from different domains such as developers, game designers, players, learners, tutors, psychologists, and pedagogues. We also worked together with developers, other professionals, and researchers.

We worked with developers coming from different contexts and cultures. We also used a variety of development techniques and processes for different iterations and different games. We worked on the same questions at different points of time with the same developers. Additionally, a different researcher worked on analyzing the data.

We also examined different cases where the adaptivity method would contradict our assumptions and results. In one of these cases, for example, we developed a prototype that was adapting too fast to the player's answering speed. We conducted postproject interviews using retrospective interviewing methods to let participants reflect on the findings.

External audits were conducted to foster the accuracy and validity of the study. We let researchers and developers not involved in the research process examine both the process of the study and the results of the interviews and resulting games.

Transferability is described by Lincoln and Guba [19] as a way of achieving a type of external validity. We are confident that our results are applicable to a wide variety of domains. However, learning with serious games may differ for different domains.

6.7 TOWARD A DEFINITION OF ADAPTIVITY

In the context of serious games based on the technology that is available today, we can base the adaptivity definitions without restrictions on the social development theory.

The definition of *adaptivity* in serious game is based on the definition of ZPD. We define adaptivity in the following way:

Adaptivity in Serious Games is an approach that enables a serious game to (A) learn from learner's behavior by (A1) intelligently monitoring and

(A2) interpreting learner's actions in the game's world and (B) to intervene in the game by (B1) automatically adjusting the learning content and (B2) the game elements according to (C) the student's individual ZPD as necessary and using the principles of (D) MKO, where adaptivity is an MKO for the learner according to the social development theory.

According to this definition, the adaptivity process in a serious game consists of four stages: monitoring players (A1), learner characterization (A2), assessment generation (B1), and adaptive intervention (B2). We note here that adaptivity describes in this definition the following four factors: A, B, C, and D.

Factor (A): The adaptive serious game monitors the learner using possible sensors and the state-of-the-art technology. All observations are used for collecting user data and characterizing the user (e.g., rating his or her mathematical skills).

Factor (B): The adaptive serious game adapts both game elements and learning content. There are game elements that affect the ability to solve the tasks related to learning content (e.g., the speed of a car that moves fast over the screen, where something is written on the car, and where the goal of the learner is to interpret the content). Those *adaptable properties* can provide powerful tools to adapt to a specific learner more fluently, although changes in learning content very often lead to discreet big jumps in the level of difficulty.

Factor (C): The adaptive serious game always individually challenges each learner.

Factor (D): The adaptive serious game takes the role of the MKO in the social development theory, where the following statement can be applied: Every function in the child's cultural development appears twice—first, on the social level, and second, on the individual level. The social level can be an interaction with the serious game or with peers in the serious game.

An adaptive serious game is a serious game that implements the adaptivity approach.

We can then map adaptation approaches as used in e-learning and ITS [20,21] to the definition of adaptivity in serious games:

- Micro adaptive approach—Adaptivity with adjustments made in the game on the assessment situations and learning situations with the restriction that the adjustments are made just to the learning content.

- Macro adaptive approach—Adaptivity with the restriction that adjustments are made only on the navigational level but for both learning content and game elements (even though game elements were not considered in the previous definition).

- Aptitude–treatment interaction approach—Adaptivity with adjustments made on game elements that represent different types of instructions, user control, or media.

- Constructivistic–collaborative approach—Adaptivity with the restriction that collaboration with peers or construction of knowledge is enabled and adaptable, but the user is in charge of changes.

6.8 OUTLOOK

Adaptivity provides a great potential for the future of serious games. Even with the simple adjustments to the learners in our games, we already could observe some great results. However, during the two studies described here, we merely focus on skill-and-action games. We already identified huge differences between adaptivity for ITS and our serious games. More complex serious games, which include story line, strategy, or sandbox elements, probably require an evergrowing set of strategies for adaptivity.

In reference [17], we already started to explore some aspects of adaptivity in connection with a story line, which is intertwined with learning contents. However, we feel that more interesting types of serious games could be achieved by researching different types of adaptivity.

6.9 SUMMARY AND CONCLUSION

In the literature review, we found an explanation of the role of human tutors in theories such as Vygotsky's social development theory, Piaget's stages of cognitive development, and Erikson's developmental stages. We focused on answering the question how the serious game itself can be adaptive, based on these learning theories that already exist and that explain why the phenomenon occurred.

When we researched *the observations of learners by tutors* in the first study, we found that for characterizing the learner, human tutors observe game environments. By observing elements, we include *game elements* in the learning content of a serious game. Therefore, we argue that the *adaptive* serious game should be able to observe both game elements and learning content.

In the second study, we observed that tutors intend to change the game element properties (in addition to changing the difficulty of the learning content) when help is necessary for a learner. We found that some of the game elements, the so-called adaptable elements, *should be* adaptive and others *should not*. We also found that the adaptable elements directly influence the learners' ability to solve tasks related to learning content.

Based on this study, we argue that adaptivity should include the observation of the user's actions in the serious game and the adaptation of both game elements and learning content. We finally gave a definition of adaptivity for serious games that considers three aspects: (1) learning theories, (2) all aspects of serious games including *game elements*, and (3) existing e-learning approaches.

REFERENCES

1. Damir Ismailović, Dennis Pagano, and Bernd Brügge. weMakeWords—An adaptive and collaborative serious game for literacy acquisition. In *IADIS International Conference—Game and Entertainment*, Rome, Italy, 2011.
2. Lev Semenovich Vygotsky. *Mind in Society: The Development of Higher Psychological Processes*. Harvard University Press, Cambridge, 1978.
3. Jean Piaget. *The Essential Piaget*, vol. 18. Jason Aronson, New York, 1977.
4. Rolf Eduard Helmut Muuss (Ed.) Erik Eriksons's theory of identity development. In *Theories of Adolescence*, pp. 42–57, 1994.
5. Kurt VanLehn, Collin Lynch, Kay Schulze, Joel A. Shapiro, Linwood Taylor, and Don Treacy. The Andes physics tutoring system: Five years of evaluations. In Gord McCalla and Chee-Kit Looi (Eds.), *Artificial Intelligence in Education*. IOS Press, Amsterdam, the Netherlands. 2005.
6. Richard Niemiec and Herbert J. Walberg. Comparative effects of computer-assisted instruction: A synthesis of reviews. *Journal of Educational Computing Research*, 3, 19–37. 1987.
7. Benjamin S. Bloom. The 2 sigma problem: The search for methods of group instruction as effective as one-to-one tutoring. *Educational Researcher*, 13(6), 4–16. 1984.
8. John A. Anderson, Albert T. Corbett, Kenneth R. Koedinger, and Ray Pelletier. Cognitive tutors: Lessons learned. *Journal of the Learning Sciences*, 4(2), 167–207. 1995.
9. Damir Ismailović, Barbara Köhler, Juan Haladjian, Dennis Pagano, and Bernd Brügge. Towards a conceptual model for adaptivity in serious games. In *IADIS International Conference—Game and Entertainment*, Lisbon, Portugal, 2012.
10. Burrhus Frederic Skinner. *Science and Human Behavior*. Free Press, New York, 1953.
11. Burrhus Frederic Skinner. *Contingencies of Reinforcement: A Theoretical Analysis*. Appleton-Century-Crofts, New York, 1969.

12. Sharan B. Merriam, Rosemary Shelly Caffarella, and Lisa Baumgartner. *Learning in Adulthood: A Comprehensive Guide*, vol. 2. The Jossey-Bass higher and adult education series. Jossey-Bass, San Francisco, CA, 2007.
13. Svein Sjoberg. Constructivism and learning. 2007. *International Encyclopedia of Education,* third edition, Elsevier, Oxford.
14. Peter E. Langford. *Vygotsky's Developmental and Educational Psychology.* Psychology Press, New York, 2005.
15. Dietrich Albert, Cord Hockemeyer, and Toshiaki Mori. Memory, knowledge, and e-learning. In L.G. Nielson and N. Ohta (Eds.) Memory and Society: Psychological perpectives (pp. 87–109). UK Psychology Press, Hove.
16. Cord Hockemeyer. Competence based adaptive e-learning in dynamic domains. In *The Joint Workshop of Cognition and Learning through Media-Communication for Advanced E-Learning,* pp. 79–82, Berlin, Germany, 2003.
17. Barbara Köhler, Damir Ismailović, and Bernd Brügge. Adaptivity in story-driven serious games. In *IADIS International Conference—Game and Entertainment,* Rome, Italy, 2011.
18. Owen Conlan, Ian O'Keeffe, Cormac Hampson, and Jürgen Heller. Using knowledge space theory to support learner modeling and personalization. In *Proceedings of World Conference on E-Learning in Corporate Government Healthcare and Higher Education,* pp. 1912–1919. AACE, Honolulu, HI, 2006.
19. Yvonna S. Lincoln and Egon G. Guba. *Naturalistic Inquiry.* SAGE, Beverly Hills, CA, 1985.
20. Christian Gütl, Felix Mödritscher, and Victor Garcia-Barrios. The past, the present and the future of adaptive e-learning. In *Proceedings of ICL,* 2004.
21. Felix Mödritscher. Towards formalising adaptive behaviour within the scope of e-learning. *Lecture Notes in Computer Science,* 4018, 362, 2006.

II

Conducting Fundamental Software Engineering Research with Computer Games

CHAPTER 7

RESTful Client–Server Architecture

A Scalable Architecture for Massively Multiuser Online Environments

Thomas Debeauvais, Arthur Valadares, and Cristina V. Lopes

CONTENTS

7.1	Introduction	154
7.2	Overview of Techniques for Scaling Up Multiuser Games	156
	7.2.1 Space Partitioning	157
	7.2.2 Other Game-Specific Techniques	158
	7.2.3 Data Management	159
	7.2.4 Network and System Approaches	160
7.3	Restful Client–Server Architecture	161
	7.3.1 Representational State Transfer	162
	7.3.2 RCAT Architecture	164
7.4	RCAT Reference Implementation	166
	7.4.1 WebSockets	168
7.5	RCAT Reference Application: Jigsaw Puzzle	168
7.6	Experiments and Results	170
	7.6.1 Experiment 1: Proxy and Database Bottlenecks	170
	7.6.2 Experiment 2: Scaling Up the Number of Players	172
	7.6.2.1 Experimental Setup	172
	7.6.2.2 Results	173

7.7   Discussion   176
7.8   Conclusion   178
References   178

7.1 INTRODUCTION

Massively multiuser online games (MMOs) such as *World of Warcraft,* *EVE Online,* and *Second Life* are virtual 3D environments in which players interact in real time with each other inside a virtual world. However, interactions in current MMOs are not truly massive: designers craft the games so that users can only interact with at most around a hundred other users at the same time. When more than the expected number of players gather together, the game usually crashes.[*]

The demand for high user concurrency is now going well beyond games. Applications such as Facebook and Twitter distribute massive numbers of events among massive numbers of users. Although these applications are not exactly real time, the updates are relatively fast paced, and therefore present similar challenges to those seen in online games. As web technologies become more capable of supporting rich 2D and 3D media, the line between online games and (serious) web applications will become fuzzier. The goal of our work is to be able to support the next generation of cloud-based massively multiuser online environments, such as massive online open courses [1], and social environments for medical applications [2].

Looking at how MMOs have approached scalability can provide insights to scale other types of multiuser applications. MMO players are generally seen as event producers and consumers: each player generates a stream of events that other players are interested in. For example, if a player orders his or her character to move forward, other players should be notified or the character's movement, update their local state of the world, and render the updated state. If all the players subscribe to all the other players, the number of event messages to deliver increases quadratically with the number of players [3]. Quickly, the system is overwhelmed by the number of events, and the latency (i.e., the time taken to forward an event) increases. The game becomes much less responsive. Thus, there is a trade-off between scalability and responsiveness. That is, as the number of users increases, so does the latency.

---

[*] See a virtual flash mob in *World of Warcraft* at http://www.youtube.com/watch?v = m7FW0BK2fUo.

To give the illusion that players can interact with thousands of other players, MMOs use interest management techniques [4]. They assume that players are only interested in events happening near them in the virtual world. The world is therefore partitioned in self-contained regions (e.g., a city or a forest), and each region is handled by a different process. Systems implementing space partitioning assume that players are interested in events generated in their current region, and maybe also in the adjacent regions, but never in the entire world. Using this partitioning strategy, MMOs have been able to support hundreds of users while keeping the latency relatively low.

Space partitioning works well until too many players decide to meet in the same region. For example, the maximum number of directly interacting users ever achieved in a commercial MMO is around 3000 in the game *EVE Online.*[*] This record was achieved thanks to very expensive hardware infrastructure, a tiered software architecture, and a game design solution called *time dilation*. Time dilation compensates for the server load by slowing down the region's time. Regions may support more players, but some have found time dilation "absolutely unplayable."[†] MMOs that cannot afford this kind of infrastructure, architecture, or game design tricks have much lower player limits: *World of Warcraft* supports around 120 users per region[‡] and *Second Life* up to 100.[§]

Research has tried to dynamically adapt the shape and size of regions to the distribution of players. However, solutions such as dynamic binary space partitioning suffer from a high overhead due to synchronization and data handover between regions [5]. In fact, the CAP theorem (for Consistency, Availability, and Partitioning) states that a partitioned system cannot be both highly available (i.e., responsive) and strongly consistent [6,7]. Because a scalable MMO system involves multiple partitioned processes, the MMO developer inherently has to trade some consistency to stay responsive.

In the past two decades, the number of MMO players has tremendously increased, but so as the number of web users. To scale, web applications follow a very constrained architectural style called representational state transfer (REST) [8]. One of the pillars supporting REST is the statelessness of the Hypertext Transfer Protocol (HTTP) protocol: web servers do

---

[*] See http://themittani.com/news/asakai-aftermath-all-over-cobalt-moon.
[†] See https://forums.eveonline.com/default.aspx?g = posts&t = 108331.
[‡] See http://www.wowwiki.com/Wintergrasp#Queuing.
[§] See http://wiki.secondlife.com/wiki/Limits#Land.

not remember any client data between two requests. This way, it is easy to scale a web application by adding more machines running the exact same application code.

In this work, we explore how REST could be applied to scale MMOs. Even though some game developers doubt that REST can be applied to MMOs [9], the suitability of REST for MMOs remains an open question. Moreover, recent web technologies such as HTML5 WebSockets or WebGL show serious opportunities for browser-based MMOs.

Although scalability is our main concern, we keep in mind the trade-off with consistency and responsiveness. Other requirements such as fault tolerance (if a machine falls, it is at minimal cost for the system) or resilience (recovering quickly from peaks or crashes) are desirable, but they are not the main focus of this chapter.

The contributions of this work are as follows:

- We make a first attempt at conceptually harmonizing REST principles with MMOs.

- We develop an architecture (RCAT) and its reference implementation, which is based on those principles.

- We report performance characteristics of a prototypical RCAT application that allow us to estimate upfront the resources necessary to deploy these applications on the cloud given specific concurrency targets.

In the rest of this chapter, we first cover the current techniques used to scale MMOs to large numbers of users. Then we introduce RCAT, our own architecture designed to scale to large number of users without being bound to a particular type of application. We then detail the reference implementation and an application based on this architecture. Finally, we report our laboratory experiments, discuss the implications, and conclude the chapter.

7.2 OVERVIEW OF TECHNIQUES FOR SCALING UP MULTIUSER GAMES

A large body of academic literature, and several practical techniques seen in the industry, focuses on scalability, consistency, and responsiveness for MMOs. These techniques are scattered in various fields of computer science and target different parts of the scalability problem. This section revisits some of the most well-known techniques for scaling up these systems.

Probably the most popular current technique for scaling MMOs is space partitioning. We detail space partitioning in the next subsection. We also describe other game-specific techniques that help scaling while maintaining consistency and responsiveness. Then we look at scaling techniques applicable to MMOs from the database community and finish with approaches from the network and systems communities.

7.2.1 Space Partitioning

Space partitioning consists of splitting the game world in to multiple regions and assigning each region to a process of the MMO system. In client–server architectures, the processes in charge of regions are game servers, whereas in peer-to-peer architectures, each peer is in charge of one region. Even though the practical feasibility of peer-to-peer architectures is subject to debate (e.g., Miller and Crowcroft [10] say "not feasible" and Hu et al. [11] say "feasible"), client–server and peer-to-peer really are two sides of the same coin: they both partition a game state over multiple machines.

The assumption behind space partitioning dates back from the seminal virtual world of the early 1990s called *DIVE* [12]. In the Distributed Interactive Virtual Environment (DIVE), users can transfer from region to region, but they only need to know what happens in their current region. DIVE follows a client–server architecture. Each server is in charge of processing the client requests concerning the virtual objects in its region, as well as the handover of users from and to other regions. This model works well until a server has to handle too many users or objects in its region. There has been a lot of academic work on space partitioning [13,14]. Most current commercial MMOs use this static space partitioning model. To prevent server crashes, game operators have resolved to *instancing*: they instantiate replicas of a particularly popular region and cap the number of players in the region. The *World of Warcraft* dungeon raids are a current example of instancing.

However, instancing replicas of a region does not make that region scale. Moreover, in virtual worlds such as *Second Life*, where users can create objects at run time, the distribution of objects and users is nonuniform, and the behavior of objects and users is hard to predict [15]. Dynamic space partitioning aims at solving this problem by adapting the size and shape of regions to the object and user distribution so as to balance the computational and bandwidth load across peers (in peer-to-peer architecture) or servers (in client–server architecture). There are several approaches to dynamic space partitioning. One approach treats regions as cells of a Voronoi diagram in either peer-to-peer [16] or client–server architecture [17]. Another approach treats regions as a set of adjacent microcells [18–20]. Yet recent work suggests that the amount of interactions between two regions can result in a high load for the two regions, thereby making spatial partitioning not suitable for all object or player distributions and behaviors [21]. In short, space partitioning is an optimization that is only efficient in certain MMO use cases, but not all.

7.2.2 Other Game-Specific Techniques

Interest management consists of notifying users and objects only about the users, objects, locations, or events they are interested in. For example, an avatar could be interested in only avatars and objects within 100 m or in chat messages directly addressed to that avatar. In academia, interest management has often involved publish–subscribe infrastructures [4], through spatial queries in peer-to-peer infrastructure [22], communication channels maintained by a centralized server [23], or a cloud-based infrastructure [24]. Commercially, interest management is central in EVE Online, a futuristic MMO. EVE's servers conceptually group nearby spaceships in self-contained and isolated spheres. Each sphere has a particular channel, to which all players in the sphere subscribe to. This is an improvement over the traditional space partitioning, as region servers now only need to compute spheres and broadcast messages within spheres rather than to the entire region [25]. Sirikata [26] uses a twist on interest management: rather than computing it spatially, they compute it based on the avatar's view of the world. Thus, clients receive more updates concerning objects in their frustum than updates concerning hidden objects. Once again, not all MMOs may be able to use interest management, visibility, or publish–subscribe techniques efficiently due to their design.

Data prioritization is a mechanism frequently used in MMOs to reduce the bandwidth between peers or from the server(s) to the clients. It assumes that some messages are critical, whereas others are not. When bandwidth or computational resources become scarce, only critical messages need to be forwarded. This has been abundantly studied in peer-to-peer academic research [27,28].

Time dilation is a technique commonly used in commercial MMOs. It consists of slowing down the simulation time, mostly because the server's physics engine cannot keep up with the load. Although time dilation is more graceful than a complete server crash, it remains game specific and severely reduces the responsiveness of the game. *EVE Online* and *Second Life* are two MMOs using time dilation.*

Finally, some online games such as first-person shooters place a strong emphasis on latency. For these games, it is better to be wrong but on time, than right but late [29]. Commercially, the Source Engine from Valve follows an *optimistic* client–server architecture†: If player A hits player B, A actually only predicts that B is hit. Client A sends the hit message to the server. If the server determines that player B was indeed hit when A fired, that is, several frames ago, it forwards the hit to B. However, B could have reacted faster than the latency between A and the server. In that case, A's view would be slightly inconsistent with B's and the server's. Thus, the server would determine that A actually missed his or her shot. The server notifies A of the missed shot, and A rollbacks its state. This rollback results in local inconsistencies [30]. In academic research, Gupta et al. [31] suggest that each client should run the game logic, and the server should only act as a message forwarder and be in charge of persistence. Clients apply their own actions to an optimistic model, and actions are received from the server to a stable model. If applying the same action to the optimistic and stable models results in two different models, the system needs to roll back. The client asks the server to broadcast a fix it proposes; all other clients execute the fix and, if they conflict, send their own fix to the fix. This can result in long chains consuming a lot of bandwidth and CPU. Thus, the server rejects fixes past a certain chain length. Both academic and commercial approaches are examples of the consistency–responsiveness trade-off mentioned earlier.

7.2.3 Data Management

The commercial MMO *Guild Wars 2* has had trouble scaling the number and complexity of *AI scripts* handled by its servers [32]. A research group at Cornell also observed this trade-off between the complexity of AI scripts and their quantity. They proposed a data-driven declarative language that factors similar queries together [33], thereby reducing the AI computations from quadratic to linear with the number of entities in the world. Pikko and BigWorld, two commercial middleware platforms for MMOs, recommend offloading AI scripts outside of the server, as if they were normal clients [34,35]. This way, the server can dedicate more CPU

---

* See http://community.eveonline.com/news/dev-blogs/3412 and http://wiki.secondlife.com/wiki/LlGetRegionTimeDilation.

† https://developer.valvesoftware.com/wiki/Source_Multiplayer_Networking.

processing client requests rather than complex AI scripts. However, there may be a significant bandwidth increase compared to the case where AI is run within the server.

Persistence wise, a *central database* is usually a bottleneck in client–server architectures. This problem has been solved in commercial MMOs in three ways: first, they only persist the state of all connected avatars to the database in a batch every few minutes. Although this alleviates the load on the database, avatar states have to roll back when a server crashes. The second technique addressing the database bottleneck in commercial MMOs is the use of a query manager: a machine stands between the database and the game servers as a buffer and a cache, as in the MMO *Tibia* [36]. A third approach consists of investing in expensive hardware for the database, also known as *vertical scaling*. For example, as of March 2011, each of the two machines hosting the database of *EVE Online* had 512 GB of RAM, 32 logical cores, and 18 solid-state drives, and used a 32 Gbps InfiniBand link to communicate with the tier of game servers.*

We saw earlier that spatial partitioning was not always the best data partitioning scheme. In *Darkstar* (now called *RedDwarf*†), an entity's data are stored on a node independent of the entity's location in the game world [37]. In this way, *Darkstar* resembles the distributed memory caching of memcached.‡ However, the main feature of *Darkstar* is its transactional tasks. Server reads can be performed on the local cache, but writes must be sent to a central server to check for conflicts with other writes. If no conflicts are detected, the transaction is executed; otherwise, the transaction fails and runs again after a period of time. This approach may add latency to some transactions, and particularly to those related to popular entities (e.g., thousands of players attacking the same boss). *Darkstar* clearly stands on the consistency side of the consistency–responsiveness spectrum.

7.2.4 Network and System Approaches

Several system architectures have been proposed for MMOs. A very common architecture seen in client–server academic prototypes and commercial MMOs alike is the *tiered architecture*. Clients connect to a tier of client managers (also known as *proxies*). Proxies forward messages between clients and the tier of game servers, running the game logic. Game servers

---

* See http://community.eveonline.com/devblog.asp?a = blog&nbid = 2292.
† See http://sourceforge.net/apps/trac/reddwarf/.
‡ See http://memcached.org.

persist their state in the database tier. Proxies are useful to externalize the load due to client handling on the server (e.g., socket management and data prioritization) [38]. Even though the average MMO packet size is less than 30 bytes [39], the number of messages to send is between linear and quadratic with the number of players. Tiered architectures were already mentioned in research in the early 2000s [40,41] and have been used in Intel's Distributed Scene Graph (DSG) [42] and many commercial MMOs [25,43,44].

Intel's DSG does more than just a tiered architecture. It aims at breaking down the monolithic simulator-centric architecture and offloading *services* to external processes [42]. Although external services provide a nice separation of concerns, they add extra latency due to the extra hop in forwarding tasks to services. Once again, we see the responsiveness–scalability trade-off. Carlini et al. mixed peer-to-peer and cloud networks by using virtual nodes as an abstraction layer for the physical node location. Virtual nodes allow for transparent node relocation, are cheaper than a pure client–server solution, and are more reliable than a pure peer-to-peer solution [45]. S-VON is a peer-to-peer Voronoi-based overlay network with super peers. Although a pure peer-to-peer Voronoi-based overlay network only accounts for in-game proximity, the super peers also take into account the network proximity to reduce the latency [11].

Another system approach consists of using *lockless* tasks to avoid deadlocks between cores. This has been tried academically in Reference [46] and commercially in the MMO called The Exiled Realm of Arborea (*TERA*) [47]. Compared to offloading services to other machines, lockless game servers do not suffer from additional latency due to the extra hop. However, lockless game servers can only scale up to the number of cores in one machine. We see once again the trade-off between scalability and responsiveness.

7.3 RESTFUL CLIENT–SERVER ARCHITECTURE

The spectrum of solutions for scaling up MMOs is large and includes many application-specific optimizations, some of which were not covered in the previous section. We seek to develop a middleware that has the following characteristics:

- It is application independent and can support a variety of massive multiuser applications, from social networks to synchronous online education to real-time 3D games. This way, the knowledge gained in developing one type of application is not lost when having to develop another type of application.

- It can scale horizontally, that is, the demand for larger number of interacting users can be met simply by adding more servers doing the same functions.

In order to meet these goals, we approach the problem from an architectural perspective. Architectures, or more precisely architectural styles, are constraints over all things that can be done [48]. By setting constraints on applications in specific ways, we establish a set of principles that, on the one hand, disallow many potentially valid application-specific shortcuts, but that, on the other, ensure that the goals of knowledge sharing and horizontal scaling are met.

In this section, we first describe some of the foundations of RCAT, and then describe RCAT itself.

7.3.1 Representational State Transfer

Before the web established itself as the main platform for Internet applications at the global scale, many other platforms had been proposed during the 1980s and the 1990s [49,50]. The web has given us two very important advantages over the competition at the time:

1. It created a common foundation for the development of a variety of applications. Web developers can create many applications in many different domains using many different frameworks, languages, and tools, but the architectural foundations are all the same.

2. It allowed web applications to start small (one web server) and gracefully grow to server farms if the businesses are so demand.

We would like MMOs to have these same properties. As such, RCAT is inspired by the architecture of web applications, in particular REST [8]. REST stipulates five main architectural constraints that we adapt to the context of MMOs:

1. *Client–server*: The state of the system is stored on the server side, not on the client side. Client–server architectures are commonplace in MMOs.

2. *Tiers*: Hardware proxies, load balancers, and software-level intermediaries are recommended to decouple clients from servers. Tiered architectures are not a new topic in the MMO architecture [51].

3. *Stateless protocol*: No client-specific information (i.e., context) can be stored on the server between two client requests. Our intuition is that servers that contain the state cannot scale because of the overhead of potentially synchronizing the parts of the state that they need to share. This is a problem we mentioned in the previous section. REST recommends persisting the state to a database or the clients. This way, the tier of application servers can scale by simply adding more hardware running the application.

4. *Uniform interface*: This involves two parts: first, a RESTful server interface should be able to receive messages with different formats and answer client requests in the format they ask for. Thus, metadata should accompany the client request to help the server understand how to interpret and answer the request—timestamps, for example. Second, each resource should have a unique address (a uniform resource identifier). For example, the host machine's IP and port, and the globally unique identifier of an object suffice to identify and access that object uniquely.

5. *Caches*: They are intermediaries between system components. Their use is highly recommended, because they can reduce computations and traffic considerably. Caches contain information that changes infrequently. In MMOs, players' positions are generally not cacheable, but textures and assets are. We saw earlier that several academic and commercial approaches replicate/cache game entities in adjacent regions for performance reasons.

We must be cautious when applying REST naively to MMOs: at first sight, the statelessness of the protocol between clients and application servers seems to be conflicting with the requirements of MMOs. A stateless protocol implies that either (1) clients have to enclose with their request all the required data for the server to process their requests or (2) the server has to retrieve the necessary data from the database. In MMOs, clients clearly cannot enclose all necessary data with their request, because this can potentially mean the whole game state. Enclosing the whole game state is doable for a two-player game of *Tic-Tac-Toe* or even Chess, but not reasonable for an MMO: bandwidth will quickly become limiting [9]. Thus, servers need to fetch data from the database for each client request. As our evaluation shows in section 7.6, compared to the current monolithic architecture of commercial MMOs, REST can result in a higher latency to process client requests, more bandwidth consumed between server and database, and the database can become a computational bottleneck.

7.3.2 RCAT Architecture

RCAT consists of four tiers: proxies, game servers, caches, and database. We first introduced this architecture in Reference [52]. RCAT is very similar to the architecture shown in Figure 7.1. Proxies handle communication with clients, game servers handle computation of the game logic or simulation, and the database ensures persistence. Each tier isolates a different performance requirement, and therefore a potential bottleneck. This architecture aims at being game agnostic, that is, it does not embed any notion of a virtual space in it.

Proxies isolate the quadratic broadcast problem from the game servers. As mentioned before, proxies are common components in MMO architectures and on the web. Clients and game servers hold permanent connections with the proxies. Their role is simply to forward messages between clients and game servers. The game operator or developer can decide how the proxy forwards client requests to the servers: round-robin, fixed (a given proxy always forwards messages to the same game

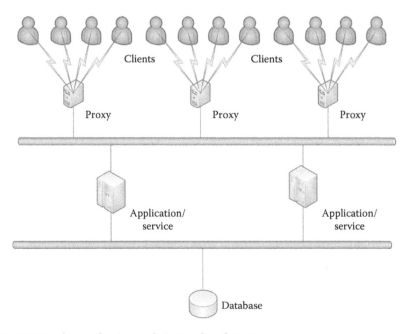

FIGURE 7.1   (**See color insert.**) A tiered architecture.

server), or per-client/"sticky" (all the messages from a given client are sent to the same server). Besides message forwarding, proxies can prioritize, bucket, piggyback, or filter messages based on certain network heuristics (e.g., upload rate or Transmission Control Protocol [TCP] window size). However, they do not have any knowledge whatsoever about the game (e.g., areas of interest or friend lists). Proxies can also help mitigating denial of service attacks against game servers.

Game servers receive and process client requests according to the game logic. When a server receives a request from a client (through a proxy), it computes which clients have to be notified and broadcasts to all the proxies the response to forward as well as the concerned clients. Servers can perform any game logic treatment, from low-latency state updates (e.g., avatar movement) to more reliable bulk transfer content delivery (e.g., textures or streaming the world state when a client first logs in). Servers can be added on the fly to the server tier at no synchronization cost. They only have to notify the proxies when they join in, and retrieve data from their cache.

Caches live on the same machines as the game servers so as to provide for the game servers a quick access to the data and to alleviate the load on the database. Determining which object lives in which cache, so as to optimize data accesses, is the concern of the developer. For example, in space partitioning, two objects that are close to each other in the game world would live in the same cache. Other types of partitioning include by users, as is currently done by Zynga [53], or by data types.

Caches are only a temporary storage to improve performance; it is up to the developer to specify which objects can be cached, the delay for cached objects to become stale, and whether replicas should be instantiated on other machines for faster reads. Basically, the cache tier is the place where the developer specifies the degrees of latency and consistency he or she needs for which objects.

Finally, the bottom tier is the database. It ensures persistence and may still be directly accessed by the game server for transactional operations that must be atomic, consistent, isolated, and durable. When a cached object expires, the cache may retrieve the object's state from the database. If an object living in the cache must be strongly consistent, all the writes performed on the object should also be forwarded to the database. However, if latency is important, the object's state can be flushed to the database only periodically.

7.4 RCAT REFERENCE IMPLEMENTATION

To be able to implement several games, and test which strategies would work best in which cases, we implemented RCAT as a middleware in Python, running on the Linux operating system. This reference implementation of RCAT supports clients running as JavaScript applications on regular web browsers and interacting with regular web servers on the backend. The source code of RCAT, as well as two games built on top of it, is available at https://github.com/gentimouton/rcat. The components of the middleware are shown in Figure 7.2. The two higher level components are the proxy and the game server.

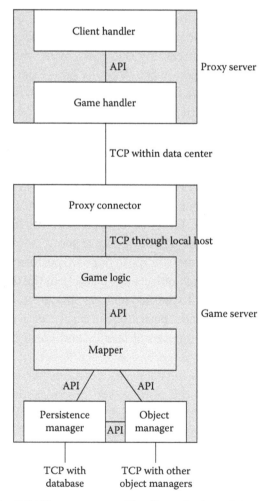

FIGURE 7.2 The RCAT components. The Game logic and Mapper components are game specific and implemented by the game developer.

The proxy communication is performed by Tornado, a nonblocking, single-threaded web server supporting WebSockets.* The proxy has two URL access points: /client and /server. Clients connect to /client, where the client handler component generates a session user ID. The game handler then forwards client messages to a game server. Servers reply to the clients through the /server URL access point of the proxy. Messages sent to /server are treated by the game handler component, which determines the clients that should receive the message.

In the game server, the game logic and mapper components are the game-specific modules of the game server. The game logic contains the game rules. The mapper provides data services to the game logic through an application programming interface (API). Both are plugged into the RCAT's middleware and interface with components from the proxy layer (the proxy connector) and the data layer (the persistence manager and the object manager).

The proxy connector provides two abstractions to the game logic. First, it demultiplexes the WebSocket connections from the game server to the proxies into a single one. Second, it hides from the game logic the location of proxies and clients. If the game logic component wishes to message users, it simply sends the message and the set of recipients (i.e., a set of user IDs). The proxy connector parses the set, checks which proxies those users are connected to, and forwards the message to the appropriate proxies.

The persistence and object managers abstract away the database-specific protocols and the handling of objects in local and remote caches. Each provides an API to the mapper. Both are implemented in Python. Any database supported by SQLAlchemy can be used, but for our implementation, we only tried MySQL.

The persistence manager provides a centralized, available, and consistent data access through SQLAlchemy,† a database object-relational mapper.

The object manager provides a distributed data access and the tools for managing data availability or consistency. The object manager was implemented by us and provides an API to (1) manipulate data stored in local or remote caches and (2) relocate data stored in remote caches to the local cache.

---

* Tornado has been used extensively in real-time web applications such as FriendFeed and Facebook's timeline. See http://www.tornadoweb.org.
† See http://www.sqlalchemy.org/.

7.4.1 WebSockets

The RCAT reference implementation uses WebSockets in order for the clients to receive messages from the servers. Here, we give a brief description of WebSockets.

A WebSocket is a standard TCP connection initiated over HTTP and growing in popularity for real-time web applications. The use of TCP in MMOs is a controversial debate in both research and industry. Some game developers would even rather implement a reliable protocol on top of the User Datagram Protocol (UDP) rather than using TCP.* We opt for TCP for three reasons:

1. TCP removes the effort of controlling packet ordering and retransmission. Adequately configuring the TCP retransmission rate can greatly reduce the latency [38].

2. MMOs generally use TCP, probably because clients send only between 1 and 10 messages per second [21,38]. Using TCP makes our approach more valid and applicable.

3. TCP has many congestion control mechanisms, such as Nagle's algorithm, that may help on the server side when broadcasting the same message to many connections. Such solutions generally trade latency for bandwidth or vice versa. They are yet another illustration of the scalability–responsiveness trade-off in MMOs.

7.5 RCAT REFERENCE APPLICATION: JIGSAW PUZZLE

In order to study the performance characteristics of applications built with the RCAT architecture, we have implemented a multiplayer client–server game using the reference RCAT implementation described above. Our virtual jigsaw puzzle does not impose any limit on the number of players. Moreover, a multiplayer jigsaw puzzle provides an interesting set of requirements:

- Players may scroll from one end of the board to another instantly.

- Players may grab any piece at any time.

---

* See http://gafferongames.com/networking-for-game-programmers/udp-vs-tcp/.

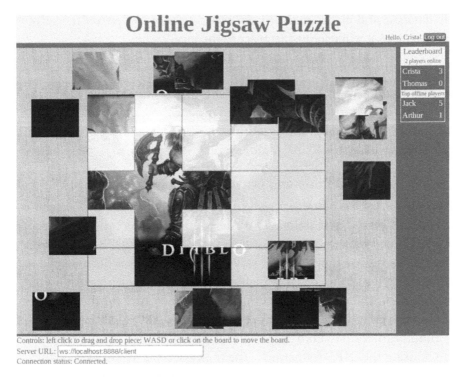

FIGURE 7.3 **(See color insert.)** Multiplayer jigsaw puzzle with 25 pieces.

- Players must know immediately the pieces that are grabbed, moved, and dropped by other players.

- Players may zoom in or out to see the overall picture, or to check for small details.

A screenshot of the HTML5 client is shown in Figure 7.3. Clearly, space partitioning will not be as effective for a multiplayer jigsaw puzzle as for MMOs with clearly defined regions such as *World of Warcraft*. However, interactions between players are minimal, and players may be likely to pick the same piece again. Thus, we configure the proxy to "stick" each client to a server: all the messages sent by that client are forwarded to the same server. Clients are stuck to game servers in a round-robin fashion. We also configure the mapper to partition by players. When a game server receives a message concerning a particular piece from a particular player, it checks if the piece is cached in another server. If it is, the server retrieves the remote piece and places it in the local cache. If the piece is not cached anywhere, the server retrieves it from the database and places it in the local cache. In short, whenever the server needs a piece, it will relocate that piece to the local cache.

7.6 EXPERIMENTS AND RESULTS

In this section, we confirm that the bottlenecks we anticipated on the proxy and database tiers actually exist in practice. We show how we scaled the number of players in the jigsaw puzzle with the number of cores and machines by using the RCAT middleware.

7.6.1 Experiment 1: Proxy and Database Bottlenecks

To confirm that the bottlenecks we anticipated on the proxy and database tiers actually exist in practice, earlier on we developed a proof of concept of a full-broadcast multiplayer movement game following the RCAT architecture, but using a much simpler server side. This study is documented in Reference [54] and the code is available at https://github.com/gentimouton/rcat-gs. We include the main findings of that study here for the purposes of illustrating the basic performance characteristics of RCAT applications.

In this earlier study, both the proxy and the game server are implemented in C# using the .NET framework. The proxy accepts WebSocket connections through the multithreaded Alchemy WebSockets server.* A graphical client was implemented in JavaScript using the HTML5 canvas for rendering and the WebSocket API to connect to the proxy. We used bots, implemented in Java, to stress test the system. Everything ran in Windows 7.

We are not trying to show that our architecture scales, but rather whether the proxy can be a bottleneck. To validate this hypothesis, we only need, and use, one proxy and one server. The commodity machines we use are Optiplex 980, with eight 2.8-GHz i7 cores. We launch up to 50 bots, in increments of 5, to the proxy. Each bot sends 20 position messages per second. The proxy and database run on one machine, the server on another, and bots run on three other different machines (five machines total). As shown in Figure 7.4, the bandwidth from the proxy to the clients increases quadratically. Thus, we cannot expect to be able to scale the number of proxies linearly with the number of clients.

In this simple game, every time the game server receives a position message from a client, it updates in the database the position of the client's avatar, retrieves the list of connected clients, and sends to the proxy, in a single message, (1) the message to be forwarded to the clients, containing

---

* See http://alchemyWebSockets.net/.

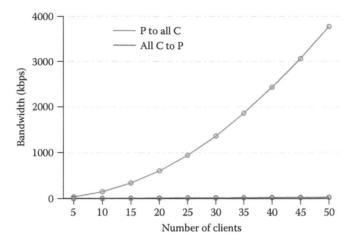

FIGURE 7.4   Bandwidth between all clients (all C) and proxy (P).

the avatar's new position, and (2) the list of clients to send the message to (i.e., everyone currently connected). To estimate the magnitude of the database bottleneck, we compare a scenario where the game server has to retrieve the list of all connected users for every client message and another scenario where the game server caches the list of users and does not have to ask the database every time.

As shown in Figure 7.5, the bandwidth from the server to the database increases linearly with the number of users and decreases slightly when

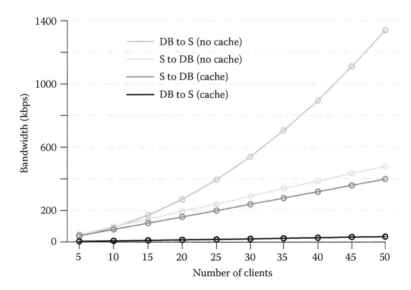

FIGURE 7.5   Bandwidth between database (DB) and server (S) with or without cache.

the list of current clients is cached (compare the two *S to DB* curves). More strikingly, the bandwidth from the database to the server increases quadratically with the number of clients. By caching the list of users, we have reduced a quadratic increase into a linear increase (compare the two *DB to S* curves). This proves that the database can be a central bottleneck and that caching can be an effective strategy.

7.6.2 Experiment 2: Scaling Up the Number of Players

The experimental results reported in this section are based on our RCAT reference application, the multiplayer online jigsaw puzzle.

7.6.2.1 Experimental Setup

Because all players must know about the jigsaw pieces that all other players are acting on, we let TCP delay and piggyback the transmission of ACKs (TCP_QUICKACK socket flag kept at 0). We keep the default value of 40 ms of delay before sending an ACK.* We also enable Nagle's algorithm (TCP_NO_DELAY socket flag kept at 0). The bots, proxies, and servers apply Nagle's algorithm and delayed ACKs.

The bots follow a scripted behavior. On both machines, a new bot joins the game every 10 seconds. Each bot starts by grabbing one piece and moves it by several game units X times per second, with X a configurable parameter. This bot behavior results in no piece having to be relocated between caches. We acknowledge that with real users, piece relocations will happen. However, unless many users fight for the same piece, these relocations should happen relatively rarely. We stop the script manually when we observe that the CPU capacity of the proxies or game servers is completely used. For example, the sum of the CPU capacity of the proxies may reach 400% if there are four proxies. However, Tornado recommends offloading tasks consuming considerable CPU to a thread pool. In our case, the game server keeps processing messages through Tornado, but offloads the game logic tasks to other threads. Consequently, the CPU for a single game server may reach more than 100% if the game logic threads are allocated to another core.

Bots measure the round-time-trip latency (latency, for short) using game messages containing globally unique identifiers. Each proxy and game server instance measures its (user plus system) CPU consumption, and the frequency of voluntary and involuntary context switches every

---

* See http://lwn.net/Articles/502585/.

5 seconds using the Linux getrusage command.* We want to check how the number of proxies and the number of game servers scale with the number of bots for different message frequencies. We define the *maximum capacity* of the system as the highest number of connected clients when the 99th percentile of the latency is below 100 ms.

The commodity machines used for the experiments are Dell Core i7 2600, each with four hyper-threaded 3.4-GHz processors. Up to two machines run proxy instances, up to two others server instances, another the database, and two others the bots. All machines reside on the same 1-Gbps LAN and are one hop from each other. Experiment names follow the format X/Y/Z, standing for X cores running one proxy each, Y cores running one game server each, and bots sending Z messages per second. For example, in the scenario 2/2/5, there are two proxy instances running on the same machine and two game servers sharing another machine, and bots on two other machines send five messages per second. In the scenario 4 + 4/4 + 4/2.5, there are four proxies running on one machine, four proxies on another, four game servers on a third machine, and four game servers on a fourth machine.

7.6.2.2 Results

Figure 7.6 shows that the maximum capacity is reached at 229 clients for the scenario 4 + 4/4 + 4/2.5. In this scenario, the proxy is the bottleneck, and the server reaches slightly past half of its total CPU capacity (400% out of 800% available). On the one hand, the total CPU consumed by the game servers increases linearly with the number of clients. On the other hand, the CPU consumed by the proxies increases quadratically at first, then flattens around 100 clients, and finally seems to increase linearly. We remark this behavior in most of the scenarios where the proxy is a bottleneck.

Figure 7.7 shows that the number of voluntary context switches also reaches a plateau around 100 clients. Voluntary context switches occur when Tornado polls the client sockets, whereas involuntary context switches are triggered by the kernel scheduler.† Thus, there may be a bottleneck on the proxy well before the maximum capacity is reached. On the plus side, this bottleneck does not seem to impact the latency observed on the client side. It is possible that the TCP congestion control

---

* See http://linux.die.net/man/2/getrusage.
† See http://www.lindevdoc.org/wiki/Involuntary_context_switch.

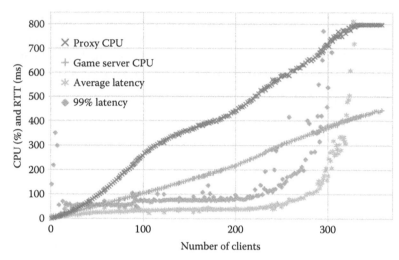

FIGURE 7.6 Evolution of the proxies' central processing unit (CPU), game servers' CPU, average latency, and 99th percentile of the latency with the number of clients when using 4 + 4 proxies and 4 + 4 game servers. The last 99th percentile of the latency to be below 100 ms is the maximum capacity: 229 clients.

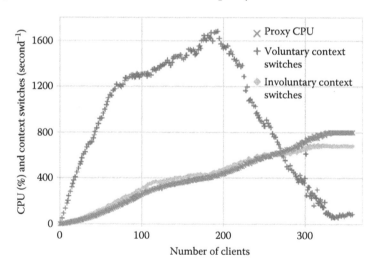

FIGURE 7.7 Evolution of the proxies' CPU and context switches with the number of clients when using 4 + 4 proxies and 4 + 4 game servers.

mechanisms (e.g., piggybacks and ACK delays) buffer the extra delay taken by the proxy.

However, these mechanisms are not enough to prevent the number of voluntary context switches to fall and the latency to spike around 200 clients. Context switches remain the principal reason: because each core ticks 250 times per second,* the maximum number of context switches, voluntary or not, for a system with eight proxies is 8 × 250 = 2000 per second. This is the cap reached around 190 clients. The proxies' cores are overwhelmed.

Interestingly, the proxies are only using half of their CPU capacity when this happens. Clearly, the proxies' CPU capacity is not a sufficient metric by itself to assess the quality of experience of the players, or even the load on the system.

Figure 7.8 plots the maximum capacities for various scenarios. Simply put, to be able to handle twice more players, the system needs 4 times more cores. And this is independent of the message frequency. It is not because a game is slower paced that it scales more linearly. Yet slower paced games can handle more players per core.

Finally, Figure 7.9 illustrates that message frequencies can result in different bottlenecks. We take the scenario with eight proxies and eight game servers as an example. At 2.5 messages per second, the maximum capacity (229 clients) is reached, whereas the game servers only consume around 250% CPU. Meanwhile, the proxies consume twice as much CPU. By contrast, when clients send 10 messages per second, the game servers consume more CPU than the proxies when reaching the overall system's maximum capacity (125 clients). In this scenario, it is difficult to know

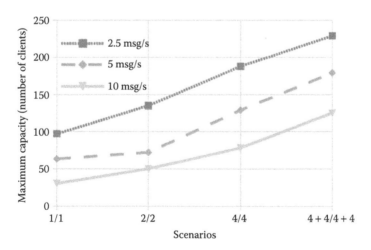

FIGURE 7.8 Scaling the number of clients with the number of cores and machines, when bots send 2.5, 5, and 10 messages per second (msg/s).

---

* The default value of a jiffy is 250 Hz. See http://man7.org/linux/man-pages/man7/time.7.html.

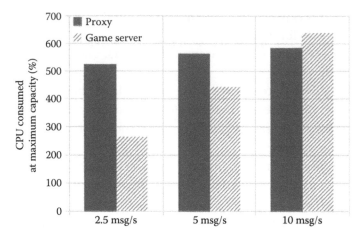

FIGURE 7.9 CPU consumed when maximum capacity is reached with 4 + 4 proxies and 4 + 4 game servers. msg/s, messages per second.

which of the proxies or the game servers is the bottleneck. Yet it seems, surprisingly, that handling many slow-paced connections is more costly than handling few active connections.

Thus, for slow message rates, the proxy is the bottleneck. However, for fast message rates, the game server may be limiting. In fact, the game logic of our jigsaw puzzle is very simple (e.g., no collision detection). Therefore, the server CPU may actually increase faster with the message frequency than shown in Figure 7.9. Provisioning how many proxies and game servers are needed for a given game is not trivial: 1-to-1 ratios may rarely be optimal.

7.7 DISCUSSION

Research has paid much attention to MMOs that are easy to partition spatially. We showed one example of MMO where space partitioning does not apply: a multiplayer jigsaw puzzle. We partitioned the data by user, but did not try other partitioning schemes. Which type of partitioning is best for a multiplayer jigsaw puzzle remains an open question. In fact, this question is not specific to MMOs: developers of other multiuser online applications, such as massive open online courses, are facing the same challenges. We are actively looking for more examples of massively multiuser online applications, as they may highlight new scalability challenges and solutions.

However, space partitioning may still be appropriate for many MMOs. In fact, picking the appropriate load partitioning algorithm is a problem common to any massively multiuser application. In our jigsaw puzzle, we originally considered a space partitioning scheme for the jigsaw puzzle MMO: cutting the board into square regions and assigning a server per region. We quickly realized that this approach would be very inefficient, because users would move pieces between regions as often as within regions. This would cause data handovers too often and result in poor performance.

Thus, we opted for a pair (client, puzzle piece) for load balancing. Whenever a client attempts to move a piece, the piece is relocated to the server treating the client's request. This way, the data for the piece is always located where the client's request is being treated. Another successful approach may have been to move the clients' messages to the application server where the jigsaw piece is cached.

The implementation of RCAT is in active development. Although some parts are application independent, the game developer needs to write the application-specific parts. We use Python for the mapper, and therefore also for the game logic, as the persistence and object managers only provide a Python API. As the middleware development progresses, different implementations of the object manager and persistence manager will provide more flexibility and choice for a wider range of applications.

Currently, each game server instantiates its own object manager. However, game servers running on the same machine could use the same object manager. Implementing this feature may require game servers to be able to tell whether other game servers are local or remote, or to slightly change our architecture.

We noted throughout our experiments that a bottleneck may hide another. Context switches on the proxies may be the limiting factor to scale, and not the proxies' CPU. Moreover, the number of voluntary context switches seems to spike right before the latency starts spiking. Thus, context switches may prove to be a more adequate indicator than the CPU to gauge whether the current load on the system actually impacts the players' experience. It may also prove to be a useful metric for provisioning.

More generally, our work informs the provisioning of massively multiuser online environments. For an application to support twice more users, the operator needs to deploy 4 times more hardware. In the case of the jigsaw puzzle, and assuming the test conditions of our experiment (i.e., all users moving pieces all the time), we estimate that we would be able to support nearly 1000 users with 256 cores. Being able to do these upfront estimations is a major engineering feat with business implications.

Operators may also need to provide a sufficient network infrastructure to support the client connections as well as communication between proxies and application servers. In our experiments, a single 1-Gbps switch was sufficient. Thus, network provisioning may only be a concern well after the 200-user mark.

7.8 CONCLUSION

In this chapter, we have presented RCAT, a scalable and adaptable three-tiered architecture for MMOs. RCAT aims at delivering the flexibility of choosing the individual trade-offs found in the extensive variety of MMOs, while providing a solid infrastructural middleware that abstracts the complexities of scaling through a distributed system. It also provides a common platform for developers and researchers to develop applications and compare results of different partitioning schemes.

We have demonstrated the potential of the architecture by presenting a multiplayer jigsaw puzzle, featuring full broadcasting of events, data locality, and massive number of users. Despite the unavoidable and essential quadratic event distribution, we can support 229 concurrent clients sending 2.5 messages per second and 125 clients sending 10 messages per second, using commodity servers with 16 cores total. Scaling to higher numbers of clients is possible simply by deploying more proxies and game servers such that a target of twice the number of users requires 4 times the number of cores.

As the web becomes more supportive of rich interactive applications, we believe that our work can be the foundation for a variety of massively multiuser online applications.

REFERENCES

1. Pierre Baldi and Cristina Lopes. The universal campus: An open virtual 3-D world infrastructure for research and education. *eLearn*, 2012(4), 2012.
2. Hossein Mousavi, Maryan Khademi, Lucy Dodakian, Steven C. Cramer, and Cristian V. Lopes. A spatial augmented reality rehab system for post-stroke hand rehabilitation. *Studies in Health Technology and Informatics*, 184:279, 2013.
3. Huaiyu Liu, Mic Bowman, Robert Adams, John Hurliman, and Dan Lake. Scaling virtual worlds: Simulation requirements and challenges. In *Winter Simulation Conference*, Baltimore, MD, December 2010.
4. Jean-Sébastien Boulanger, Jörg Kienzle, and Clark Verbrugge. Comparing interest management algorithms for massively multiplayer games. In *Proceedings of the 5th ACM SIGCOMM Workshop on Network and System Support for Games*. ACM, New York, 2006.

5. Huaiyu Liu and Mic Bowman. Scale virtual worlds through dynamic load balancing. *Proceedings of the 14th International Symposium on Distributed Simulation and Real Time Applications*, pp. 43–52. Fairfax, VA, October 2010.

6. Eric Brewer. Towards robust distributed systems, Principles of Distributed Computing (PODC), Portland, OR, July 2000.

7. Eric Brewer. Cap twelve years later: How the "rules" have changed. *Computer*, 45(2):23–29, 2012.

8. Roy Thomas Fielding. Architectural styles and the design of network-based software architectures. PhD thesis, University of California, Irvine, CA, 2000.

9. John Watte. REST and games don't mix. http://engineering.imvu.com/2010/12/18/rest-and-games-dont-mix/.

10. John L. Miller and Jon Crowcroft. The near-term feasibility of P2P MMOG's. In *2010 9th Annual Workshop on Network and Systems Support for Games*, Taipei, Taiwan, November 2010.

11. Shun-Yun Hu, Chuan Wu, Eliya Buyukkaya, Chien-Hao Chien, Tzu-Hao Lin, Maha Abdallah, Jehn-Ruey Jiang, and Kuan-Ta Chen. A spatial publish subscribe overlay for massively multiuser virtual environments. In *International Conference on Electronics and Information Engineering*, vol. 2, pp. V2-314–V2-318. Kyoto, Japan, August 2010.

12. Christer Carlsson. DIVE—A multi-user virtual reality system. *Proceedings of Virtual Reality Annual International Symposium*, pp. 394–400, 1993.

13. Takuji Iimura, Hiroaki Hazeyama, and Youki Kadobayashi. Zoned federation of game servers: A peer-to-peer approach to scalable multi-player online games. In *Proceedings of the 3rd ACM SIGCOMM Workshop on Network and System Support for Games*, Portland, OR, pp. 116–120. ACM, New York, 2004.

14. Shinya Yamamoto, Yoshihiro Murata, Keiichi Yasumoto, and Minoru Ito. A distributed event delivery method with load balancing for mmorpg. In *Proceedings of the 4th ACM SIGCOMM Workshop on Network and System Support for Games*, Hawthorne, NY, pp. 1–8. ACM, New York, 2005.

15. Laura Itzel, Florian Heger, Gregor Schiele, and Christian Becker. The quest for meaningful mobility in massively multi-user virtual environments. In *Proceedings of the 10th Annual Workshop on Network and Systems Support for Games*, pp. 1–2. Ottawa, Canada, October 2011.

16. Eliya Buyukkaya and Maha Abdallah. Data management in Voronoi-based P2P gaming. In *Proceedings of the 5th Consumer Communications and Networking Conference*, pp. 1050–1053. IEEE, Las Vegas, NV, January 2008.

17. David Almroth and Christian Lonnholm. PikkoTekk—Technical summary. Technical report, MuchDifferent, Uppsala, Sweden, February 2011.

18. Bart De Vleeschauwer, Bruno Van Den Bossche, Tom Verdickt, Filip De Turck, Bart Dhoedt, and Piet Demeester. Dynamic microcell assignment for massively multiplayer online gaming. In *Proceedings of the 4th ACM SIGCOMM Workshop on Network and System Support for Games*, Hawthorne, NY, pp. 1–7. ACM, New York, 2005.

19. Alexandre Denault, César Cañas, Jörg Kienzle, and Bettina Kemme. Triangle-based obstacle-aware load balancing for massively multiplayer games. In *Proceedings of the 10th Annual Workshop on Network and Systems Support for Games*, Ottawa, Canada, pp. 4:1–4:6. IEEE Press, Piscataway, NJ, 2011.

20. Bruno Van Den Bossche, Bart De Vleeschauwer, Tom Verdickt, Filip De Turck, Bart Dhoedt, and Piet Demeester. Autonomic microcell assignment in massively distributed online virtual environments. *Journal of Network and Computer Applications*, 32(6):1242–1256, 2009.

21. Kuan-Ta Chen and Chin-Laung Lei. Network game design: Hints and implications of player interaction. In *Proceedings of the 5th ACM SIGCOMM Workshop on Network and System Support for Games*. ACM, New York, 2006.

22. Ashwin R. Bharambe, Sanjay Rao, and Srinivasan Seshan. Mercury: A scalable publish-subscribe system for internet games. In *Proceedings of the 1st Workshop on Network and System Support for Games*, pp. 3–9. ACM, New York, 2002.

23. Stefan Fiedler, Michael Wallner, and Michael Weber. A communication architecture for massive multiplayer games. In *Proceedings of the 1st Workshop on Network and System Support for Games*, pp. 14–22. ACM, New York, 2002.

24. Mahdi Tayarani Najaran and Charles Krasic. Scaling online games with adaptive interest management in the cloud. In *Proceedings of the 9th Annual Workshop on Network and Systems Support for Games*, pp. 9:1–9:6. IEEE Press, Piscataway, NJ, 2010.

25. David H. Brandt. Scaling EVE Online, under the hood of the network layer. Technical report, CCP Games, Reykjavik, Iceland, 2005.

26. Daniel Horn, Ewen Cheslack-Postava, Tahir Azim, Michael J. Freedman, and Philip Levis. Scaling virtual worlds with a physical metaphor. *IEEE Pervasive Computing*, 8: 50–54, 2009.

27. Ashwin Bharambe, John R. Douceur, Jacob R. Lorch, Thomas Moscibroda, Jeffrey Pang, Srinivasan Seshan, and Xinyu Zhuang. Donnybrook: Enabling large-scale, high-speed, peer-to-peer games. In *Proceedings of the ACM SIGCOMM 2008 Conference on Data Communication*, pp. 389–400. ACM, New York, 2008.

28. Jeffrey Pang. Scaling peer-to-peer games in low-bandwidth environments. In *Proceedings of the 6th International Workshop on Peer-to-Peer Systems*, Bellevue, WA, February 2007.

29. Martin Mauve. How to keep a dead man from shooting. In *Proceedings of the 7th International Workshop on Interactive Distributed Multimedia Systems and Telecommunication Services*, pp. 199–204. Enschede, the Netherlands, October 2000.

30. Eric Cronin, Burton Filstrup, Anthony R. Kurc, and Sugih Jamin. An efficient synchronization mechanism for mirrored game architectures. In *Proceedings of the 1st Workshop on Network and System Support for Games*, Braunschweig, Germany, pp. 67–73. ACM, New York, 2002.

31. Nitin Gupta, Alan Demers, Johannes Gehrke, Philipp Unterbrunner, and Walker White. Scalability for virtual worlds. In *Proceedings of the 2009 IEEE International Conference on Data Engineering*, pp. 1311–1314. IEEE Computer Society, Washington, DC, 2009.

32. Mike Lewis. Managing the masses. In *Game Developers Conference*, San Francisco, CA, March 2012.

33. Walker White, Alan Demers, Christoph Koch, Johannes Gehrke, and Rajmohan Rajagopalan. Scaling games to epic proportions. In *Proceedings of the 2007 ACM SIGMOD International Conference on Management of Data*, Beijing, People's Republic of China, pp. 31–42. ACM, New York, 2007.

34. David Almroth and Christian Lonnholm. PikkoTekk—Horizontal scalability. Technical report, MuchDifferent, Uppsala, Sweden, February 2011.

35. BigWorld. Server overview. Technical report, BigWorld, Sydney, Australia, 2009.

36. Matthias Rudy. Inside tibia—The technical infrastructure of an MMORPG. In *Game Developers Conference Europe*, Cologne, Germany, August 2011.

37. Jim Waldo. Scaling in games and virtual worlds. *Communications of ACM*, 51:38–44, 2008.

38. Carsten Griwodz and Pål Halvorsen. The fun of using TCP for an MMORPG. In *Proceedings of the 2006 International Workshop on Network and Operating Systems Support for Digital Audio and Video*, pp. 1:1–1:7. ACM, New York, 2006.

39. Szabolcs Harcsik, Andreas Petlund, Carsten Griwodz, and Pål Halvorsen. Latency evaluation of networking mechanisms for game traffic. In *Proceedings of the 6th ACM SIGCOMM Workshop on Network and System Support for Games*, pp. 129–134. ACM, New York, 2007.

40. Carsten Griwodz. State replication for multiplayer games. In *Proceedings of the 1st Workshop on Network and System Support for Games*, pp. 29–35. ACM, New York, 2002.

41. Martin Mauve, Stefan Fischer, and Jörg Widmer. A generic proxy system for networked computer games. In *Proceedings of the 1st Workshop on Network and System Support for Games*, pp. 25–28. ACM, New York, 2002.

42. Dan Lake, Mic Bowman, and Huaiyu Liu. Distributed scene graph to enable thousands of interacting users in a virtual environment. In *Proceedings of the 9th Annual Workshop on Network and Systems Support for Games*, Taipei, Taiwan, 2010.

43. David Almroth. Pikko server. In *Erlang User Conference*, Stockholm, Sweden, 2010.

44. Seungmo Koo. How to support an action-heavy MMORPG from the angle of server architecture. In *Chinese Game Developers Conference*, Shanghai, People's Republic of China, 2010.

45. Emanuele Carlini, Massimo Coppola, and Laura Ricci. Integration of P2P and clouds to support massively multiuser virtual environments. In *Proceedings of the 9th Annual Workshop on Network and Systems Support for Games*, Taipei, Taiwan, November 2010.

46. Kjetil Raaen, Håvard Espeland, Håkon Kvale Stensland, Andreas Petlund, Pål Halvorsen, and Carsten Griwodz. A demonstration of a lockless, relaxed atomicity state parallel game server (LEARS). In *Proceedings of the 10th Annual Workshop on Network and Systems Support for Games*, Ottawa, Canada, pp. 19:1–19:3. IEEE Press, Piscataway, NJ, 2011.

47. Seungmo Koo. TERA: Evolving MMORPG combat. *Game Developer Magazine*, July 2012.
48. Richard N. Taylor, Nenad Medvidovic, and Eric M. Dashofy. *Software Architecture: Foundations, Theory, and Practice*. Wiley, New York, 2009.
49. William Grosso. *Java RMI*. O'Reilly, Sebastopol, CA, 2001.
50. Robert Orfali, Dan Harkey, and Jeri Edwards. *The Essential Distributed Objects Survival Guide*. Wiley, New York, 1995.
51. Howard Abrams. Three-tiered interest management for large-scale virtual environments. In *Proceedings of the ACM Symposium on Virtual Reality Software and Technology*, Taipei, Taiwan, November 1998.
52. Thomas Debeauvais and Bonnie Nardi. A qualitative study of Ragnarök Online private servers: In-game sociological issues. In *Proceedings of the 5th International Conference on the Foundations of Digital Games*, Monterey, CA, 2010.
53. Robert Zubek. Scalability for social games. In *Game Developers Conference Online*, Austin, TX, 2010.
54. Cristina Videira Lopes, Thomas Debeauvais, and Arthur Valadares. RESTful Massively Multi-user Virtual Environments: A feasibility study. In *2012 IEEE International Games Innovation Conference*, pp. 1–4. Rochester, NY, September 2012.

CHAPTER 8

Software Engineering Challenges of Multiplayer Outdoor Smart Phone Games

Robert J. Hall

CONTENTS

8.1 Motivation 184
8.2 Three Geocast Games 184
    8.2.1 iTron 185
    8.2.2 iTESS 185
    8.2.3 Butterflies 188
8.3 Engineering Challenges 190
    8.3.1 Architecture 190
    8.3.2 Design 191
    8.3.3 Coding 193
    8.3.4 Requirements 193
    8.3.5 Validation 194
8.4 The GGA 194
    8.4.1 Variants 195
8.5 Summary 196
References 196

8.1 MOTIVATION

Video games are extremely popular in today's world. People who spend too much time with video games, however, are prone to many health and cognitive risks, including obesity, poor socialization, and repetitive stress injuries. Children are particularly sensitive to these problems and developmental delays as well. To combat these problems, our goal in the Geocast Games Project [1] is to build attractive games that inherently incorporate vigorous physical activity outdoors and encourage multiplayer interactions.

In pursuance of this goal, if the games we build were to require additional equipment that must be bought and brought solely to support the game experience, it could harm our ability to reach a broad segment of the population. Moreover, we wish to allow as unrestricted an experience outdoors as possible; having to leave one's laptop, for example, unattended in the dirt while running off into a public park, has obvious risks and disincentives. Moreover, such supernumerary devices would need to be powered and administered, further increasing the burden and reducing the constituency for our games.

Instead, we wish to provide the games solely on equipment people are likely to carry anyway for other purposes, namely smart phones, iPods, and so on. In this way, people can play spontaneously whenever and wherever a willing group is present. More specifically, we want devices that are location aware and capable of 802.11 wireless communications (or other wireless communications technologies as may become available). Richer experiences are possible when devices have other features that are becoming prevalent today, such as azimuth sensors, accelerometers, wide area wireless (e.g., 4G [4th Generation], LTE [Long Term Evalution], GSM [Global System for Mobility]), cameras, and rich audio capabilities. For this chapter, we will term this class *smart phones*, even though not all of them necessarily have telephone capability. The decision to restrict to smart phones has major consequences for the architecture and software engineering of the games.

8.2 THREE GEOCAST GAMES

The GC1 prototype [1,2] is a smart phone application that includes three multiplayer outdoor smart phone games. All of these Geocast Games combine real-world action and movement with virtual elements implemented in a distributed fashion on smart phones. I describe them briefly here to provide context for what follows.

FIGURE 8.1 **(See color insert.)** Typical iTron game.

8.2.1 iTron

iTron [3] is a real-world "snake" game. Essentially, players must move around in the real world; while doing so, they leave a trail of "walls" in the virtual world (Figure 8.1). Players must avoid running into walls by moving so that their represented position crosses a wall on the display. Figure 8.1 shows real-world and virtual-world views of a three-person iTron game in progress. One player has crashed into the tail of another early on, whereas one is in danger of hitting the area boundary. The object is to be the last one remaining after all others have crashed. The game is both a strategy game in which one tries to surround and cut off one's opponents from territory and an athletic game involving running fast enough and accurately enough to carry out these strategies.

Note also the player using an inexpensive *Kyle Wrist Mount* to convert the smart phone into a hands-free wearable, a key innovation that reduces risk to the device and allows more freedom for the athletic activities of the game.

This game was played in a relatively small, clear area like a parking lot or football field. iTron can also be played in larger areas having complex terrain, such that climbing and terrain traversal become a significant part of the planning and athleticism. This style of iTron game is termed *iTron/ Parkour.* The final state of such a game is shown in Figure 8.2.

8.2.2 iTESS

iTESS [4] is a hide-and-seek conflict game that provides virtual weaponry and intelligence assets to players in the real world. The object of the game

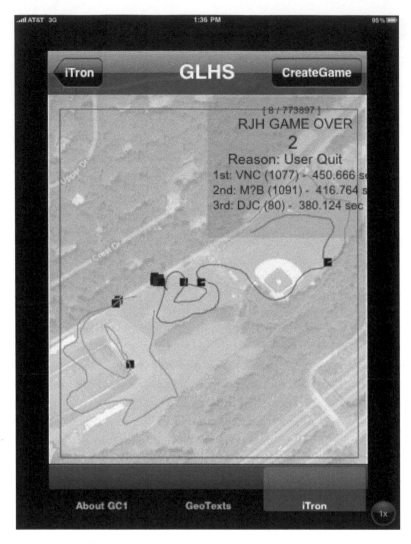

FIGURE 8.2 Final state of an iTron/Parkour game.

is for a player to last as long as possible without being hit by a weapon shot (either artillery or shotgun weapon), with one's score being the maximum of such interval achieved during an extended game session. One searches for one's opponents either in the real world or by commanding a virtual unmanned aerial vehicle (UAV) on the screen of the smart phone that "flies" over the map and paints red dots if it spots opponents (see Figure 8.3). The green-shaded (lightly shaded circle in lower right corner) circle is the UAV lookdown region. The blue dot with compass arrow is the location of the

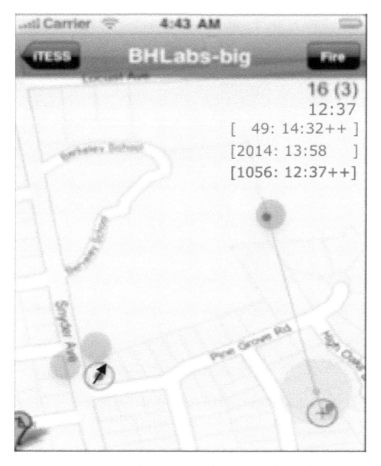

FIGURE 8.3 Screen capture from iTESS showing artillery shots. Upper right numeric display shows top three scores in game at any time.

player of the device shown, and the red dot represents the enemy players spotted by the UAV. The red-shaded circles are warnings for incoming artillery rounds, whereas the blue circle is the effect area of one's own round.

One targets artillery by moving a crosshair and then tapping the fire button. By contrast, one targets the shotgun by physically pointing the device and then doing a screen drag to pull the trigger (see Figure 8.4).

In either case, shotgun shot or artillery shot, opponents in the effect area of the weapon are notified and shown the area they must escape in the brief time before the round reaches them. iTESS is designed to have slow weapon effects to encourage and allow rapid reactions and fast running to save players (see Reference [4] for details).

(a)

(b)

FIGURE 8.4 **(See color insert.)** (a) Point-and-shoot interface for the iTESS shotgun weapon and (b) screen display during a shotgun shot animation.

iTESS operates using *ad hoc* networking to transfer geographically addressed messages among devices. Once a player is hit, his or her interval time restarts from 0.

8.2.3 Butterflies

Butterflies provides virtual creatures interacting with human players in the real world. Figure 8.5 shows a game situation, with blue dot (dark dot with arrow through it) being one's own position on the map, red dots being other human players' positions, and the other symbols representing butterflies and butterfly net acquisition areas. Essentially, the human's goal is to collect as many good butterflies as possible by running so as to move onto their bodies while avoiding being touched by (running within) bad butterflies. A butterfly net (if one has one available) can extend one's reach to capture hard to reach or fast butterflies, such as those that fly on top of

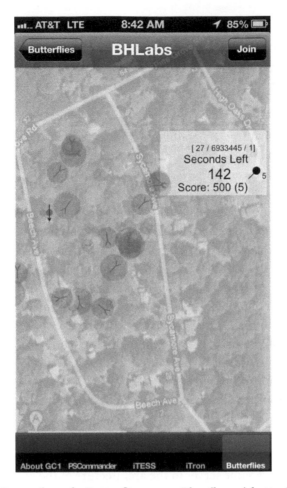

FIGURE 8.5 Screenshot of a Butterflies game. Blue (larger) butterflies are good, red (smaller) ones are bad, blue dot is my position, and red dots are other players' positions. Green lollipop symbols are positions at which a player can obtain butterfly nets.

buildings. As game level increases, butterflies gain more and more complex behaviors. At lowest levels, they move randomly in predetermined pseudorandom patterns. At higher levels, they can run away from humans or chase them, at varying speeds. Humans can find butterfly nets that help catch or defend against them. This game therefore involves a lot of movement, planning, and social interaction as, for example, some butterflies are so fast and clever that often the only way to catch them is for humans to coordinate their actions.

8.3 ENGINEERING CHALLENGES

Outdoor multiplayer games as discussed earlier bring challenges to software engineering in at least five phases: architecture, design, coding, validation, and requirements.

8.3.1 Architecture

Outdoor play in natural environments such as parks, beaches, and remote camps will often involve play without or weak network coverage, with no WiFi hot spots or even 3G coverage available. The devices, however, are capable of device-to-device *ad hoc* networking. This will generally mean that communications between distant players will become disconnected unpredictably and for extended periods. For example, two iTESS players might run off into a valley while continuing to shoot at each other, yet still be out of network contact with the other players due to terrain. Similarly, subsets of iTron or Butterflies players can move apart, to opposite sides of a building, for example. Because to be successful the game experience must continue (to the extent physically possible) even when out of infrastructure coverage areas and even when partitioned from distant players, I term this first major problem in architecting an outdoor smart phone game the *communication problem.*

Following from this first problem is the fact that any two devices can become unpredictably partitioned from one another for extended periods. This means that *game experience must not require a central controller.* That is, for games intended for play in remote areas, not only can we *not* require a console or Internet game server in the architecture of the game, but also we cannot even designate one of the smart phones as the controller. If we did so, any time devices become partitioned away from it, they lose game experience until contact is reestablished. I term this the *full distribution problem.*

Finally, another architecture issue, *the long-range play problem* concerns games playable at long distances. It makes perfect sense for a group in California to play iTESS against groups in New Jersey, the United Kingdom, and Tokyo. Obviously, this requires Internet connectivity, because device-to-device relaying is clearly inadequate. If we assume that enough players have devices that *are* in coverage of an Internet access point (e.g., receiving 3G/GSM coverage), we would like our game architecture to support the communications necessary as seamlessly as possible.

My initial progress on attacking these problems is captured in the *Geocast Games Architecture (GGA)* (see Section 8.4).

8.3.2 Design

When designing games involving virtual structures, objects, or creatures that can have evolving states, there is a need for the game system to manage state evolution in a way that yields the desired game experience to all players. As an example, consider virtual creature control. A butterfly that reacts to human proximity by flying away changes state in response to environment events. But how do players located away from this butterfly's location, maybe even network partitioned from the area, gain a coherent view of its state? The problem is compounded when events from *multiple* different devices cause state changes, as we must be concerned with how the different players view the creature, given that different subsets of players will have been made aware of different subsets of the events. Figure 8.6 shows screen captures from two Butterflies players at nearly the same time; the two players have been out of network contact due to being on opposite sides of a building. Consequently, their devices have different views of what the butterflies have been doing. Positions of butterflies and even positions of other players are significantly different. This

 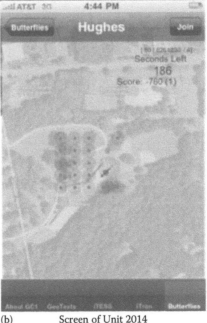

(a)   Screen of Unit 80   (b)   Screen of Unit 2014

FIGURE 8.6   (a,b) Two device screens at nearly the same time (13 seconds apart) in a Butterflies game with radio obstacles.

is because players have moved while out of radio contact due to the intervening school building.

Now, we cannot hope to defeat the Physics of the situation; given the presence of communications partitions due to terrain, there is no way to keep all devices having identical states at all times. Fortunately, we do not need this to provide playable and fun game experiences. Instead, we can demand that once devices come back together (i.e., reestablish contact), they come to agree as quickly as possible on a common coherent view of the state. I term this property *rapid recoherence (RRC)*. Figure 8.7 shows the same Butterflies game as earlier, approximately 90 seconds later in time, after the players have met up and the devices have undergone RRC. The two displays differ only in that the dot representing one's own position is different for the two devices.

This issue goes beyond the question of rapidity into how to recohere in a way that seems fair to players; for example, if one works hard to gain points, can points be taken away just because someone far away did something in the past of which one was unaware? Similarly, if the process of recoherence involves retracting state changes, how far into *alternate history extrapolation*

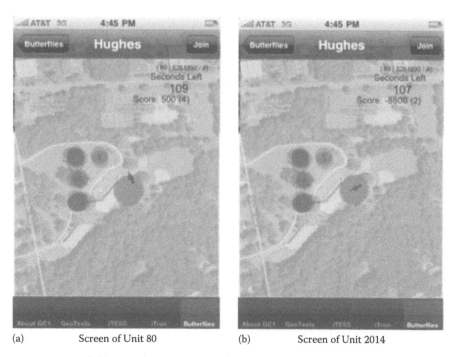

(a)   Screen of Unit 80   (b)   Screen of Unit 2014

FIGURE 8.7   (a,b) Two device screens after RRC in the same Butterflies game.

can or should a system delve to reconstruct what would have happened had the newly discovered information been known earlier? In aggregate, I group all these issues under the term the *distributed joint state problem*. Specifically, can we come up with a design methodology that allows a coherent creature behavior to be implemented on top of a fully distributed architecture subject to sporadic communication? The Butterflies game is an initial experiment in RRC and distributed joint state management, but there is still room for future research in this area.

8.3.3 Coding

Pursuing our goal of appealing to (and thereby benefiting) as large a cross section of the population as possible, we cannot provide our games on merely one brand or model of smart phone. Therefore, we must seek abstractions and tool support in cross-platform development that not only helps with cross-compilation of source code, but can help the developer compensate for differences in hardware performance, sensor capabilities, communications systems differences, and operating system and language differences.

Cross-platform code development frameworks such as Cocos2d-x [5] for iOS, Android, Windows, and Blackberry smart phones are a promising start in this area.

8.3.4 Requirements

It is clear that not every possible game semantics that is implementable in a central server architecture is achievable in a fully distributed outdoor gaming context. This is simply because of the sporadic communications problem: if I capture a creature at time t, but there is no way for your device to hear about this for a delay $\Delta > 0$, from your viewpoint, the creature is still available to be captured prior to $t + \Delta$. If my game requirements included the notion that all players shall have a consistent description of which creatures are captured and which are not at every instant of time, it would simply not be implementable in this architecture. I term this the (*outdoor games*) *requirements restriction problem*. Specifically, we need to develop a domain-specific set of *meta-requirements* applicable to outdoor game design. Such meta-requirements would comprise guidelines and constraints on requirements models to help developers better understand when they are posing impossible or impractical requirements for new games. Prior work on tolerating inconsistency [6] would seem relevant here.

As an example, a hypothetical requirements tool could notice when a requirement statement implied global consistency in the joint state at all times, flag this as unrealizable, and even suggest replacing it with an RRC-based criterion.

8.3.5 Validation

Testing and formal validation of distributed systems is well known to be difficult; however, fully distributed smart phone games exacerbate this difficulty. The requirements one is validating are often relative to the distributed joint state of the system, so validating means to understand the relaxed semantics of systems designed and specified to allow temporary network partitions leading to inconsistent state views. For example, two devices disagreeing on who captured a creature due to being out of network contact is no longer indicative of a validation failure unless the condition remains well after the devices have reestablished network contact. How can one express such a notion of correctness and test for it, or formally validate compliance with it? I term this the *(outdoor games) semantic validation problem*.

On a more pragmatic level, tests will often involve many to tens of devices. Simply gathering, merging, synchronizing, and cleaning test data in order to even start analyzing a run is now quite complex, because it would seem to need a substantial tool infrastructure to gather and analyze the data from the devices and the wireless medium. The *Capture Calculus Toolset* (CCT) [7] is one such tool suite that can capture, transform, combine, analyze, and animate real-world test data.

Scale and load testing requires even more devices, seemingly requiring some sophisticated tool support or else an army of willing helpers. I term this the *(outdoor games) pragmatic testing problem*. Just maintaining a lab with tens of devices involves a lot of charging, app loading, configuring, and tracking of devices. The CCT provides combinators for combining and enlarging captured test run data with procedurally generated scenarios to increase the scale of the data. This can then be animated, analyzed, and simulated. However, one future work problem is a tool capable of taking such synthesized large-scale scenarios and actually executing them on real devices automatically.

8.4 THE GGA

In my previous work, I have documented my approach to implementing outdoor smart phone games. The three games discussed in Section 8.2 are all built using the GGA [2]. I recap here its three principles.

1. *Fully distributed architecture*: This is motivated by the reasons given above. All games shall be designed without central controller running only on the devices worn or carried by players.

2. *Geographic communications*: The GGA defines that communications among devices will use scalable geographic addressing framework (SGAF) [8], with the *Scalable* Ad Hoc *Geocast Protocol* (*SAGP*) [9] used, where applicable, within the *ad hoc* field communications tier. SAGP is *ad hoc*, in that it propagates from peer device to peer, not requiring base stations or infrastructure support. It is a geographic addressing protocol, meaning that the application addresses network messages *geographically*, by the area of space to which they should be transferred, rather than by device identifier, IP address, cell phone number, or anything else. This allows it to avoid the scalability and robustness pitfalls of traditional IP networking. It is scalable in the sense that its overhead is low and does not increase dramatically with device density in an area. This allows game playing in crowded venues as well as outdoor venues.

3. *Optional long-range extension*: If devices do have access to infrastructure networks, such as wide area networking such as 4G/LTE/GSM service, geographically addressed communications can exploit this via the *Tiered Geocast Protocol* [10], the long-range framework part of SGAF, to allow long-range communications efficiently. For example, it allows iTESS play between people on opposite coasts, a scenario that has been enacted on multiple occasions.

8.4.1 Variants

The above definition is a bit of an idealization in that there can be situations where one needs or desires to alter the GGA somewhat to accommodate restrictions or changed requirements. For example, one may wish to incorporate devices that do not have a compatible 802.11 (WiFi) capability; such could be incorporated as a separate, non-*ad hoc* tier within the SGAF. Similarly, one may wish to interface to low-cost networked sensors that do not have their own location sensing capabilities or may have low memory or CPU resources. In such cases, we may compromise the ideal of *full* distribution and allow some devices to offload computation, sensing, and/or storage to other devices.

Extensive testing and trial experience (over 175 users have played at least one of the three geocast games) show that the GGA-based games meet our goals for fun and athletic play outdoors. See References [3] (iTron) and [4] (iTESS) for descriptions of the implementations of games according to GGA principles. However, the GGA is only a foundation. In particular, much future work needs to be done to address the challenges discussed in Section 8.3.

8.5 SUMMARY

I have briefly overviewed the motivation for healthy outdoor multiplayer smart phone games and the challenges they bring for software engineering. I have also provided overviews of three implemented games that have allowed experimentation with the concepts and provided initial trials of the GGA and RRC.

In scratching the surface of the many challenges brought by this game domain, I have touched on five facets of software engineering:

1. Architecture—Communications and full distribution problems

2. Design—Distributed joint state problem and RRC

3. Coding—Cross-platform coding problem

4. Requirements—Requirements restriction problem

5. Validation—Semantic validation and pragmatic testing problems

In short, this is a rich and challenging area that is ripe for research that can contribute toward worthwhile social goals.

REFERENCES

1. Scalable ad hoc wireless geocast project. www.research.att.com/projects/ Geocast/.
2. R. J. Hall. Cheating attacks and resistance techniques in geogame design. In *Proceedings of ACM FuturePlay Conference*, Vancouver, BC, May 2010.
3. R. J. Hall. The iTron family of geocast games. *IEEE Transactions on Consumer Electronics*, **58**(2), 2012.
4. R. J. Hall. A point and shoot weapon design for outdoor multiplayer smartphone games. In *Proceedings of the 2011 International Conference on the Foundations of Digital Games*, Bordeaux, France, June 2011.
5. Cocos2d-x.org. n.d. www.cocos2d-x.org.
6. R. Balzer. Tolerating inconsistency. In *Proceedings of the 13th International Conference on Software Engineering*, Austin, TX, September 1991.
7. R. J. Hall. The capture calculus toolset. In *Proceedings of the 26th IEEE/ ACM International Conference on Automated Software Engineering, Research Demonstrations Track*, Lawrence, KS, November 2011.

8. R. J. Hall. Scaling up a geographic addressing system. In *Proceedings of 2013 IEEE Military Communications Conference*, San Diego, CA, November 2013.
9. R. J. Hall. An improved geocast for mobile ad hoc networks. *IEEE Transactions on Mobile Computing*, **10**(2):254–266, 2011.
10. R. J. Hall and J. Auzins. A tiered geocast protocol for long range mobile ad hoc networking. In *Proceedings of the 2006 IEEE Military Communications Conference*, Washington, DC, October 2006.

CHAPTER 9

Understanding User Behavior at Three Scales

The AGoogleADay Story

Daniel M. Russell

CONTENTS

9.1	Introduction	200
9.2	Background	201
9.3	Our Game: AGAD	201
9.4	Three Views of the User: Micro, Meso, and Macro	203
	9.4.1 Micro Level: How Players Behave over Short Timescales	204
	9.4.2 Meso Level: How Humans Behave Minute by Minute	206
	9.4.3 Macro Level: How Humans Behave over Days and in the Large	208
	9.4.4 Integrating Research and Design across the Three Levels	210
9.5	Summary	212
	References	212

Abstract: How people behave is the central question for data analytics, and a single approach to understanding user behavior is often limiting. The way people play, the way they interact, and the kinds of behaviors they bring to the game are factors that ultimately drive how our systems perform and what we can understand about why users do what they do. I suggest that looking at user data at three different scales of time and sampling resolution shows us how looking at behavior data at the micro, meso, and macro levels is a superb way to understand what people are doing in our systems and why. Knowing this lets you not just understand what is going on, but also how to improve the user experience for the next design cycle.

9.1 INTRODUCTION

Although there are many motivations for creating games, *serious games* are usually vehicles for teaching and learning. Although serious games are important in many educational settings, they sometimes suffer from a lack of attention to the details of game design. Although the goal is to teach and instruct, the *game* experience sometimes suffers. Face it, some of those serious games are not so much fun to play. How is it possible that a game can be created and deployed without anyone noticing that it has some playability issues?

Many people have reported on ways to instrument and monitor a game. We have found that a particularly useful approach to understand the overall user experience has been to analyze game player behavior at three different timescales of behavior, from very short millisecond-by-millisecond behaviors, up to the timescale of millions of players as they use the game to learn over weeks and months.

The AGoogleADay.com (AGAD) game had a simple goal. We simply wanted to show the public some more sophisticated ways to use the Google search engine. Although Google is simple to use, there are many features within Google that are not widely used. By building a "trivia question" style game where the use of Google was *required* (and not prohibited, as in most such games), we hoped to introduce new features to the players by creating questions that were difficult (and obscure) enough to motivate their use.

Originally planned as a 3-month experiment, the AGAD game continues to run more than 2 years after its launch, serving millions of game players each month and improving players' ability to seek out answers to questions by searching.

Here we describe some of the analyses we did to understand what was happening with the players—what they did and what effect changes to the game would have.

Although this chapter is about AGAD, the game, the approach of understanding complex user behavior at these three different timescales, and using three different kinds of studies, is applicable to software systems with complex user interfaces (UIs) in general.

9.2 BACKGROUND

There has been a practice of developing games with an eye toward testing and analysis (Pinelle 2008; Nacke 2009; Koeffel 2010). Typically, the analysis of games has followed traditional usability analysis methods or logging player behavior.

Human computer interaction (HCI) researchers have grown increasingly interested in studying the design and experience of online games, creating methods to evaluate their user experience (Bernhaupt 2010), "playability" heuristics for their design (Schaffer 2008), and models for the components of games (Schaffer 2008) and game experience (Sweetser and Wyeth 2005). Each of these approaches, although useful, is primarily situated within a single scale of analysis—playability heuristics are defined at the microscale, whereas game experience is primarily studied at the mesoscale. Likewise, the work of Bell et al. (2006) is definitely a macroscale study (by means of diaries), but does not take into account the behavior of players across the scales.

However, in an age when online games are played by a large number of gamers, from potentially many places around the world, a more comprehensive method for understanding game use early on in the design process is often fruitful. This desire to bridge the gap between the lowest levels of use and the behavior of players in the very large led us to apply a broad-spectrum analysis to our game.

9.3 OUR GAME: AGAD

The AGAD game was originally developed with a dual purpose in mind: (1) to be a serious game to teach people more advanced search skills, such as how to use the **filetype:** or **site:** or **filter-by-color** search methods, and (2) to also be a marketing presence for Google search in new markets in which we wanted to experiment. Although Google has a good deal of experience in advertising, this was the first attempt at creating an engaging experience with such a dual purpose.

The goal from the outset was to create a very visual game that would be "sticky," but not all consuming. In other words, it had to be the kind of game one would play for a relatively short amount of time, be exposed to the message, and learn a bit along the way.

We designed a "trivia question" game that would be significantly more difficult than ordinary trivia answering games. Typical trivia games walk a delicate balance between being too difficult to answer (except by a small fraction of the game-playing population) and being too easy (and therefore unsuitable for competitive play). For AGAD, we selected questions that are purposefully unlikely to be known by even a small fraction of the gamers, yet answers that are discoverable with a few Google searches. The questions also had to be of some intrinsic interest—truly trivial questions, such as what is the 23rd digit in the decimal expansion of pi?—are unsuitable for game play.

AGAD is a fairly simple game to construct. The UI presents a few questions each day, with daily updates to the set. Players work through the questions, doing Google searches in a separate iframe that allows the search engine to be visible alongside the question. Each question has a simple answer that can be recognized by a regular expression. Writing the `regexp` is slightly tricky, as most questions have multiple variants on an answer (e.g., "three," "3," or "the number 3").

As shown in Figure 9.1, the questions are presented in a frame at the bottom of the page, with typical game mechanics such as unlocking subsequent questions, buttons to let the player skip a question, and ways to compare your score (and time to answer the question) with friends via the Google+ social network.

As we developed AGAD, it quickly became clear that user testing would have to be an important part of the design cycle. This is true for

FIGURE 9.1 **(See color insert.)** The AGAD game shows a search question (3), then lets you search for the answer with Google (1). You work through the questions (2) scoring points as you unlock and solve additional questions.

all games, but as we proceeded, it became clear that we actually had to do more than standard usability testing in the lab. One large bias was that in the lab setting, people are highly motivated to perform to the best of their ability. As a consequence, we were seeing a divergence between the lab testing and what we anecdotally observed when watching people in the wild. How could we improve the accuracy of our design-driven testing?

To make our understanding of the players more accurate, we needed to understand what they are doing when they started up the game, how they played the game, and what happened over a broad population. This is what led to the idea that the studies should encompass three different approaches. We needed to not just understand the low-level usability issues but also verify that the game was fun to play and would leave people with a positive attitude about Google.

Thus, the goal of our design testing strategy became to observe the players in three different ways in order to create a fully rounded picture of what they are doing in (and how they are enjoying) the game.

9.4 THREE VIEWS OF THE USER: MICRO, MESO, AND MACRO

After a bit of iteration, we settled on three different analyses of player behavior. We wanted to understand the play behavior at a second-to-second timescale. As useful as that is for usability issues (e.g., why do players sometimes never click on a particular game option), this level of analysis is too detailed for understanding user reactions to the game and does not provide any information about their affective responses. To provide that kind of information, we ended up doing analyses of game play over the period of minutes to hours. And similarly, that level of analysis (while useful) would not provide the kind of large population data we also wanted to collect and understand—data that would tell us from weeks to months what was happening.

We realized that our three scales of analysis were very similar to Newell's timescales of human behavior (Newell 1994). Newell's analysis framework has four bands: neural (1–10 ms), cognitive (10 ms–10 seconds), rational (minutes to hours), and social (days to months). His division of cognitive behaviors along different timescales was to emphasize that different kinds of effects can be explained by fundamentally different mechanisms. I take a similar approach here.

1. *Microscale* measures the behaviors from milliseconds up to minutes of behavior, usually with a small number of people, usually in a lab setting. With these studies, we want to gain insight into the mechanics of the game—where players look, how they perceive the game elements, and what is left unnoticed and unexplored.

2. *Mesoscale* measures the behaviors from minutes to hours. This is the realm of field studies, watching people play the game in natural settings (e.g., at home or in the coffee shop). The mesoscale provides insights into why people choose to play and why they end up stopping their play, as well as understanding about what makes the game interesting (or not).

3. *Macroscale* measures the behaviors from days to weeks and months. Typically, this involves large numbers of players and is usually an analysis of the logs of many people playing the game.

Logs of user behavior have been a standard practice for some time. Traces of behavior have been gathered in psychology studies since the 1930s (Skinner 1938), and with the advent of web- and computer-based applications, it became common to capture a number of interactions and save them to log files for later analysis. More recently, the rise of web-based computing platforms has made it possible to capture human interactions with web services on a large scale. Log data let us observe how to compare different interfaces for supporting e-mail uptake and sustained use patterns (Dumais et al. 2003; Rodden and Leggett 2010).

Let us look at each of these timescale analysis methods in more detail.

9.4.1 Micro Level: How Players Behave over Short Timescales

Although there are many methods to study human behavior over short periods of time, the simplest and most practical method for usability studies is eye tracking (also known as *eye gaze*) studies (Bergstrom et al. 2014).

Eye tracking studies require bringing a subject into the lab to use a special monitor that has an eye tracking system built into the bezel of the monitor (there are many companies that sell such systems, e.g., Tobii, or Senso Motoric Instruments[SMI]). These systems calibrate the game player's eye movements on the monitor and output where the eye moves on the screen at time resolutions down to the milliseconds. Essentially, they create X, Y, and T data streams (X and Y positions of the gaze focus on the display, where T is the amount of time the eye dwells on those X and Y locations), along with any user actions taken (such as a click, typing, or scroll event).

As shown in Figures 9.2 and 9.3, perhaps the most useful way to visualize the millisecond-by-millisecond behavior stream is as either eye tracks on the display.

With this kind of very detailed information about what the player is doing, we can identify distractors and invisible portions of the interface. For instance, in an earlier version of the game, we did not have the Learn How to Play and Tips & Tricks tabs in the upper right corner. As can be seen by the eye movement chart in Figure 9.2, although they were rarely used, they would be scanned by game players from time to time, ensuring that they knew about their presence, even if only rarely actually used in game play.

More importantly, understanding how a player visually scans the display, and where they spend most of their time (especially when game play is proceeding poorly), is a valuable resource for tuning the game play mechanics. When the player gets stuck, does he or she exhibit visual search behaviors, or is he or she able to quickly determine what the next plausible course of action should be?

The lab setting is useful, allowing demographic and other data to be easily collected about participants and allowing control over variables that are not of interest, while allowing instrumentation of novel systems that could not be easily deployed broadly. However, we have found that in the lab, researchers ask behavioral questions that do not originate with the

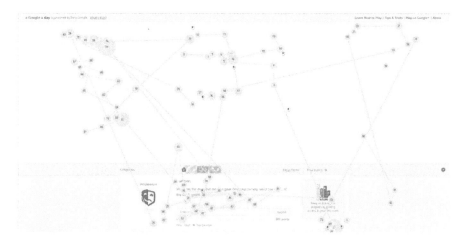

FIGURE 9.2 **(See color insert.)** The movement of the eye on the display is shown by a connected graph. The numbers indicate which fixation, or pause, it represents and the size of the circle represents the duration of the eye fixation at that point. The number 1 is near the bottom right, where the player clicked the button on the previous page.

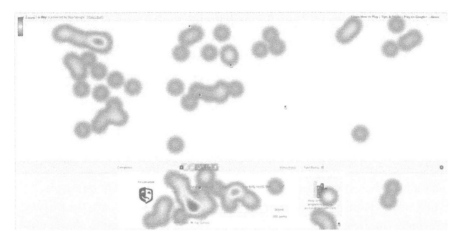

FIGURE 9.3 **(See color insert.)** The heat map display shows how much time the eye spent at any one spot during the sample time. Here we can see the player spent most of the time reading the question (next to the theatrical mask glyph at the bottom and near the top at the search query).

study participant. Although it seems like a small thing, in fact, questions and behaviors that are natural to ask the participant may never arise in a lab setting (Grimes and Russell 2007). Researchers can learn a good deal about participants and their motivations in this way, but the observed behavior happens in a controlled and artificial setting and may not be representative of behavior that would be observed "in the wild."

In the lab setting study, a person may invest more time to complete a task in the lab than he or she might otherwise to please the investigator (Dell et al. 2012). In addition, laboratory studies are often expensive in terms of the time required to collect the data and the number of different people and systems that can be studied.

The micro level of study is useful, but does not answer all of the questions one might have about game play in a more ordinary setting.

9.4.2 Meso Level: How Humans Behave Minute by Minute

At the meso level of study, research is done to determine how system users perform tasks of interest (play the game) and to collect information that cannot be gathered in any other way (e.g., direct observation of affective responses to a computer game).

The meso-level research approach is primarily to perform field studies of user behavior, that is, to collect data from participants in their natural environments as they go about their activities. Data collected in this manner tend to be less artificial than in lab studies, but also less controlled, in both positive ways (as when the participant does something completely unexpected) and negative ways (as when the presence of the researchers influences their natural behaviors).

In particular, we were interested in natural use phenomena (the full complex of interactions, ads, distractions, multitasking, etc.) in the AGAD game. Unlike a more deeply engaging game such as quest game, AGAD was always intended to be a short-duration, low-overhead, small-investment game play. Therefore, we wanted to understand how people would play the game, that is, what would cause them to start the game, why would they stop playing, what did they find engaging about the game, what was disruptive during game play, and what were the drivers for returning to the game?

In a series of studies, we would interview AGAD players as they used the game for the first time (to identify initial reactions and learnability questions), and later we interviewed repeat players to identify reasons for returning to the game.

The 15 interviews (fortunately) identified almost no learnability issues—the game was simple enough that the design was straightforward.

However, the interviews also asked various AGAD questions of varying degrees of difficulty. One question we asked was as follows: This member of the Lepidoptera increases its weight nearly 10,000-fold in a fortnight. What is its name?

As we watched, we learned quickly that this question (as it was for many others) had challenging vocabulary and concepts. People did not know what a Lepidoptera was or what a fortnight was. This led to interesting misreadings and varying reactions. This, we learned, is a problem for all such "question asking/trivia question" games.

In this particular case, the term *Lepidoptera* led many people to highly technical articles (e.g., from entomology journals), which in turn use words such as *instar* and *mitochrondial transformation*. However, highly motivated game players would work through these issues and get to the answer, feeling a distinct sense of victory.

Other more casual players would simply give up at that point, causing us to add in the Skip question feature and Clue feature, which would show the number of letters in the answer with one or two letters shown. (There was a Hint button from the original design, but given that so many of our observations were about people getting frustrated, this suggested the Clue modification to help people who were having difficulty, but not to disclose anything to players who really wanted to solve the full challenge.)

From a game design perspective, this kind of mesoscale user behavior in a natural setting was invaluable. It is the kind of information that can deeply influence a system design by providing feedback *during* the course of play. It is the kind of player behavior that is impossible to abstract from microscale behaviors and difficult to infer from the macro level.

9.4.3 Macro Level: How Humans Behave over Days and in the Large

Although mesoscale studies are very natural, macro studies collect the most natural observations of people as they use systems in large quantities over longer periods of time. This is generally done by logging behavior from *in situ*, naturalistic behaviors that are uninfluenced by the presence experimenters or observers. As the amount of log data collected increases, log studies increasingly include many different kinds of people, from all over the world, doing many different kinds of tasks. However, because of the way log data are gathered, much less is known about the people being observed or the context in which the observed behaviors occur than in field or lab studies.

Games also have begun using analytics over logs, especially in age of web-based games. Thawonmas (2008) used logs analysis to find bot players in massively-multiplayer online role-playing games (MMORPGs), whereas Itsuki et al. (2010) looked for "real-time money trading" in games. Dow et al. (2010) used a mesoscale interview approach in conjunction with a macroscale logs analysis to demonstrate how interactive game operators changed their use preferences over time.

In the case of AGAD, we closely examined logs for behaviors we expected, but also kept an eye open for behaviors we did not anticipate. (This become particularly important for behaviors that are impossible to see in our micro- or mesoscale studies. Marketing events and system errors are the most common and most interesting [see Figure 9.7].)

There were several unexpected behaviors that were found through macroscale logs analysis—behaviors that were, by definition—only possible to see once the game had been available for some time. One instance of this was the cumulative effect of people returning to the game, and then backing up to play previous days' games. (This feature was removed when the game was redesigned to support social play.)

This led to a roughly 2-week rolling sliding window in the game data as players would go backward in time. We noticed this when the log data for

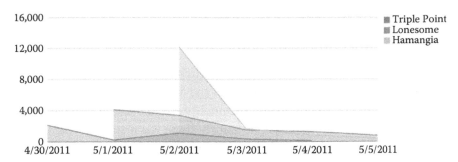

FIGURE 9.4 **(See color insert.)** Tracking data on questions by day. The graph shows player volume for 6 days for three different questions ("Triple Point," "Lonesome," and "Hamangia"). "Triple Point" was introduced on 4/30/2011, yet players kept backing up to that question 4 days later.

a given day's challenge would strangely change *after the fact*. In essence, what this did was to give a very long tail of data for any particular search question (Figure 9.4).

We also found through logs analysis that players were doing a significantly larger number of queries/visit. Players had a nearly 2× query volume increase overall in distinct queries (Figure 9.5). This increase in total search volume would not be explained simply by playing the game, but due to additional searches outside the scope of AGAD. Because one of the goals of the game was to help people become more effective users, this

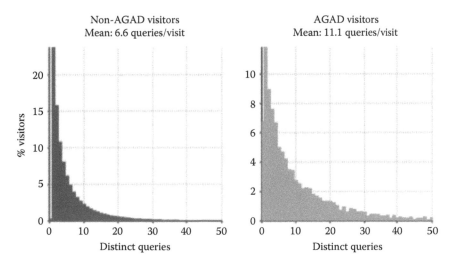

FIGURE 9.5 The number of distinct queries/search session, comparing AGAD players matched with comparable non-AGAD players.

might seem to be evidence that searchers were becoming *less* effective, not more. However, in a survey of 200 AGAD players in September 2011, we discovered that after playing for several days, the perception was that they were taking on much more sophisticated search tasks, requiring additional searches. In fact, this was suggestive that the approach of additional time spent practicing actually improved the quality of their search skills.

Surprisingly, several months after launch, there was a start-of-year error in the way our co-marketing ads were being launched (in particular, in the 2011 New Year, our partners were not getting the feeds that were set up) (see Figure 9.6). As this was over the holiday, we only checked the logs every 2 weeks; it was a fortnight before the error was noticed in the logs. It was through this error that we discovered that although AGAD has a large returning visitor rate, the genesis of their return was the presence of a reminder in a media stream. Once a player saw the reminder, he or she would go to the site and play (and often, as noted above, play more than one day at a time).

9.4.4 Integrating Research and Design across the Three Levels

Each of the three levels of analysis gives a particular kind of data to drive development. Micro-level data inform decisions about the UI and the operation of game play. For AGAD, this validated the particulars of the UI and guided item placement on the display.

FIGURE 9.6 An example of the unexpected. The Analytics view of AGAD over the 2011 New Year's holiday. A mistake in advertising leads to a huge drop in players for several weeks.

Meanwhile, meso-level data give designers critical feedback information about how a game is perceived and used in the real world. Some games (especially mobile games) function very differently depending on the physical and social context in which they are played.

From this kind of information, we learned that it is difficult to write questions that would be engaging without being intimidating. Player reactions are crucial. As a side effect of the meso-level data analysis, we decided to add a Feedback button on the UI so players could connect directly with the design team. Although it generates a fair number of empty messages (when people click on the button but do not enter any commentary), we found that complaints about mistakes in the questions/answers could be fixed rapidly, once we knew about the issue. In effect, the Feedback button became a meso-level data feed that helped to improve the game's quality overall, as well as providing a base-line sense for how the game was performing.

Macro-level data tell the story of how the game is performing in the large and in the wild. With macro-level data, we knew that the game began performing well almost immediately. We understood the ways in which players returned to the site, how often they returned, and how long they would engage. As shown in Figure 9.7, we could see the effects of various marketing efforts. Plateaus and spikes in the data indicated to us that we were on the right track as we tested various ways of getting the word out.

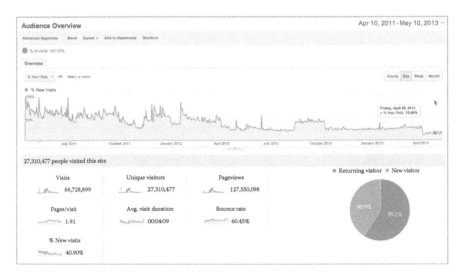

FIGURE 9.7   Total audience participation in AGAD over a 2-year period. Various spikes and plateaus correspond to marketing events. Note the returning visitor rate in the lower right; this is an extremely high-returning player rate.

9.5 SUMMARY

A useful way to look at user behavior is at three different cognitive levels—first, the fast/rapid/millisecond level; second, the minute-to-minute behavior; and third, the effect of long/slow cognition over days/weeks. Each timescale reveals substantially different kinds of information about how the user/player uses, thinks about, and responds to the game.

Examining user behavior across these three levels is as productive for understanding applications as it is for games. The same underlying user experience research methods apply and can be immensely useful when developing a game.

The design space for a complex game is huge. User experience research, seen from a multiscale perspective, gives insights into what opportunities and issues will arise in the game. What is more, looking at insights found at one scale often gives insights into behaviors at another.

In general, a good software engineering practice is to tightly weave together not just great software engineering but also great attention to the user experience moment to moment as well as play experience over an extended period.

Great games have these characteristics, performing on all of these levels of design simultaneously. They have great visuals; they have great audio; they have great backend engineering, interactions, controllers, and stories. Great games go on to have multiple editions and last for years. You can see how analyzing the game at multiple levels, with attention to different kinds of user interactions, will lead to improved design and user enjoyment overall.

REFERENCES

Bell, M., Chalmers, M., Barkhuus, L., Hall, M., Sherwood, S., Tennent, P., Brown, B., Rowland, D., Benford, S., Capra, M., and Hampshire, A. Interweaving mobile games with everyday life. In *Conference on Human Factors in Computing Systems*, pp. 417–426, Montreal, Quebec, Canada, 2006.

Bergstrom, Jennifer Romano, and Andrew Schall, eds. *Eye Tracking in User Experience Design*. Elsevier, 2014.

Bernhaupt, R. (ed). *Evaluating User Experience in Games: Concepts and Methods*. Springer, London, 2010.

Dell, N., Vaidyanathan, V., Medhi, I. Cutrell, E. and Thies, W. "Yours is better!": Participant response bias in HCI. In *Proceedings of CHI*, pp. 1321–1330, 2012.

Dow, S.P., Mehta, M., MacIntyre, B., and Mateas, M. Eliza meets the wizard-of-oz: Blending machine and human control of embodied characters. *Proceedings of the SIGCHI Conference on Human Factors in Computing Systems*. ACM, New York, 2010.

Dumais, S.T., Cutrell, E., Cadiz, J.J., Jancke, G., Sarin, R., and Robbins, D.C. Stuff I've Seen: A system for personal information retrieval and re-use. In *Proceedings of SIGIR*, pp. 72–79, Toronto, Canada, 2003.

Itsuki, H., Takeuchi, A., Fujita, A., and Matsubara, H. Exploiting MMORPG log data toward efficient RMT player detection. *Proceedings of the 7th International Conference on Advances in Computer Entertainment Technology*. ACM, Taipei, Taiwan, 2010.

Koeffel, C., Hochleitner, W., Leitner, J., Haller, M., Geven, A., and Tscheligi, M. Using heuristics to evaluate the overall user experience of video games and advanced interaction games. In *Evaluating User Experience in Games*, pp. 233–256. Springer, London, 2010.

Nacke, L.E., Drachen, A., Kuikkaniemi, K., Niesenhaus, J., Korhonen, H.J., van den Hoogen, W.M., Poels, K., IJsselsteijn, W., and Kort, Y. Playability and player experience research. In *Proceedings of DiGRA*, Brunel University, London, UK, 2009.

Newell, A. Putting it all together. In Klahr, D. and Kotovsky, K. (eds.), *Complex Information Processing: The Impact of Herbert A. Simon*. Psychology Press, New York, 1989.

Newell, A. *Unified Theories of Cognition*. Harvard University Press, 1994.

Pinelle, D., Wong, N., and Stach, T. Heuristic evaluation for games: Usability principles for video game design. *Proceedings of the SIGCHI Conference on Human Factors in Computing Systems*. ACM, New York, 2008.

Rodden, K. and Leggett, M. Best of both worlds: Improving Gmail labels with the affordance of folders. In *Proceedings of CHI*, pp. 4587–4596. Atlanta, GA, 2010.

Russell, D.M., and Grimes, C. Assigned tasks are not the same as self-chosen web search tasks. System Sciences. HICSS. *40th Annual Hawaii International Conference on IEEE*, IEEE, Hawaii, 2007.

Schaffer, N. Heuristic evaluation of games. In Isbister, K. and Schaffer, N. (eds.), *Game Usability: Advice from the Experts for Advancing the Player Experience*, pp. 79–89. Morgan Kaufman, Amsterdam, the Netherlands, 2008.

Skinner, B.F. *The Behavior of Organisms: An Experimental Analysis*. Appleton-Century, Oxford, 1938.

Sweetser, P. and Wyeth, P. GameFlow: A model for evaluating player enjoyment in games. *Computers in Entertainment* 3(3):3, 2005.

Thawonmas, R., Kashifuji, Y., and Chen, K.-T. Detection of MMORPG bots based on behavior analysis. In *Proceedings of the 2008 International Conference on Advances in Computer Entertainment Technology*. ACM, 2008.

CHAPTER 10

Modular Reuse of AI Behaviors for Digital Games

Christopher Dragert, Jörg Kienzle, and Clark Verbrugge

CONTENTS

10.1	Introduction	216
10.2	Background and Related Work	218
	10.2.1 Layered Statechart-Based AI	219
	10.2.1.1 Sample AI for a Squirrel NPC	220
10.3	AI Module	222
	10.3.1 AI Module Interaction	223
	10.3.1.1 Event-Based Interaction	223
	10.3.1.2 Synchronous Communication	223
	10.3.1.3 Miscellaneous AI Module Properties	224
	10.3.2 AI Module Interface	225
10.4	Reuse and Component Integration	226
	10.4.1 Event Renaming	227
	10.4.2 Associated-Class Connection	228
	10.4.3 Functional Groups	229
	10.4.3.1 Group-Private Events	230
10.5	Case Study: Squirrel to Trash Collector	231
	10.5.1 Trash Collector Specification	231
	10.5.1.1 Exploring	232
	10.5.1.2 Collecting Trash	232
	10.5.1.3 Using Trash Receptacles	233

10.5.2	Building the NPC	233
10.5.3	Case Study Summary	234
10.6	Scythe AI Tool	235
10.6.1	Workflow and Key Features	235
	10.6.1.1 Importing Modules	235
	10.6.1.2 AI Construction	236
	10.6.1.3 Outputting the AI	237
10.7	Conclusions and Future Work	237
References		238

10.1 INTRODUCTION

Complex and ubiquitous artificial intelligence (AI) has become a staple of modern computer games; players expect nonplayer characters (NPCs) to intelligently react to player actions while exhibiting appropriate behaviors depending on their role within the game context. Developing a good AI for a real-time game environment, however, is a difficult task. Although a variety of formalisms are employed, practical AI designs typically resort to strongly customized approaches closely connected to the underlying game architecture and the NPC type. This results in a relative lack of reuse in game AI, increasing development costs and requiring the repetitive development of often quite similar AI behaviors.

The narrow game-by-game focus is a source of consternation for game developers. At GDC 2011, Kevin Dill raised this issue, arguing that the lack of behavioral modularity was stymieing the development of high-quality AI [1]. Previous work has argued that the fundamental cause for this lies within the formalisms employed [2]. The applicability of software engineering practices becomes limited due to the use of nonmodular custom approaches. As an alternative, the layered statechart-based approach [3] provides inherent modularity with nesting capabilities.

Our approach to AI reuse builds from layered statechart-based AI. Here, we provide a formalism and structure that encapsulates behaviors; we are able to define a development strategy that allows the extensive reuse of different AI components, including both high- and low-level elements. Partial behavioral composition is enabled by the introduction of *functional groups*, providing an efficient way to reuse groups of related behaviors. Clear identification of code dependencies further permits analysis and the tool-based presentation required to ensure proper integration into the actual game code. This yields a faster development process with the ability to employ a library of AI behaviors to construct complex AIs, while at the same time simplifying adaptation of the AI to an actual game context.

We illustrate our approach by creating a garbage collector NPC through the reuse of large portions of the AI designed for a squirrel NPC. These are different game AI contexts, and would typically be approached as unique development tasks. By treating the AI as a collection of interacting modules, many behavioral similarities emerge. By expressing and reusing AI behaviors at a suitable level of abstraction, our approach is able to capture many of these commonalities: fully two-thirds of the *AI modules* in the garbage collector are reused from the squirrel.

Our development and reuse approach is made practical through our tool *Scythe AI*. This software framework directs and facilitates the development workflow, taking in statecharts and associated classes, providing an interface for producing novel AIs from a library of behaviors, and exporting code that can be directly incorporated into a game. By formally representing and understanding the game code associated with specific behaviors, Scythe AI is able to perform basic analysis of the constructed AI, ensuring code and functional group dependencies are properly satisfied and thus the AI is well constructed. Scythe AI represents a useful illustration of the practical value and general feasibility of our approach.

Major contributions of our work include the following:

- Extending the reuse strategy for developing game AIs based on statecharts presented by Dragert et al. [2]. The work further demonstrates the feasibility of statecharts for game AIs [3], by defining efficient development, component definition, and porting strategies.

- A demonstration of reuse by reusing AI modules from a squirrel NPC to build a new AI for a garbage collector NPC.

- Concretizing the approach through the design of a software tool, *Scythe AI*. As part of a practical workflow for AI generation, it simplifies component reuse and allows for nontrivial analysis, helping to ensure that AI components are properly composed and integrated.

We begin the next section with a basic background to our approach, as well as appropriate related work. Section 10.3 then describes our general design, whereas Section 10.4 presents our reuse strategy. Section 10.5 details a case study of reuse. Section 10.6 discusses the tool we developed and used to perform this task and reifies our general design. Finally, we offer conclusions and discuss future work in Section 10.7.

10.2 BACKGROUND AND RELATED WORK

AI in modern computer games focuses upon controlling NPCs such that they exhibit behaviors fulfilling that character's role in the game. This type of AI is referred to as *computational behavior*, distinguishing it from classical AI approaches. In the context of game development, efficiency and testability are paramount, strongly constraining design approaches. The easiest approach is to employ an arbitrary code expressed through a custom scripting context [4,5] or a relatively simple tree or graph structure, such as a decision tree.

Industrial research into AI reuse focuses on modularizing code artifacts [6] or on modifying an existing AI system [7,8] with incremental improvements rather than modularizing and porting behaviors to a fundamentally new context. Our approach aims to shed light on this relatively unexplored space, by demonstrating how behaviors themselves can be modularized and reused in new game contexts.

Finite state machines (FSMs) are the oldest and most commonly used formalism to model game AIs, wherein states represent behaviors and transitions are triggered to change the behavior exhibited [9,10]. Hierarchical FSMs (HFSMs) incorporate aspects of statecharts [11] by allowing states to contain substates with internal transitions. In the context of reuse, superstates in HFSMs can be treated as modules and exported to new AIs [12]. This approach is valuable, but omits important details such as code portability and has no provision for interaction with internal states. The strict hierarchical nature of HFSMs can be limiting, as they place restrictions on how transitions between states can be modeled. This limitation is shared by behavior trees [13], which, although they more clearly delineate how the system chooses behaviors, are strongly hierarchical, and further suffer from a lack of modal states encapsulating different behavioral groupings. Modularizing behavioral components is based upon pruning and reusing branches, an idea that has been previously explored [14]. In a practical sense, the extent of reuse in behavior trees is limited as individual tree nodes are often highly game- or AI-specific—code actions and abstract, high-level behavior are intimately entwined in behavior tree models.

In theory, planning approaches seem ideal for reuse. Goal-oriented action planners, popularized by the game F.E.A.R. [15], choose behaviors using a heuristic search through a library of behavior modules with pre- and postconditions. In practice, getting the planner to select appropriate behaviors requires a proliferation of variables encapsulating the basic knowledge, along with considerable tweaking of weights and heuristics. As a result, the modules become highly customized to the game context and the general-purpose reuse becomes more difficult as a result.

Behavior trees offer a reuse model based on pruning and reusing branches [14]. In a practical sense, however, the extent of reuse is limited as individual tree nodes are often highly game- or AI-specific—code actions and abstract, high-level behavior are intimately entwined in behavior tree models. Although behavior trees delineate clearly how the system chooses behaviors, they suffer from a lack of modal states encapsulating different behavioral groupings. Reuse, in practice, has been demonstrated primarily in terms of modifying an existing AI [7] with incremental improvements rather than porting AI logic to a fundamentally new context.

10.2.1 Layered Statechart-Based AI

Our work adopts the formalism developed by Kienzle et al. [3], who introduce an AI based on an abstract layering of statecharts. This approach is inspired by the *sense-plan-act architecture* common in robotics. Here, each statechart implements a single behavioral concern, such as sensing the game state, memorizing data, making high-level decisions, and so on. Due to the clear demarcation of duties, the statecharts are ideal for reuse. An AI is built from multiple statecharts, each embodying a specific concept, with the exhibited behavior being a function of the superposition of states. Importantly, communication can occur at lower levels without involving higher levels, meaning the formalism employs a subsumption architecture [16]. This allows for improved modularity; higher levels of abstraction do not require a full set of knowledge to make decisions, which also reduces crosscutting concerns.

Under this model, the lowest layer contains *sensors*, which read the game state typically through `listeners` or observers that generate events as changes are detected. Events are passed up to *analyzers* that interpret and combine sensing data to form a coherent picture of the game state. The next layer contains *memorizers*, which store the analyzed data and complex state information for later reference. The highest layer is the *strategic decider*, most typically a single statechart, which reacts to analyzed and memorized data to decide upon a high-level goal. Becoming less abstract, the goal triggers a *tactical decider* to determine how it will be executed.

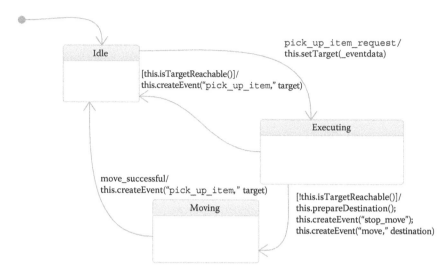

FIGURE 10.1   A Sample AI statechart governing the `pickup` behavior.

The next layer provides *executors* that enact execution decisions, translating goals into actions. Depending on the current state of the NPC, certain commands can cause conflicts or suboptimal courses of action, which are corrected by *coordinators*. The final layer contains *actuators*, which execute actions by modifying the game state.

In Figure 10.1, a sample `Pickup Executor` statechart is presented. It reacts to `pick _ up _ item _ request` events by determining if the item is reachable. The guard condition `[this.isTargetReachable()]` only allows the guarded transition to fire when the guard evaluates to true. The transition then fires the event to either `pick up` the item or first move to the appropriate location and then `pick up` the item. Statecharts have become of interest relatively recently to the game development industry, with initial designs focusing on low-level issues such as efficient interpretation within a game context [17].

10.2.1.1 Sample AI for a Squirrel NPC
We first introduce an existing AI created in the layered statechart formalism. This will help clarify AI structure and provide us with a set of modules available for reuse. We describe here a layered statechart-based AI for a squirrel, a simple background NPC. For game purposes, a high level of abstraction is sufficient in modeling the squirrel behaviors—a detailed simulation would overshoot the mark for the typical game AI.

Each squirrel NPC has a physical size, a movement speed, a position, and an energy level. In our game, energy has an initial high value that gradually decreases as the squirrel moves about, but that can be restored by eating acorns. A squirrel can also carry a game item, such as an acorn. Thus, our basic squirrel behavior involves moving about with the aim of collecting and eating acorns, while maintaining a healthy distance from nonsquirrel creatures. This allows for the squirrel to observably perform basic behaviors, while providing the possibility of interaction with the player through fleeing.

Our full squirrel behavior is composed of 13 statecharts that individually model the sensors (objects, players, and energy), analyzers (threat), memorizers (items), the strategizer (brain), deciders (flee and eat), executors (wander, eat, and `pickup`), and actuators (eat, `pickup`, and move). Figure 10.2 gives an overview of the squirrel AI.

The high-level brain is shown in Figure 10.3. This statechart is the highest level decision maker in the AI, as it chooses the current high-level goal from one of wandering, getting food, or fleeing. Initially, the squirrel will always begin wandering. During this time, the squirrel will flee from all threats. Once the squirrel becomes hungry, the high-level goal of getting food will be selected. If the squirrel is close to starving, it will ignore low threats in its desperation for food.

Although this AI is small in scale, it is not atypical when compared to AIs in popular massively multiplayer games or arcade-style games, where NPC behavior can be as simple as running at the player and attacking until defeated. The squirrel AI is a reasonable representative of game AI, and thus provides useful behaviors for reuse. For those interested, a more detailed exploration of the squirrel architecture can be found in [18].

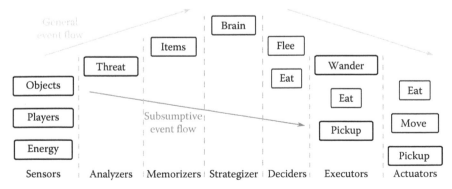

FIGURE 10.2 Overview of the squirrel AI showing event flow.

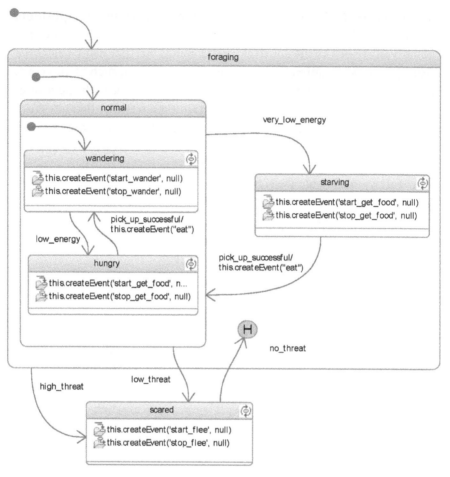

FIGURE 10.3   The high-level brain governing the squirrel behavior.

10.3 AI MODULE

Layered statechart-based AI is built around combining individual statecharts to produce the overall behavior. This implies that the fundamental module is the statechart itself. We define an *AI module* as a statechart along with its associated class and will use this as our fundamental module in the reuse process. This is similar to game graphics, wherein models built from texture-mapped triangles form the basic reusable component. Models can easily be reused in new contexts, and by clearly defining the reusable component, we provide a method for AI modules to be just as reusable when building new game AIs.

The pairing of statechart and the associated class is a highly appropriate choice for two reasons. First, statecharts act independently, and only cooperate due to higher level coordination. This means that the statechart itself has a contained execution environment, allowing for execution in any context. Second, each statechart has a link to an individual associated class, providing an elegant approach to the inclusion of source code. This pairing is advantageous as we can now reason at a high level about AI behavior without neglecting the implementing code.

10.3.1 AI Module Interaction

As modules are reused, they are removed from one context and placed into another. For reuse to be successful, the new context must be able to interact with the reused AI module. To enable reuse, there needs to be a clear description of how modules interact. Having this will allow us to build up an interaction profile for each module, supplying the information needed to correctly insert an AI module into a new context.

10.3.1.1 Event-Based Interaction

The statechart portion of an AI module communicates using an event-based message passing. Using the cooperative approach, statecharts generate events that are broadcast to all other statecharts in the system.

Events generated by a statechart and consumed by other statecharts are classified as *output* events from the perspective of the generating statechart. These same events become *input* events when viewed by the consuming statechart. If an event is neither generated nor consumed by a statechart, then that event is irrelevant to that statechart and is ignored.

In some rare cases, a statechart may both generate and consume an event, or the associated class may generate an event (such as the health sensor in the *HALO* AI) that is intended only for the statechart in the module. These self-communication events express logic internal to a single statechart, and so these are classified as *private*.

10.3.1.2 Synchronous Communication

Associated classes in AI modules communicate through synchronous method calls directly between modules. When reusing a module that makes synchronous method calls to other classes, any target modules must also be reused, or the associated class edited to update the call with a valid target.

Otherwise, the associated class will give a compilation error as a method call cannot be resolved.

When compared with an event-based communication, synchronous communication leads to tightly coupled modules. This reduces the ease of reuse, as the module cannot be reused on its own without modification. Because of this, we recommend limiting the use of synchronous methods calls as this favors reusability.

An easy approach to limiting synchronous calls is to employ events with payloads. Payloads can carry pertinent information to satisfy upstream data requirements, resulting in fewer synchronous method calls. This allows for a more loosely coupled system overall, better suited for reuse. An event with a payload can be given a *signature* stating the type of the payload, much like a function or method signature, making it clear the information that is contained in that payload.

As an example, a common task in the layered statechart module is for analyzers to refine information collected by the sensors. The sensor could store the data and make it available by synchronous method call; however, the reuse of the analyzer would be complicated if the sensor is also not reused. Instead, the event notifying the analyzer of the data collection could be given relevant data as the payload. Now, when the analyzer is reused, no modification of the associated class would be required, and the reuse is simplified.

10.3.1.3 Miscellaneous AI Module Properties

In addition to event-based communication and synchronous communication, there are three additional properties of an AI module that impact reuse, all of which derive from the associated class. Although statecharts are represented in language-independent Statechart Extensible Markup Language (SCXML), the associated class is a code artifact. Because it is programmed in a specific language (e.g., Java or C++), the AI module can only be reused in games programmed in the same implementation language.

The next property important to reuse is the set of links between the associated class and the game at large. Any imports in Java or includes in C++ create dependencies in the code. Although references to core libraries (such as `java.*`) are always resolvable, references to custom libraries or to game-specific classes may cause issues. Successful reuse demands that such calls be updated to appropriate targets in the new context or referenced classes must also be reused such that the associated class can compile correctly. If an AI module has no game imports, then it is *game agnostic* and can be safely reused in a different game without issue.

The final property relates to nonmodal properties of the AI module. Such properties, stored as variables in the associated class, allow for customization as the module is reused. An example comes in the form of the KeyItemMemorizer module, found in the definition of the squirrel AI. The associated class has a type parameter. If a spotted item is of the same type as the type parameter, then it is a key item (type Acorn, in the case of the squirrel). A game implementing several important items (such as flowers, shirts, and boxes) could have a KeyItemMemorizer for each item relevant to the AI. When a KeyItemMemorizer receives an item _ spotted event from a sensor, the payload would be inspected and compared against the key item parameter, and then memorized if it is a matching type. By exposing parameters in the interface, it makes it possible to modify them at time of reuse, and thus customize the module to the new context.

10.3.2 AI Module Interface

The motivation behind an AI module interface is to collect information relevant to reuse in a single location. This is similar to the Application Programming Interface (API) for an application or library. Proper use of a library requires that the API be followed; proper reuse of an AI module demands that the module interface be followed.

The interface for an AI module collects and presents information on events, synchronous calls, parameters, and any imports. Pertinent information, such as a name for the module, an outline of the behavior, and the intended layer, can optionally be added to the interface. This means that all the information relating to the reuse of a module is found in a single location, making the usage of module interfaces a valuable tool when performing reuse. A straightforward depiction of a generic interface is given in Figure 10.4.

By filling in descriptions and additional information, the interface effectively communicates the functionality of the module. Figure 10.5 presents the AI module interface for the Key Item Memorizer presented in the squirrel AI, and clearly describes how the module works, and how it communicates.

Statechart Name	

Game: Mammoth *Language:* Java
Description:
  –Description of the statechart and its behavior
Parameters:
  –Type :: Description	

Events	**Calls**

Input:
  –EventIn (PayloadType)
  –Event2In
Output:
  –EventOut
  –Event2Out (PayloadType)
Private:
  –InternalEvent
	Game imports:
	  –import Game.Element
	  –import Library.Class
	Available synch. calls:
	  –method(signature)
	
	External synch. calls:
	  –Module.method(signature)

FIGURE 10.4   A generic AI module interface.

KeyItemMemorizer	
Game: Mammoth *Language:* Java *Description:* Filters item spotted events to memorize key items that have been spotted *Parameters:* –ItemObject keyItem :: The item type to be memorized as the key item	
Events	**Calls**

Input:
  –*i_see_item (ItemObject)*
  –*i_dont_see_item (ItemObject)*
Output:
  –*key_item_visible*
  –*no_key_item_visible*
	Game imports:
	  –Mammoth.AI.NPC.Role,
	  ".PhysicsEngine.PhysicsEngine,
	  ".WorldManager.ItemObject,
	  ".WorldManager.WorldManager
	Available synch. calls:
	  –Vector<ItemObject> getKeyItemList()

FIGURE 10.5   The module interface for the Key Item Memorizer.

10.4 REUSE AND COMPONENT INTEGRATION

Integrating modules correctly and easily is fundamental to effective AI reuse. Each reused module must be *connected* to the other modules in the new AI, through either an event-based communication or a synchronous communication. Here we describe how modules can be reused and correctly connected in a new context.

10.4.1 Event Renaming

For event-based connections, modules communicate by pairing an input event and an output event. Under a broadcast model, event renaming allows connections to be formed by renaming the output event, so that it matches the input event (or vice versa). Mechanically, this means modifying the source of the statechart to use the new event names.

To ensure correctness, existing connections should be respected. If a new module uses event names that are already present in the new system, and no connection is intended, then events in the new module should be renamed to prevent the formation of unintended connections.

As a rule, private events are not appropriate for use in forming connections. By definition, a private event is used internally by a statechart, and encapsulation implies that the event should be invisible to the rest of the system. Generation of the event may depend on the internal logic of the statechart in a nonobvious fashion, meaning that the generation of the private event by another statechart may break that internal logic.

Technically speaking, the consumption of a private event by another statechart cannot break the internal logic. Because this breaks notions of encapsulation, such a connection would complicate future reuse and modification. However, it could be the case that an event intended as output merely happens to be consumed by an orthogonal region in the same statechart. Here, the designer should classify that event as output, so that it is clear that the event can indeed be used as a connection point.

In the special case where multiple statecharts are connected using the same event, renaming may create unintended connections. Consider Figure 10.6, where a statechart A outputs event α that is received by

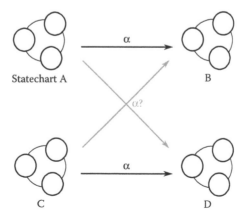

FIGURE 10.6   Reuse scenario with unintended connections.

statechart B. New statecharts C and D are added to AI with a preexisting communication that also uses α. Because broadcast communication is name based, A will connect to D and C will connect to B on the event α. If these new connections are not intended, then renaming could be applied, by modifying C and D to communicate on β instead of α, for instance.

Renaming can break the existing connections and can fail entirely in certain corner cases. Continuing our example in Figure 10.6, imagine only one of the two cross connections is desired. For example, A should connect to D on α but C should not connect to B. If C outputs β, breaking the connection to B, then D will also lose connection. Renaming the input in D would break the intended connection to A. There is no broadcasting renaming solution in this scenario. As a rule, multiple statecharts cannot connect to different subsets of receivers using the same event. Renaming is unable to resolve this. Such situations should be avoided.

As an alternative to broadcasting with event renaming, narrowcasting can be employed. This means that each event generation specifies target statecharts, and only the targets receive the event. Although this would resolve the event-renaming corner cases, it adds additional complexity at the design level by forcing developers to specify targets for each transition. Reuse of a module would force the respecification of all event targets to match the modules in the new AI. In our experience, corner cases are quite rare and easily avoided during design, and thus do not justify the extra effort required to model event targets. Broadcast communication is more appropriate in the context of AI module reuse.

10.4.2 Associated-Class Connection

Integration relating to the associated class is less forgiving, as an unsatisfied import or synchronous method call will prevent compilation or cause run-time errors. In the case of unsatisfied method calls, either the target AI module must be included or the associated class must be modified to point to a new implementing module.

In general, synchronous calls are more restrictive than event passing, and limiting the number of synchronous calls simplifies integration. Event passing occurs at the modeling level and is easily addressed there using renaming. The following guideline helps to clarify when each approach should be used: when a module receives an event and takes action immediately, that event should include relevant information as payload. When a module needs complex and dynamic state information at some undetermined point in the future, then a synchronous call is appropriate.

Module reuse across different games is constrained by imports and implementation language. The simplest case is when an AI module is purely behavior driven and has no imports (aside from core libraries supplied with the language). Such modules are *game agnostic* and may be freely moved between games. If a module has noncore imports, then reuse in a new game will require updating all imports, copying libraries, and other more drastic rewrites. This may not always be trivial or possible, and thus designing for reuse implies that modules be made game agnostic whenever possible. The process is much more complicated if the target game is coded in a different programming language. In that case, only the statechart could be reused, whereas the associated class would require a total rewrite.

10.4.3 Functional Groups

Reuse of AI modules allows for behavioral aspects of an AI to be exported, but the typical module is too fine-grained to fully capture a higher level behavior. For example, a fleeing behavior would encompass spotting enemies with a sensor, analyzing threat, deciding on a fleeing tactic, and moving using an actuator. These modules are connected, and through their cooperative actions, realize a behavioral goal.

To allow the reuse of module connections, and provide a way to modularize high-level behaviors, we introduce *functional groups*. A functional group comprises at least two AI modules that are connected either by an input–output event pairing or through synchronous calls.

A functional group interface can be built from the AI module interfaces of the contained modules. Input events that pair with output events can be reclassified as private to protect logic internal to the group. Unpaired events are copied to the new interface without change and act as the connection points when the group is reused. Synchronous calls, parameters, and game calls can all be added to the group interface. The end result is that member interfaces are subsumed, giving a single interface for the functional group.

Importantly, the resulting interface is identical in form to the interface for individual modules, and thus can be used interchangeably. Thus, a functional group interface is simply a special case of an AI module interface, and wherever an AI module can be reused, a functional group could instead be employed.

Mammoth `Listener`	
Game: Mammoth *Language:* Java *Description:* –A `listener` that maps area of interest game events into statechart events *Parameters:* none	
Events	**Calls**

Input: none
 	
 Output:
   –i_see_item (ItemObject)
   –i_dont_see_item (ItemObject)
   –i_see_player (Player)
   –i_dont_see_player (Player)
 	
 Private: none
	Game imports:
	   –Mammoth.AI.NPC.NPCEvent;
	   –".AI.NPC.Role;
	   –".AI.NPC.TaskImpl;
	   –".WorldManager.ItemObject;
	   –".WorldManager.Player;
	   –".WorldManager.PointOfView.
	     PointOfViewListener;
	   –".WorldManager.PointOfView.
	     PointOfViewManager;
	 Available synch. calls: none
	 External synch. calls: none

FIGURE 10.7   The module interface for the Mammoth `Listener`.

As an example, we create a functional group for identifying key items, called the `Key Item Tracker`. This will use the `Key Item Memorizer`, responsible for memorizing item locations and filtering key items, along with the `Mammoth Listener` for the squirrel with interface shown in Figure 10.7.

10.4.3.1 Group-Private Events

Combining the `Listener` and `Key Item Memorizer` gives the interface shown in Figure 10.8. Note how the i _ see _ item and i _ dont _ see _ item events have been reclassified as *group-private* events. This indicates they are now part of the internal logic of the functional group, and being classified as private prevents interference from other statecharts.

Reclassification is optional, however, and decided upon by the designer creating the group. In some cases, it would be reasonable for other statecharts to generate a group-private event. Continuing our example, we assume that our `Listener` works on line of sight. If another statechart was added that worked on sense of smell, then it too could create i _ see _ item events to easily included smell data into the decision-making process of the AI.

Key Item Identifier Functional Group	
Game: Mammoth *Language:* Java	
Description: Spots items and players. If they are key items, they are memorized and a notification is created.	
Modules: KeyItemMemorizer, `MammothListener`	
Parameters:	
–ItemObject keyItem :: The item type to be memorized as the key item	

Events	Calls
Input: none	*Game imports:*
Output:	–Mammoth.AI.NPC.Role,
–key_item_visible	–".AI.NPC.NPCEvent,
–no_key_item_visible	–".AI.NPC.TaskImpl,
–i_see_player (Player)	–".PhysicsEngine.PhysicsEngine,
–i_dont_see_player (Player)	–".WorldManager.ItemObject,
	–".WorldManager.Player,
	–".WorldManager.PointOfView.
	PointOfViewListener,
Private:	–".WorldManager.PointOfView.
–i_see_item (ItemObject)	PointOfViewManager,
–i_dont_see_item (ItemObject)	–".WorldManager.WorldManager
	Available synch. calls:
	–Vector<ItemObject> getKeyItemList()

FIGURE 10.8   The module interface for a functional group.

10.5 CASE STUDY: SQUIRREL TO TRASH COLLECTOR

To demonstrate the validity and usefulness of the presented approach, this section gives a concrete example of AI reuse. Here, we take the AI developed for the squirrel and reuse its components to create a new AI for a trash collector. Using the described reuse techniques coupled with good modular design practices, we find that many elements of the squirrel can easily be repurposed, greatly simplifying the development of the new AI.

This process is greatly streamlined by the fact that the source and target game are the same. Thus, the associated classes can be reused without modification, as the implementation language is the same and all game imports are valid.

10.5.1 Trash Collector Specification

The purpose of the trash collector NPC is to clean up the Mammoth game world. This is done by collecting pieces of rubbish left by other players, then depositing the trash into garbage bins. The requirements for the NPC are to explore the game world, spot garbage bins and pieces of trash, `pick up` pieces of trash, and drop trash into receptacles.

The high-level behavior of the trash collector differs from that of the squirrel. While the squirrel has four high-level goals (wandering, gathering food, eating, and fleeing), the trash collector only has three: searching, picking up trash, and depositing trash. Searching and wandering seem similar, and gathering food and picking up trash are also similar; we start our reuse from there.

10.5.1.1 Exploring

In the squirrel, wandering is performed by means of a `start _ wander` event that is received by the `Wander Executor`. In turn, the `Wander Executor` uses the `Move Actuator` to effect movement plans. These already perform a wandering behavior, and thus can be directly reused in the trash collector.

In order to preserve the existing connection, we create a new functional group called `Wander Move`, comprised of the `Move Actuator` and the `Wander Executor`. This new group is connected through the `move`, `move _ successful`, and `move _ failed` events. However, other parts of the squirrel AI connect to the `Move Actuator`, and so in creating the group, we will not reclassify these events as being group-private events.

10.5.1.2 Collecting Trash

To collect acorns, the squirrel performs two separate functions. First is finding them, and then next is collecting them. Finding requires object identification, handled by the `Key Item Tracker` group introduced in Section 10.4.3. This group can be reused by updating the key item parameter to use a *Trash* item object instead of *Acorn*. This allows the trash collector to spot and identify trash objects.

Once the squirrel brain has decided to collect food, the `Eat Decider` translates the goal into actions, including picking up food. Only the picking up portion of this behavior is useful for the trash collector, and so we build a `Pick Up` functional group for reuse. Included are the `Pick Up Executor` and the `Pick Up Actuator`, connected via the `pick _ up _ item` event. The `Pick Up Executor` can also move to targets, and connects with the `Move Actuator` to accomplish this. Because the `Move Actuator` has already been added to the new AI through the inclusion of the `Wander Move` group, this connection does not need modification.

The `Pick Up Executor` makes a synchronous call to the `Key Item Memorizer`, but this module is in place and so the call is satisfied.

10.5.1.3 Using Trash Receptacles

The new behavior in trash collector is to use trash receptacles. Because the reused `Mammoth Listener` notifies on every spotted item, the AI is already aware of garbage cans. We can add a new instance of the `Key Item Memorizer`, called a `Trash Can Memorizer` to receive these notifications and track garbage cans. However, this creates an unintended connection on the `key _ item _ visible` event. Event renaming resolves this, and so we have the `Trash Can Memorizer` generate `trash _ can _ visible` and `no _ trash _ can _ visible` events instead of key item events.

Once trash has been collected, the NPC must move to the garbage can and drop the trash in the can. Fundamentally, this is the same logic as the `Pick Up Executor`, which handles moving to and picking up an object. We create a `Drop Executor` by renaming all events with `pick _ up` into `drop`, e.g., `pick _ up _ item` becomes `drop _ item`, and by changing the target of the synchronous call to the `Trash Can Memorizer`. The `drop _ item` is currently unconnected and will form the connection to a yet-to-be introduced `Drop Actuator`.

10.5.2 Building the NPC

With most behaviors now in place, the only design task left is to fill in missing behaviors with new modules, and connect them all with a new strategizer. Because we have designed our AI in a modular fashion with clearly defined interfaces, we know the exact events available for connection, summarized in Table 10.1.

The trash collector brain will be somewhat different than the squirrel brain. The behavior desired is to `pick up` a single piece of garbage and throw it in the trash, repeating indefinitely. The brain is thus a simple two-state statechart, alternating between the two goals based upon if the NPC currently has a piece of trash.

A new decider was created to implement the high-level collect goal. The `Collect Decider`, shown in Figure 10.9, realizes the collect goal by searching for a piece of trash, then picking up a piece of visible trash. When the collection is successful, the brain will stop collection, and start the `Discard Decider`. It is identical in form to the `Collect Decider`, searching for a garbage can, then throwing the trash in the can, with the

TABLE 10.1   Unconnected Events in the New Trash Collector AI

Unconnected Inputs	Module/Functional Group	Unconnected Outputs
start_wander stop_wander	Wander Move FG	—
—	Key Item Tracker FG	key_item_visible no_key_item_visible
pick_up_item_request	Pick Up FG	pick_up_successful pick_up_failed
—	Trash Can Memorizer	trash_can_visible no_trash_can_visible
drop_item_request	Drop Executor	drop_item

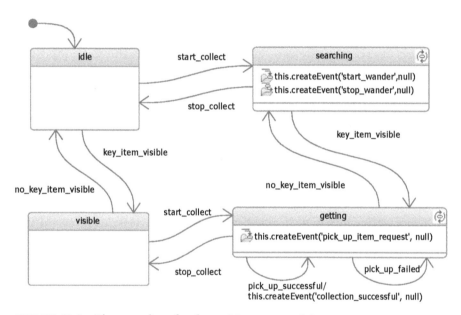

FIGURE 10.9   The statechart for the Collect Decider.

events renamed to match the connections in Table 10.1. In addition, a new Drop Actuator was created to receive the drop _ item event and have the NPC actually drop the carried trash into the can.

10.5.3 Case Study Summary

In total, the new AI is comprised of 12 modules, of which 8 have been reused. This means that only one-third of the modules in the new AI were newly designed. Of these four, one had only two states, and the other had only a single state. By avoiding the redevelopment of the existing AI logic, the workload to develop the new AI was dramatically reduced. The reuse process itself does take some effort. However, by representing module connections in a clearly defined fashion, and through the use of functional groups, the act of module integration was greatly simplified. Based upon this case study, we can conclude that our reuse techniques are a valuable approach for AI designers.

10.6 SCYTHE AI TOOL

With a formal AI module interface, it becomes possible to add tool support to the reuse process. Our tool, Scythe AI, allows a user to grow and manage a library of AI modules, and create new AIs through the described reuse approach. The tool includes a streamlined importing process to introduce new modules, library management of modules, an error and warning system to assist in new AI construction, and can export directly to a defined target game.

At a high level, Scythe AI allows users to build a library of AI modules by importing statecharts and associated classes. These modules are then reused to build new AIs. Like a standard IDE, warnings and errors are generated to guide users through the process of connecting modules to ensure proper interaction. When an AI is completed, it can be exported directly from Scythe AI into a target game. The workflow is illustrated in Figure 10.10.

10.6.1 Workflow and Key Features

10.6.1.1 Importing Modules

Importing an AI module into Scythe AI consists of building the AI interface by working through a highly guided process. Event-based communication details are recovered directly from the statechart itself, supplied in the SCXML format. Scythe AI scans the statechart for all events that are generated or transitioned upon and suggests these as output or input events, respectively. Any event that is both created and consumed is an internal event, and is inappropriate for any type of connection.

The remainder of the AI module interface comes from the associated class. Currently, Scythe AI supports Java files and could be extended to support C++. When importing, the associated class is parsed and information relevant to reuse is extracted. The user is given the list of class imports, where the user determines which imports come from, and thus link the module to, the source game. As well, any parameters in the

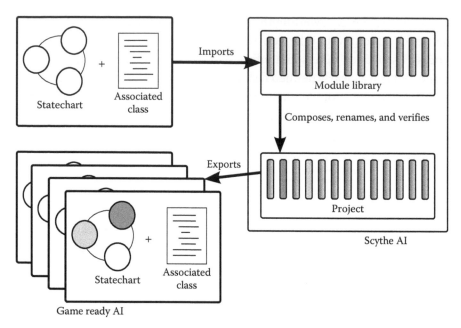

FIGURE 10.10   Scythe AI workflow.

class are extracted, so that values can be specified when that AI module is reused. Synchronous calls are addressed next, covering calls made to other classes, and calls made available for other classes to utilize. When this guided process is complete, the new AI module is added to Scythe AI's module library, and copies of the associated class and statechart are made and stored.

10.6.1.2 AI Construction

The building process consists of adding modules from the library to the new AI. Assuming that a module's logic is internally correct, that is, the statechart correctly does what it claims to do, the task for the user is to coordinate module communication such that the modules in the new AI will cooperate as desired. Most frequently, this means ensuring that events sent by a statechart are correctly received by target statecharts, while not being incidentally received by nontarget statecharts. This is done by event renaming as described in Section 10.4.1. Once a module is added, values for parameters should be specified.

A number of issues can arise while constructing a new AI. These are classified as *errors* if they will prevent the AI from running (e.g., a synchronous call is not satisfied), and must be corrected before completion.

TABLE 10.2   Warnings and Errors Generated by Scythe AI

Severity	Problem	Description
Error	Event interference	Event e is private in module x, but is used by module y
Warning	No input	Module x has input event e, which is not generated by any module
Warning	No receiver	Module x outputs event e, which is not received by any module
Warning	Game conflict	Module x has input event e sourced by the game, but module y generates e
Error	Game mismatch	Module x has game imports for g when target game is j
Error	Unsatisfied call	Module x calls m in *class*, which does not exist
Warning	Unused call	Module x provides method m which is never called
Warning	Null parameter	Parameter p in module x is null
Warning	No actuators	Project has no actuators

An issue is classified as a *warning* if it is a likely source of behavioral error, but would not prevent the AI from running. Each issue is listed in the main interface, so that the user has a continual description of potential problems. Table 10.2 gives Scythe AI's current listing of warnings and errors.

10.6.1.3 Outputting the AI

Once the AI is complete, the final step is to output the AI. For a typical game, this will be in the form of a class or .xml file defining the AI. Scythe AI automatically builds this file from the constructed AI. Output also includes both the .scxml statechart and the source Java file for each AI module. Scythe AI will modify output.scxml files to account for any event renaming that has occurred. The source game must be able to accept these files as input.

In our experimentation, we output to the game Mammoth, an massively multiplayer online (MMO) research framework. Importantly, Mammoth allows NPCs to be defined externally using XML files, written in Java, and has an SCXML execution environment. Thus, our output profile for Mammoth writes the external XML definition, which delineates the exact SCXML/Java pairings and provides specific values for parameters.

10.7 CONCLUSIONS AND FUTURE WORK

There is strong commonality within game AIs, even between apparently different character classes—certainly at a high level, NPCs have many similar behaviors. Historically, however, reuse has been complicated by a focus on context-dependent reactive behavior, and the need to express the AI in terms of strong code dependencies. As we have shown here, a statechart-based approach greatly helps in exposing the reuse opportunities, encapsulating the reuse at an appropriate level that encompasses not just a specific mechanic, but the high-level, behavioral abstraction. By composing functional groups of behaviors, novel AIs can then be directly constructed from a library of AI modules, a very practical strategy we demonstrate in the design of the Scythe AI development tool.

A primary benefit of formalizing reuse as we have done is in further being able to validate and perhaps even procedurally generate new AIs. Our design facilitates model checking and verification, and as part of future work, we are developing analyses that help in identifying and avoiding some of the more intricate logical errors that may arise in combining larger and more complex AI modules. Implicit state or message dependencies, for example, are a potential concern that may be addressed through deeper analysis of functional group behaviors, as well as through more formal means of specifying statechart interactions, such as found in protocol state machines.

Application of this reuse approach to more complex AIs is certainly possible. For example, NPCs in first-person shooter games employ tactical movement and cover, squad behaviors, and extensive combat behaviors such as ranged and melee weapons, vehicle-based combat, and fleeing. The *HALO* AI, taken from the successful *HALO* line of games, was reworked into the layered-statechart approach [19], and found to require 48 statecharts. This granularity affords considerable flexibility to the developer practicing reuse and provides an excellent start to any reuse library.

REFERENCES

1. Brian Schwab, Dave Mark, Kevin Dill, Mike Lewis, and Richard Evans. GDC: Turing tantrums—AI developers rant. http://www.gdcvault.com/play/1014586/Turing-Tantrums-AI-Developers-Rant, 2011.
2. Christopher Dragert, Jörg Kienzle, and Clark Verbrugge. Toward high-level reuse of statechart-based AI in computer games. In *Proceedings of the 1st International Workshop on Games and Software Engineering*, pp. 25–28. Honolulu, HI, May 2011.
3. Jörg Kienzle, Alexandre Denault, and Hans Vangheluwe. Model-based design of computer-controlled game character behavior. In *MODELS*, vol. 4735, *LNCS*, pp. 650–665, 2007.
4. Unreal Technology. The Unreal Engine 3. http://www.unrealengine.com, 2007.

5. Curtis Onuczko, Maria Cutumisu, Duane Szafron, Jonathan Schaeffer, Matthew McNaughton, Thomas Roy, Kevin Waugh, Mike Carbonaro, and Jeff Siegel. A pattern catalog for computer role playing games. In *GameOn North America*, pp. 33–38. Eurosis, August 2005.

6. Brent Laming, Joel McGinnis, and Alex Champanard. Creating your building blocks: Modular component AI systems. http://www.gdcvault.com/play/1014573/Creating-Your-Building-Blocks-Modular, 2011.

7. Max Dyckhoff. Evolving Halo's behaviour tree AI. Presentation at GDC. http://halo.bungie.net/inside/publications.aspx#pub15065, 2007.

8. John Walker, Robert Zubek, and Phil Carlisle. Little big AI: Rich behavior on a small budget. http://www.gdcvault.com/play/1012483/Little-Big-AI-Rich-Behavior, 2010.

9. Daniel Fu and Ryan T. Houlette. Putting AI in entertainment: An AI authoring tool for simulation and games. *IEEE Intelligent Systems*, **17**(4):81–84, 2002.

10. Sunbir Gill. Visual Finite State Machine AI Systems. http://www.gamasutra.com/features/20041118/gill-01.shtml, November 2004.

11. David Harel and Hillel Kugler. The Rhapsody semantics of Statecharts (or, on the executable core of the UML). *LNCS*, 3147:325–354, 2004.

12. John Krajewski. Creating all humans: A data-driven AI framework for open game worlds. http://www.gamasutra.com/view/feature/1862/creating_all_humans_a_datadriven_.php, 2009.

13. Damian Isla. Handling complexity in the Halo 2 AI. *Game Developers Conference*, p. 12. San Francisco, CA, March 2005.

14. Chong-U Lim, Robin Baumgarten, and Simon Colton. Evolving behaviour trees for the commercial game DEFCON. In *Applications of Evolutionary Computation*, vol. 6024, *LNCS*, pp. 100–110. Springer, 2010.

15. Jeff Orkin. Three states and a plan: The AI of F.E.A.R. In *Proceedings of the Game Developer's Conference* http://alumni.media.mit.edu/~jorkin/gdc2006_orkin_jeff_fear.pdf, 2006.

16. Rodney Brooks. A robust layered control system for a mobile robot. *IEEE Journal of Robotics and Automation*, **2**(1):14–23, 1986.

17. Philipp Kolhoff. Level up for finite state machines: An interpreter for statecharts. In Steve Rabin (ed.), *AI Game Programming Wisdom 4*, pp. 317–332. Charles River Media, Hingham, MA, 2008.

18. Christopher Dragert, Jörg Kienzle, and Clark Verbrugge. Reusable components for artificial intelligence in computer games. In *Proceedings of the 2nd International Workshop on Games and Software Engineering*, pp. 35–41. Zurich, Switzerland, June 2012.

19. Christopher Dragert, Jörg Kienzle, and Clark Verbrugge. Statechart-based AI in practice. In *Proceedings of AIIDE*, Palo Alto, CA, October 2012.

CHAPTER 11

Repurposing Game Play Mechanics as a Technique for Designing Game-Based Virtual Worlds

Walt Scacchi

CONTENTS

11.1	Overview	242
11.2	Related Research on the *What* and *How* of Repurposing Game Play Mechanics	242
11.3	Case Studies in Repurposing Game Play Mechanics	243
	11.3.1 Case 1—Producing Functionally Similar Games	244
	11.3.2 Case 2—Modding an Existing Game via New Game Play Levels, Characters, and Play Objectives	246
	11.3.3 Case 3—Replacing Multicharacter Dialogs and Adding Rashomon-Style Role-Play	248
	11.3.4 Case 4—Recognizing Resource Allocation Challenges with Uncertainty in Problem Domain	251
	11.3.5 Case 5—Choosing Meta-Problem Solving Domains for Game Development, Extension, and Play	254

11.4   Comparative Case Analysis: The Emerging Technique of
        Repurposing Game Play Mechanics for Game Design   256
11.5   Conclusions   257
Acknowledgments   258
References   258

11.1 OVERVIEW

This chapter examines the concept and practice of repurposing game play mechanics as a game design technique. Section 11.2 begins with a review of related research that informs this view of repurposing as a game design technique that may be adopted and practiced by new game developers or game players who want to engage in end-user game software development. Next, the chapter describes five game design case studies where different forms of repurposing are employed. These case studies include the identification of the example games and play mechanics that served to inform the resulting game designs from each. Each case study also categorizes the kinds of repurposing methods that were employed in reusing and adapting the source game mechanics into those employed in the new game design. Finally, the chapter includes a simple comparative analysis and a summary of these repurposing methods, as a basis for generalizing the method as a reusable and adaptive game design technique.

11.2 RELATED RESEARCH ON THE *WHAT* AND *HOW* OF REPURPOSING GAME PLAY MECHANICS

Designing computer games or game-based virtual worlds is a challenging problem (Bartle 2004). Such a problem has the complexity of both software systems design and designing the fun interactive play experiences (Fullerton et al. 2004; Howard 2008; Schell 2008). For the software engineering specialist new to game development, a clean-sheet game design can be a daunting challenge. Therefore, developers are wise to first start by examining the existing games and game play experiences as a basis for designing future games. Such an approach relies on some form of informal domain analysis (Prieto-Diaz and Arango 1991) to identify recognizable game features and capabilities, and game objects; functional operations; game play rules; and relationships between objects, operations, rules, features, and capabilities, as game play mechanics (Sicart 2008).

A formal domain analysis might have the potential to give rise to a persistent set of reusable game components, play mechanics, and eventually a meta-design theory for games (cf. Koehne et al. 2011) that could enable the (semi)automated generation of playable computer games (Scacchi 2012a). However, we are not yet at that point. Instead, we first seek a simpler contribution; that is, we explore how observation and informal analysis of the existing games can lead to the identification and conceptual reuse of game play mechanics (cf. Frakes and Kang 2006). Such an approach is already available in part through game modding tools and techniques that allow end users (game players or aspiring game developers) to learn how to modify an existing game product (El-Nasr and Smith 2006) to create functionally equivalent game variants, functionally similar game versions, or total conversions of the game into an entirely new game (Scacchi 2012b). Such forms of game modding are a widespread form of end-user software engineering (cf. Ko et al. 2001) that rely on user-interface customization, use of domain-specific scripting languages, or game-specific software development kits (Scacchi 2012b). Modding, as an approach to game development, can, however, also be extended across games through informal *mashups* (cf. Cappiello et al. 2011; Nelson and Churchill 2006) that compose game play mechanics from multiple games, or from other online applications, into a new game conversion.

In this chapter, we utilize a collection of case studies of game-based virtual worlds that we have produced across a number of game development projects. Our goal is to describe our experience in recognizing and reusing game play mechanics found in the existing games (including those we have developed) as the basis for articulating a new approach to game design. Five cases are presented, where each identifies the game (or games) that preceded or precipitated the design of a new game. In many of these cases, the explicit reuse of game play mechanics was not our goal, but appeared in our review so, we use this chapter to highlight our experience and findings. We then provide a comparative case analysis to identify an emerging set of generalizations that arise from our experience. Such generalizations are intended to serve as a starting point for a more fully articulated approach to the design of computer games or game-based virtual worlds through either opportunistic repurposing or the systematic reuse of game play mechanisms.

11.3 CASE STUDIES IN REPURPOSING GAME PLAY MECHANICS

In this section, five case studies are presented that identify and describe different techniques or strategies for repurposing game play mechanics. The case studies arise from observation of practices that gave rise to different computer game development projects produced or directed by the author. Each is described in turn.

11.3.1 Case 1—Producing Functionally Similar Games

One of the first game R&D projects focused on producing games for young students in grades K-6 that focused on informal life science education (Scacchi et al. 2008). These games were envisioned as part of a science learning game environment called *DinoQuest Online* for free-to-play, web-based deployment. It was designed to complement and interoperate with an on-site interactive, hands-on science exhibit called *DinoQuest*, located at the Discovery Science Center (a family-friendly science museum) in Santa Ana, California (Scacchi et al. 2008). Our starting point was to develop games for learning life sciences appropriate for primary/elementary school students, focusing on dinosaurs as prehistoric living creatures. Such creatures, like other living animals or humans, have basic body systems (e.g., skeletal, nervous, digestive, reproductive, cardiopulmonary), and an understanding of what these system are, what they do, and how they do it; interrelationships of these body systems is fundamental, as is the understanding of the ecologies in which these creatures thrive, survive, and die. The ecologies include relationships among creatures of different species, such as relationships indicating prey–predator, food chains, and *circle of life*, all of which are foundational to contemporary life science in the worlds in which people and animals live. So how might we design a game or a play mechanic that would highlight these ecological relationships? Our inspiration came from the core play mechanics of *Tetris* and *Dr. Mario*, displayed in Figure 11.1.

Tetris and *Dr. Mario* are tile-matching puzzle games, where sets of geometric colored tile patterns (sometimes called, *tetrominoes* in homage to dominoes) arrive/fall into the game play space (the playing field), and

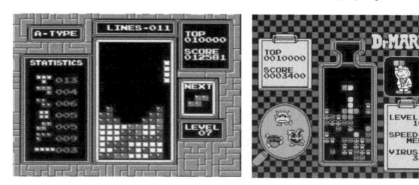

FIGURE 11.1 Screenshot of *Tetris* (left) and *Dr. Mario* (right) games. (*Tetris*: Courtesy of http://en.wikipedia.org/wiki/Tetris; *Dr. Mario*: Courtesy of http://en.wikipedia.org/wiki/Dr._Mario. Accessed on July 1, 2014.)

must be matched to fit in with other tile patterns already in place (*Tetris*), or form a repeated pattern like three-in-a row (*Dr. Mario*). The arriving tile patterns may be rotated or slid across the playing field in order to align and match the in-place patterns. Game play is motivated by time, as the patterns fall into and progress across the playing field at a certain pace, so that rapid recognition matching patterns and geometric spatial reasoning are helpful cognitive skills for an effective game play.

This game encourages and relies on such cognitive skills as game play increases in complexity and repetition. As the few people involved in the game project team were all experienced in Tetris game play, we quickly began to see how the basic Tetris play mechanic could be repurposed by substituting a carnivore, herbivore, plant, and mulch as the four (color) kinds of tiles. The resulting prey–predator food chain game is seen in Figure 11.2. However, we elected to rotate the Tetris/food chain game

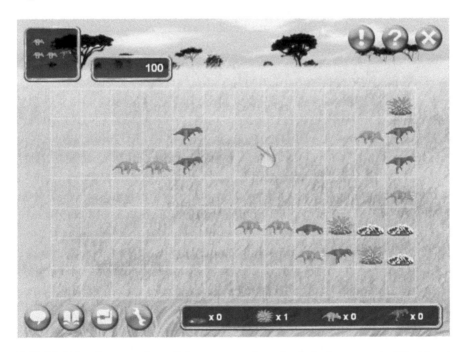

FIGURE 11.2 A screenshot of the prey–predator food chain games in *DinoQuest Online* that repurpose familiar *Tetris* play mechanics, from left-to-right instead of top-to-bottom. (With kind permission from Springer Science+Business Media: *New Frontiers for Entertainment Computing, Proceedings of the 1st IFIP Entertainment Computing Symposium*, P. Ciancarini et al., Eds., A collaborative science learning game environment for informal science education: DinoQuest online, Scacchi, W. et al., Springer, Boston, MA, Vol. 279, 2008, 71–82.)

board 90°, so that prey–predator tetrominoes emerge and flow left to right, rather than top to bottom.

When carnivores (predators) are aligned with herbivores (prey), they form a simple food chain, allowing the survival of the carnivore and the consumption of the prey. Similarly, when herbivores are aligned with plants, the herbivore survives, as the plant is consumed. When plants are aligned with mulch, they thrive and the mulch is consumed. When one or more carnivores are aligned with plants or mulch, they will eventually die and turn into mulch. Therefore, our game enacts a prey–predator food chain relationship where mulch contributes to plants, plants to herbivores, herbivores to carnivores, and carnivores to mulch as the circle of life (or food web), and game play enables players to score points as they recognize and reenact the prey–predator and food chain relationships through their game play moves. As such, we were fortunate to recognize that Tetris and Dr. Mario could serve as functionally similar games and game play, whose game play mechanics could be abstracted, reused, and tailored as part of our game design.

11.3.2 Case 2—Modding an Existing Game via New Game Play Levels, Characters, and Play Objectives

Another project arose in response to our presentation of *DinoQuest Online* at the Game Developers Conference (GDC) in 2007. We had a chance encounter with people from Intel Corporation who inquired of us if or how games might be employed to provide an interactive game-based training environment targeted to adult technicians as the player/trainee. These technicians operate, diagnose, and service semiconductor fabrication operation facilities in advanced manufacturing systems factories (Scacchi 2010). We took up this challenge. At the time, the then new first-person shooter (FPS) game, *Unreal Tournament 2007 (UT2K7)*, was being demonstrated at the GDC (prior to its release later that year), as a new version succeeding *Unreal Tournament 2004 (UT2K4)*. Both UT2K4 and UT2K7 were among the early generation of FPS games that could be modded using a game editor (UnrealEd), which we were already familiar with (cf. Scacchi 2002). Figure 11.3 displays UnrealEd.

Our challenge entailed the understanding of what a semiconductor fabrication facility looks like, what kinds of fabrication machines are present, and their basic operation, along with technician procedures and practices for operating, diagnosing, and servicing the machines, including dealing with material spills that *contaminate* a fabrication clean room. Much of this

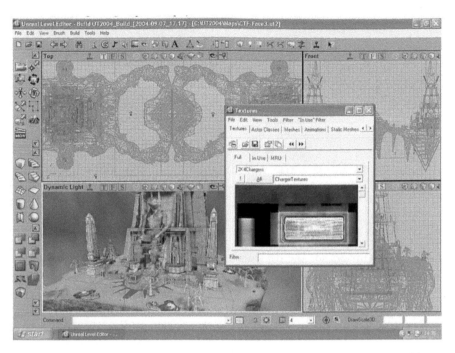

FIGURE 11.3   A screenshot of UnrealEd software development (game modding) kit operating with *Unreal Tournament 2004* game environment. (UnrealEd: Courtesy of http://en.wikipedia.org/wiki/UnrealEd. Accessed on July 1, 2014.)

information could be found in the information acquired through copious web searches, along with visits to a local semiconductor and nanotechnology systems fabrication facility located at the University of California, Irvine (UCI)—the UCI Integrated Nanosystems Research Facility. We then constructed the object, character, and fabrication machine models and associated textures (skins) using tools such as Autodesk 3DStudio and Photoshop. Visualizing and simulating materials spills were a priority interest of our sponsors, as training technicians in diagnosing and cleaning up such spills was a critical challenge of interest to our sponsors. Similarly, we recognized that fabrication technicians were attired in full-body suits (*bunny suits*), and modeling and simulating how they put on such suits (*gowning*) became a separate follow-on game-based training simulation project with our sponsor. So once we acquired knowledge about semiconductor fabrication operations and diagnostic servicing, we were able to rapidly design and prototype a new game called *FabLab* through a mod of UT2K4. A sample of images is shown in Figure 11.4.

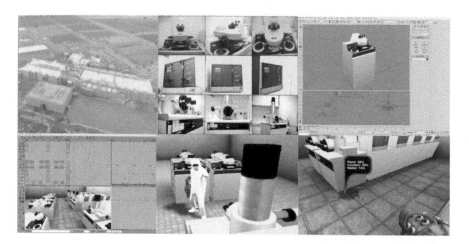

FIGURE 11.4 Images for the development and use of the FabLab game mod developed with UnrealEd and *Unreal Tournament 2004*. (With kind permission from Springer Science+Business Media: *Online Worlds: Convergence of the Real and the Virtual*, W.S. Bainbridge, Ed., Game-based virtual worlds as decentralized virtual activity systems, Scacchi, W., Springer, New York, 2010, 225–236.)

Among the noteworthy details of the modding-based game development effort was that it was performed by a single undergraduate student researcher (directed by the author), and initially released within three months of the start of the project. Similarly, feedback from the project sponsor included additional challenge tasks to develop other game prototypes for different manufacturing and business operation processes. Nonetheless, the networked multiplayer game play capabilities provided by UT2K4 and UT2K7 were inherently available within the FabLab game mod, and thus could be reused as-is at no additional software development effort.

11.3.3 Case 3—Replacing Multicharacter Dialogs and Adding Rashomon-Style Role-Play

Another game development challenge posed by Intel was for our group to rapidly develop a new game from scratch using low-cost tools and a total development schedule, including global deployment and end-user play evaluation, of less than two months. This would be a training game, rather than a game-based operations simulator such as FabLab, and it would need to be deployable on low-cost personal computers or mobile devices (e.g., smart phones). Part of the sponsor's goal was for us to articulate and document the game design and development process in ways that might be reused by corporate eLearning specialists who develop on-the-job training materials for newly hired business process personnel. Also, our development budget was limited to be comparable to that available for these specialists to develop conventional training materials (e.g., PowerPoint presentation slide decks). The selected business process was *order management,* which focuses on the activities of business specialists who handle incoming customer orders for products that are manufactured either *built to external order* or *built to fill internal inventory.* The result of this internal-only game development and deployment (due to nondisclosure agreement at the time) was a simple, single-player 2D role-playing game called *Customer Business Analyst* (CBA) that covered 3–4 weeks of simulated order management problem-solving tasks in a cubicle office environment, from simple to problematic (with nagging customers making phone calls to complain, communicating with customers and manufacturing operations via email, accessing in-house corporate enterprise resource planning systems—the *Hub*—and unreliable order status information). These features are highlighted in Figure 11.5—the two figures on the left provide a *bird's eye view* of the office space, whereas

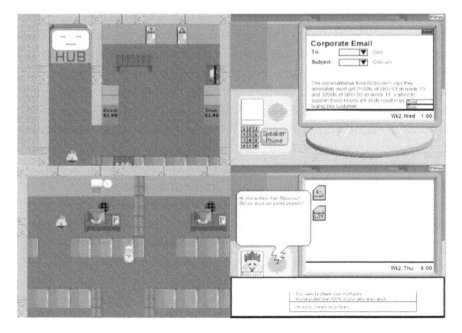

FIGURE 11.5 Four screenshots from the *Customer Business Analyst* game for training order management business analysts.

the two figures on the right provide an analyst's *desktop view* of their order management work activities.

After the delivery and retirement of the CBA game, about two years later, we received a new challenge from a large statewide government agency in California responsible for deploying state-mandated annual training for state employees in recognizing, avoiding, and reporting sexual harassment in public workplaces. Once again, our game prototyping budget and demonstration schedule was extremely limited, so this called for a game design and demonstration that could be done *quick and dirty*.

Our choice was to repurpose the role-playing CBA game through the substitution of in-game characters dialog while also providing support for the *Rashomon* effect (Heider 1988), but through in-game characters and nonplayer characters. The substitution of character dialog and situations as the basis for a new/adapted story is a common practice found in the literature, cinema, and game-based machinima. For example, the Shakespearian story of *The Tempest* was repurposed into the cinematic science-fiction story of the *Forbidden Planet*, whereas the popular *Red vs. Blue* machinima series represent the substitution of human voices over in-game character dialogs/taunts from various *HALO* FPS games. The Rashomon effect refers to the situation where multiple actors in a common situation or interaction provide differing, sometimes conflicting, interpretations of what they perceive (cf. the allegory of the blind men feeling the elephant). This exploration of characters acting in different roles encountering a common situation also appears in interactive game-based worlds, where players can switch between characters to reinterpret and reexperience a recent game play situation, as a play mechanic, appears in games such as *The Residents: Bad Day at the Midway* released in 1996 (Residents 2014). Our new game play experience was thus designed to demonstrate how to provide scenario-based character encounters that feature innocent, ambiguous, or abusive verbal interactions different/competing perspectives of in-game characters regarding whether or not they perceived multicharacter dialog or interactions as engendering sexual harassment activities. A screenshot of the repurposed CBA-into-sexual harassment game is shown in Figure 11.6.

To be clear, this game is not envisioned as a game to play to win, but instead to provide a sufficiently engaging experience, so that state employees would play through dozens of different possible sexual harassment scenarios to fulfill the state-mandated training requirement. The state's harassment liability insurance provider eventually argued against the development and deployment of the game in part because it was *a game,*

FIGURE 11.6 A screenshot from the repurposed CBA game now including substituted in-game character dialogs (here, highlighting a scenario where one character uses possibly ambiguous terms of endearment or sexual innuendo, drawn from a current sexual harassment training scenario).

though the Rashomon effect was highlighted as very original and likely well suited for sexual harassment training (though a few other reviewers objected to its value for this subject, as they preferred clear and unambiguous interpretations of what is or is not harassment).

11.3.4 Case 4—Recognizing Resource Allocation Challenges with Uncertainty in Problem Domain

A different repurposing opportunity emerged during a research project engagement with a different corporate sponsor, and later with a government sponsor. The challenge was to design and prototype a multiplayer virtual world, where different users could engage in *mission planning* problem-solving tasks found in military and civilian command and control systems. Mission planning refers to the activity of identifying and allocating available resources to remote parties who need the resources to complete their assigned mission (e.g., the search and rescue of victims in a remote location following a natural disaster). Mission planning is difficult in situations that are dynamic and constantly changing, as resource availability is characterized by uncertainty, as is the information about what is the most pressing conditions or mission variables to manage at a given time.

Mission planning is a kind of multiparty resource allocation with uncertainty problem in classical game theory. Few people are particularly adept at mission planning, and the consequences of allocation decisions may be very high. Subsequently, there is a widespread R&D effort focused on identifying *optimal* solutions to such allocation decisions, but little in the way of training simulators that situate new players in planning contexts, where they must make resource allocation decisions in the presence of private/shared information that is dynamic and uncertain.

We developed and demonstrated a game-based virtual world for conducting experiments in a multiplayer game-based mission planning that we called *DECENT* (Scacchi et al. 2012). Our world building efforts were based on the user-extensible open source software (OSS) virtual world server and *Second Life* work-alike platform, *OpenSim* http://opensimulator.org/. OpenSim operates on a scalable massively multiplayer online (MMO) and a federated wide-area network environment linking multiple interoperable virtual worlds via the *Hypergrid* (Lopes 2011; Scacchi 2012a). Once again, as in Case 2 for the FabLab game, we start by investigating and analyzing information about mission planning activities and facilities, as the basis for modeling and simulating the world of mission planning. Figure 11.7 displays a collage showing a large physical facility for mission planning; adjacent to scenes of the virtual world we modeled to simulate it [in-world agents are not shown in these scenes, but they can be seen elsewhere (Scacchi et al. 2012)]. The virtual world for experimental studies for mission planning in a decentralized command and control setting is called DECENT.

In further brainstorming with our project sponsors based on early demonstrations of the DECENT world, our sponsors asked what kind of mission planning game play would be possible in such a virtual world. *OpenSim*, much like *Second Life*, is not a game development environment, but is an open-ended, user-extensible virtual world environment. Therefore, it lacks game play primitives, score keeping, and domain-specific scripting facilities designed for game play. However, it is open to user extension. After considering and debating a number of alternatives, we decided that the popular seven-card poker tournament game, *Texas Hold'em*, would be our candidate for supporting mission planning game play. Accordingly, we extended our DECENT world to support this game, but utilizing the in-world user display screens to show both each user's card holdings, along with the table

FIGURE 11.7 Scenes from a physical facility for mission planning, and mirror virtual world for mission planning in DECENT. (Data from Scacchi, W. et al., Exploring the potential of computer games for decentralized command and control, *Proceedings of the 17th International Command and Control Research and Technology Symposium*, Paper no. 104, Fairfax, VA, June, 2012.)

cards on a large virtual wall display visible to all. We also repurposed the poker cards to now be denominated in four types of military services (land, sea, air, and cyber), with card point values expressing a corresponding quantity of military objects (e.g., tanks, ships, planes, and staff). We also added meta-game nonplayer cards drawn at random that serve to modify the value of cards held/shown, as another way to introduce uncertainty into the resource allocation game play. In multiplayer games, only the winning hand gets its resource allocation effected, based on the cards in the final round, while losing hands do not get allocations. Otherwise, game play follows the rules and procedures of the Texas Hold'em card game. Figure 11.8 displays a scene from in-world game play, and a photograph of multiple students playing the game.

Finally, we have taken the multiplayer virtual world of DECENT and have also repurposed its characters and objects for nonmilitary applications. For instance, we have repurposed from the virtual world for mission planning to adult teachers and children students in an elementary classroom setting with desks, tabletop computers, and a large-screen projector to support new experimental studies of classroom-based science and health care education.

FIGURE 11.8   Scenes of game play in the DECENT virtual world for mission planning. (Data from Scacchi, W. et al., Exploring the potential of computer games for decentralized command and control, *Proceedings of the 17th International Command and Control Research and Technology Symposium*, Paper no. 104, Fairfax, VA, June, 2012.)

11.3.5 Case 5—Choosing Meta-Problem Solving Domains for Game Development, Extension, and Play

The last case study examines an ongoing research project that focuses on developing a reusable framework for developing games about contemporary science mission research projects. Mission-oriented science projects are generally large-scale quests involving multiple characters in different roles (cf. a role-playing game) pursing both local and shared goals that include accomplishing a previously unattained destination (cf. Howard 2008).

Our interest is on mission quests that focus on new research studies that seek to travel to difficult sites, observe/sense, and retrieve objects/material results of great scientific interest. Recent NASA/space science projects include space-borne robotic travel, landing, instrumented sensing, and resource harvesting from nearby planets, moons, asteroids, and comets. Earth-centered satellite observation missions are similar, as are exploratory voyages to the bottom of the Earth's oceanic abyssal plane or deep-sea destinations. They are also missions to develop, launch, navigate, and capture/deliver nanoscale objects of interest within living systems, such as the human body. We also are examining other mission-like quest games, such as *Buzz Aldrin's Race into Space* (which recreates the competition between the United States and Russia to land a man on the moon), along with cinematic science-fiction stories such as *Fantastic Voyage* (a microscopic-scale vehicle navigation and the treatment of a human body) for mechanics for repurposing. A growing number of scientific missions like these have broader implications for both anticipating technology commercialization efforts and providing awareness and public interest to future science students. Subsequently, this effort leverages and repurposes what we had accomplished with our mission planning world from Case 4, as well as what we have learned from our other repurposing case study efforts.

What is, therefore, new in this case is our focus on meta-problem solving domains: multiple independent domains of scientific exploration where large-scale missions are focal, as are modeling and the simulation of diverse behavioral objects and multiple character roles that collectively articulate mission processes, procedures, and puzzles. In this case, the challenge for designing a reusable science game development framework through repurposing to rapidly develop new, scalable, and potentially interoperable games that are associated with scientific research missions in different science domains. Figure 11.9 displays screenshots of game play mechanics we

FIGURE 11.9 Example game objects and affordances for near-earth space exploration games for prototyping future space science missions and educational outreach. (Data from Scacchi, W., The future of research in computer games and virtual worlds: NSF workshop report, Technical Report ISR-12-8, Institute for Software Research, University of California, Irvine, CA, August. http://www.isr.uci.edu/tech_reports/UCI-ISR-12-8.pdf, 2012a.)

are currently investigating for space science missions that focus on travel to, capture, and retrieval of near-earth objects or small planetary objects, such as near-earth asteroids (Hasnain et al. 2012; Scacchi 2012a; Wall 2013).

11.4 COMPARATIVE CASE ANALYSIS: THE EMERGING TECHNIQUE OF REPURPOSING GAME PLAY MECHANICS FOR GAME DESIGN

In this chapter, we have presented five case studies of game-based virtual worlds that we have produced across a number of game development projects. Our goal has been to describe our experience in recognizing and reusing game play mechanics found in the existing games, including those we have developed, as the basis for articulating a new approach to game design. Along the way, we identified five ways for repurposing game play mechanics via (1) appropriating play mechanics from functional similar games; (2) modding game play levels, characters, and weapons through a game-specific software development kit; (3) substituting in-game character/nonplayer character dialogs along with adopting multiplayer role-play scenarios; (4) employing play mechanisms for resource allocation with uncertainty that reenact classic game theory problems; and (5) identifying game design patterns (quests and multiplayer role-playing) that can be used to develop families of games across science research problem-solving domains. All of these games repurposing mechanics are reusable, though the five cases presented find them used idiosyncratically. However, in presenting these cases, it becomes clear that it is possible to systematically observe, identify, conceptually extract, generalize, and then specialize or tailor game play mechanics that are provided capabilities (Alspaugh and Scacchi 2013) in the existing games.

Although these five repurposing cases denote a different type of repurposing, we would not say that a repurposing taxonomy or a process meta-model would only include these five classes. In contrast, we hold that repurposing is an interesting and productive family of design heuristics that can inform game design in ways that can be readily mastered by software engineers who focus on software reuse tools and techniques (Frakes and Kang 2006; Neighbors 1984; Prieto-Diaz and Arango 1991). Identification, classification, and taxonomization of repurposing heuristics would, however, appear as a promising line of research and practice in game design that is informed by modern software engineering theory and practice. It is also fair to say that repurposing is not an end-user software engineering practice, at least not at this time, as repurposing relies on insights and practices arising in the analysis and modeling of games or game play mechanics as a problem domain (Prieto-Diaz and Arango 1991). But determining which repurposing heuristics might be useful for end users seeking to engage during game modding also appears as a promising line of inquiry and practice. Thus, the existing games can serve as a rich base from which it is possible to analyze as an application design domain that utilizes diverse game play mechanics and associated objects, operations, and play experiences. Consequently, repurposing is a new and different method for identifying, analyzing, and generalizing reusable game-based software system designs that are available to game designers familiar with the existing games, or experienced in game development.

Last, it is also worth noting that repurposing is not merely copying and editing, or merely creating derivative variants of known games. Repurposing is not the same as modding, though modding practices can inform or afford the repurposing of game play mechanics (Scacchi 2012b), and as just noted, repurposing may inform game modding. Repurposing is targeted at the design level, rather than at the implementation level, of software. Reuse of source code (or OSS) is a different problem and opportunity compared to the reuse of software system designs, or the reuse of game play mechanics. Reusing game play mechanics or the design of play mechanisms is desirable and noninfringing: it does not necessarily produce or give rise to derivative works that might infringe on the copyright of an established game property. Once again, the repurposing of game play mechanics is an emerging technique for the design of computer games and game-based virtual worlds, as demonstrated in this chapter.

11.5 CONCLUSIONS

This chapter examines the concept and practice of repurposing game play mechanics as a game design technique. In addition to a review of related research, the chapter briefly describes five game design case studies, where the different forms of repurposing were employed. These case studies include the identification of the source game and play mechanics, as well as categorizing what kinds of repurposing methods were employed in reusing and adapting the source game mechanics into those employed in the new game design. The chapter also includes a simple comparative analysis of these repurposing methods, as a basis for generalizing the method as a reusable and adaptive game design technique. Repurposing appears to be a promising new heuristic approach for identifying, rapidly designing, and making computer games or game-based virtual worlds in ways that employ informal domain analysis techniques and related methods from reusable software and end-user software engineering. It also suggests new lines of research and practice that leverage computer games and software engineer research and practice, which, therefore, merit further investigation.

ACKNOWLEDGMENTS

Support for this research was provided by grants #0808783, #1041918, and #1256593 from the U.S. National Science Foundation. No review, approval, or endorsement is implied. Only the author of this chapter is responsible for statements and recommendations made herein.

REFERENCES

Alspaugh, T.A. and Scacchi, W. (2013). Ongoing software development without classical functional requirements, *Proceedings of the 21st IEEE International Conference Requirements Engineering*, Rio de Janeiro, Brazil, pp. 165–174.

Bartle, R.A. (2004). *Designing Virtual Worlds*, New Riders, Indianapolis, IA.

Cappiello, C., Daniel, F., Matera, M., Picozzi, M., and Weiss, M. (2011). Enabling end user development through mashups: Requirements, abstractions and innovation toolkits, in *End-User Development, Lecture Notes in Computer Science*, Vol. 6654, pp. 9–14.

El-Nasr, M.S. and Smith, B.K. (2006). Learning through game modding, *ACM Computers in Entertainment*, 4(1), Article 3B.

Frakes, W.B. and Kang, K. (2006). Software reuse research: Status and future, *IEEE Transactions on Software Engineering*, 31(7), 529–536.

Fullerton, T., Swain, C., Hoffman, S. (2004). *Game Design Workshop: Designing, Prototyping and Playtesting Games*, CMP Books, San Francisco, CA.

Hasnain, Z., Lamb, C.A., and Ross, S.D. (2012). Capturing near-Earth asteroids around Earth. *Acta Astronautica*, 81(2), 523–531.

Heider, K.G. (1988). The Rashomon effect: When ethnographers disagree, *American Anthropologist*, 90(1), 73–81.

Howard, J. (2008). *Quests: Design, Theory, and History in Games and Narratives*, A.K. Peters, Wellesley, MA.

Ko, A.J., Abraham, R., Beckwith, L. et al. (2011). The state of the art in end-user software engineering, *ACM Computing Surveys*, 43(3), Article No. 21.

Koehne, B., Redmiles, D., and Fisher, G. (2011). Extending the meta-design theory: Engaging participants as active contributors in virtual worlds, in *End-User Development, Lecture Notes in Computer Science*, Vol. 6654, pp. 264–269.

Lopes, C. (2011). Hypergrid: Architecture and protocol for virtual world interoperability, *IEEE Internet Computing*, 15(5), 22–29.

Neighbors, J.M. (1984). The Draco approach to constructing software from reusable components. *IEEE Transactions on Software Engineering*, SE-**10**(5), 564–574, 1984.

Nelson, L. and Churchill, E. (2006). Repurposing: Techniques for reuse and integration of interactive systems, *Proceedings of the 2006 IEEE Conference Information Reuse and Integration*, pp. 490–495. Waikoloa, HA, September 2006.

Prieto-Diaz, R. and Arango, G. (1991). *Domain Analysis and Software Systems Modeling*, IEEE Computer Society, Los Alamitos, CA.

Residents (2014). *Bad Day at the Midway*, Wikipedia.com, http://en.wikipedia.org/wiki/Bad_Day_on_the_Midway, accessed April 2014.

Scacchi, W. (2002). Understanding the requirements for open source software development, *IEE Proceedings-Software*, **149**(1), 24–39, February 2002.

Scacchi, W. (2010). Game-based virtual worlds as decentralized virtual activity systems, in W.S. Bainbridge (Ed.), *Online Worlds: Convergence of the Real and the Virtual*, Springer, New York, pp. 225–236.

Scacchi, W. (Ed.) (2012a). The future of research in computer games and virtual worlds: NSF workshop report, Technical Report ISR-12-8, Institute for Software Research, University of California, Irvine, CA, August. http://www.isr.uci.edu/tech_reports/UCI-ISR-12-8.pdf, accessed August 2012.

Scacchi, W. (2012b). Modding as an approach to extending computer game systems, *International Journal of Open Source Software and Processes*, **3**(3), 36–47.

Scacchi, W., Brown, C., and Nies, K. (2012). Exploring the potential of computer games for decentralized command and control, *Proceedings of the 17th International Command and Control Research and Technology Symposium*, Paper no. 104, Fairfax, VA, June.

Scacchi, W., Nideffer, R., and Adams, J. (2008). A collaborative science learning game environment for informal science education: DinoQuest online, in *New Frontiers for Entertainment Computing*, IFIP International Federation for Information Processing, P. Ciancarini, R. Nakatsu, M. Rauterberg, M. Roccetti (Eds.), Vol. 279, Springer, Boston, MA, pp. 71–82.

Schell, J. (2008). *The Art of Game Design: A Book of Lenses*, Morgan Kaufmann, Amsterdam, the Netherlands.

Sicart, M. (2008). Defining game mechanics, *Game Studies*, **8**(2), December.

Wall, M. (2013). Capturing an asteroid: How NASA could do it, *Space.com*, April 10. http://www.space.com/20591-nasa-asteroid-capture-mission-feasibility.html, accessed June 2014.

CHAPTER 12

Emerging Research Challenges in Computer Games and Software Engineering

Walt Scacchi and Kendra M.L. Cooper

CONTENTS

12.1	Overview	262
12.2	Looking Forward from the Preceding CGSE Chapters	263
12.3	Grand Challenges in Software Engineering through Computer Games	267
	12.3.1 Using Games to Solve Challenge Problems in Large-Scale Software Engineering	267
	12.3.2 Game Software Requirements Engineering	268
	12.3.3 Game Software Design	270
	12.3.4 Game Software Testing	272
	12.3.5 Teamwork Processes in CGSE	274
	12.3.6 GSD and Global CGSE	275
	12.3.7 Game-Based Software Engineering Education	276
12.4	Other Research Opportunity Areas for CGSE	277
12.5	Future Investment Opportunities in CGSE R&D Programs	280
12.6	Conclusions	281
Acknowledgments		282
References		282

12.1 OVERVIEW

There are many possible future directions for research in computer games and software engineering (CGSE). Computer games may well be the quintessential domain for computer science (CS) and SE R&D. Why? Modern multiplayer online games must address core issues in just about every major area of CS research and education. Such games entail the development, integration, and balancing of software capabilities drawn from algorithm design and complexity, artificial intelligence (AI), computer graphics, computer-supported cooperative work/play, database management systems, human–computer interaction and interface design, operating systems and resource/storage management, networking, programming/scripting language design and interpretation, performance monitoring, and more. Few other software system application arenas demand such technical mastery and integration skill. Yet, game development is expected to rely on such mastery, still provide a game play experience that most users find satisfying, fun, and engaging. Computer games are thus an excellent domain for research and development of new ways and means for (game) software engineering.

This chapter highlights future R&D opportunities in CGSE. Some are found in Chapters 2 through 11, while others are emerging research trends at the intersection of computer games (CG) and SE with each other, and with other disciplines. A starting question to ask is, "how CG development is different from SE?" (Murphy-Hill et al. 2014) More broadly, an overall question for the student or professional reading this book is "how will future computer games succeed/fail with/without SE tools, techniques, and concepts?" For example, if SE is mostly irrelevant to the successful development, deployment, and sustained evolution of computer games, then how or why is SE irrelevant? Is (1) traditional SE no longer relevant overall to the upcoming generations of game software developers, or is (2) there something about the ways and means by which computer games, game development projects, and game development organizations operate and engage players that eludes recognition and comprehension by SE researchers and educators? Although the former (1) seems unlikely and unpopular to contemplate, the latter (2) points to opportunities for future research in SE. The challenges are thus yours to consider and address.

The mainstream CG industry is a global endeavor with multibillion dollar game development companies, as well as untold numbers of independent small-to-mid-sized game studios that make games for commercial markets or specialty applications (e.g., game-based training).

Computer games are the most popular application on mobile devices, based on downloads and time spent using such apps. So what is going on with game development, and what role can or should SE play in advancing the commercial interests of game development firms, the technical challenges facing game developers, and the fun-filled experience and playful challenges that millions of players worldwide and across cultures want through game software? With this in mind, we begin to address some future arenas and issues for research that lies at the intersections of CGSE. First, we highlight example problems that are found by review of the preceding chapters. Second, we look to long-term challenges in SE that may be addressed through the lens of CGSE, to see if there is something new or different to be learned that may advance our understanding of how to better address such challenges. Last, we look to other grand challenge areas within science and engineering arenas that span global markets, to help see if there are potential opportunities for students and scholars in different geographic regions that may be specific to their industrial workforce, external research funding bases, and emerging game market opportunities. This last topic is intended to help broaden the perspective of seeing the future of research in CGSE is not just something relevant to the United States, but is, in fact, a global opportunity area that can be advanced both scientifically and socioeconomically through CGSE.

12.2 LOOKING FORWARD FROM THE PRECEDING CGSE CHAPTERS

The research presented in Chapters 2 through 11 in this book have emerged within various outlets, including the first three workshops on Games and Software Engineering (GAS) associated with the International Conference on Software Engineering. Interest in this area of research also appears in venues primarily focusing on computer game research and development (e.g., Foundations of Digital Games and Game Developers Conference). But in many ways, the intellectual home for CGSE has been based in SE. We believe that the all contributors to this first book in the emerging field of CGSE have established or emerging research accomplishments in the domain of SE, but with a growing focus of attention to the potential of CG within SE research, education, and industrial practice.

In Chapter 2, Wang and Wu provide a comprehensive review to date, describing how computer game development is being integrated into precollege and undergraduate computer science and SE coursework. Other SE and game design courses that have not yet been studied following his survey would include game playtesting, playtesting-based incremental game development, game production, and SE project management, to suggest a few. Similarly, courses designed to facilitate or complement competitive game jams (described subsequently) also represent opportunities for future CGSE research and educational practice.

In Chapter 3, Cooper and Longstreet introduce the use of model-driven SE techniques to the development of serious games for education. Their meta-model foundation explicitly represents traditional game elements (e.g., narrative and characters), educational elements (e.g., learning objectives and learning taxonomy), and their relationships. Well-established informal, semiformal, and formal requirements engineering techniques are tailored and integrated in the approach. The adoption of comic-style storyboards, for example, for different SE project efforts is likely to be popular. Future efforts in this direction can include case studies on the use of these techniques in the development of different serious games by different groups of student developers. Semiautomated transformations, with tool support for their approach, could further provide an effective, easy-to-use game development platform.

In Chapter 4, Sheth, Bell, and Kaiser from Columbia University describe their efforts in using game play motifs inspired from the massively multiplayer online role-playing games (MMORPG) to introduce students to the challenges of formal software testing process. Their use of RPG quests to perform and substantiate game progress, together with achievements acquired and experience points earned along the way, represents a playful gamification of SE processes that can be embedded within mainstream interactive development environments (IDEs) such as Eclipse. Gamification of other programming, design, debugging, multitarget source code build and release, configuration management, and other SE production tasks associated with IDEs are likely candidates for further study, as are how RPG play motifs might be integrated into different kinds of IDEs, whether for introductory or advanced skilled software students.

In Chapter 5, Xie at University of Illinois at Urbana-Champaign, along with Tillman, de Halleux, and Bishop at Microsoft Research, examines the potential for game-based SE tools for gamifying SE techniques in educational settings. Their *Pex4Fun* and its successor *Code Hunt*, provide a game-based programming environment that poses increasingly challenging program development tasks as coding duels, along with automated scoring of the results. The potential for gamifying other aspects of SE is thus a natural extension of such efforts, as might be the adoption of different kinds of game play models: paired peer-to-peer programmer duels or paired team-to-team duels. Also, alternative schemes for scoring and ranking programmer players could help to identify who is good/best at what task, as well as whether top-scoring individuals can work in teams that are also top-ranked performers.

In Chapter 6, Reichart, Ismailović, Pagano, and Brügge from the Technical University of Munich present their approach for developing serious games that employ new methods for adapting lessons and provisioning help to student playing serious games. Their work is informed by social learning theories from outside of SE. Educational and learning sciences may, there-fore, serve as a fertile ground for identifying and applying other emerging ideas and approaches for how best to adaptively guide game players at dif-ferent skill/accomplishment levels, as well as in serious games drawn from different game genres—role-playing, real-time strategy, first-person action, simulations, and others.

All these preceding efforts point to the potential of CG within SE edu-cation. This means that more SE courses in the near future may be trans-formed into games, as others are also beginning to explore and deploy in diverse education settings (Sheldon 2011). In Section I of the book (Chapters 2 through 6) all these preceding efforts point to the potential of CG within SE education. This also raises the prospect that more SE courses in the near future may be transformed into games, as others are also begin-ning to explore and deploy in diverse education settings (Sheldon 2011). In Section II of the book (Chapters 7 through 11) the remaining chapters explore new ways and means for advancing CG development through dif-ferent kinds of SE innovations that span from advanced multiplayer game play infrastructure design, geocasting, and user experience (UX) studies, through software reuse and repurposing techniques. We can, therefore, identify some future CGSE research opportunities here as well.

The development of the RESTful client–server architecture software server infrastructure by Debeauvais, Valadares, and Lopes at UC Irvine (discussed in Chapter 7) points to the challenges of engineering back-end server software architectures and networking protocols for massively multiplayer online game systems and virtual worlds. Exploration of new architectures and protocols seems like the next step for CGSE software systems R&D. Similarly, there is opportunity to engineer new representa-tions of in-game characters and objects that are designed with dynamic data (de)compression associated with network game play protocols that minimize perceived latency while scaling to ever larger, more com-plex in-game levels/worlds, interoperable meta-verses (Lopes 2011), and animated/simulated behaviors. New game development frameworks may, therefore, seek to support or provide such capabilities.

In Chapter 8, Hall, from AT&T Labs, describes advances in the provision and geocast sharing of game players and play object locations for use in outdoor mobile environments. Future augmented reality games that support visualization overlay capabilities on a player's viewport (e.g., via Google Glass or similar device) may be able to take advantage of these capabilities. Similarly, alternate or mixed reality games that support multiple heterogeneous devices (mobile health accessories, networked watches, smart cars, etc.) that can locally network with mobile devices may also be opportunity areas for geocasting system designs. Hall's work also demonstrates ways to tie back geo-located mobile games development to traditional SE concerns, which could, therefore, also be employed for future geocasting game software systems.

In Chapter 9, Russell describes how multilevel data analytics can be employed to support UX assessments during the development of the serious game, *AGoogleADay*, for research and experimental studies of end-user search practices with the Google search service. The role of UX, as a key factor driving the ongoing development and refinement of a serious game, points toward a future where such studies are part of the skills and capabilities of CGSE practitioners and may need to support the cost-effective development of large-scale web-based games. In particular, user play experiences studied by Russell at micro-, meso-, and macro-level point to the opportunity for future CGSE research in the use of data analytics to drive the continuous design and playtesting the UX of scalable cloud-based game development.

In Chapter 10, Dragert, Kienzle, and Verbrugge from McGill University focus their attention to a scheme on how to reuse AI behaviors for different in-game nonplayer characters (NPCs). Such reuse more readily enables the verification and model checking of game software modules that can be reused within and across games. This, in turn, can help reduce unexpected logical errors that may arise when diverse AI behaviors are incorporated into different game characters, whose interactions may be triggered by unusual or unexplored game play events. How best to design, assess, package, and tailor game software modules of different types (for in-game characters or other behavioral objects, for the generation of game levels populated with NPCs, etc.) for different patterns of reuse thus appear as promising new directions for future CGSE research.

In Chapter 11, Scacchi takes a complementary view of reuse, but at the level of repurposing game play mechanics found in the existing games.

Modding and repurposing are two forms of software reuse and extensibility that start from the existing games and game engines that are open to further customization, modification, or total conversion. How best to design and deploy domain-specific languages, game development frameworks, and game run-time environments (game engines) for scripting-based repurposing are promising areas for CGSE research. Similarly, how best to design or generate game content assets (e.g., NPCs, behavioral objects, and extensible rule sets for modifying game play mechanics) for modding or repurposing is open for research, along with new domain analysis and domain modeling techniques that can support them.

Overall, the Chapters 2 through 11 all point to different opportunity areas for future research into CGSE topics that merit further exploration, prototyping, and deployment to CG or SE researchers, educators, practitioners, and students. With this in mind, we can next turn to examine other opportunities for future CGSE research that arise in mainstream SE.

12.3 GRAND CHALLENGES IN SOFTWARE ENGINEERING THROUGH COMPUTER GAMES

Many traditional grand challenges in SE arise during the development of computer games as complex software systems. This includes using games to solve challenge problems in large-scale software engineering, game software requirements engineering, game software design and testing, teamwork processes in game software development, global software development (GSD) and global game development, and other problem areas for future research study. This set of challenges is intended to be suggestive rather than exhaustive or prioritized by importance. Each is examined in turn.

12.3.1 Using Games to Solve Challenge Problems in Large-Scale Software Engineering

Engineering large-scale software systems has long been recognized as a difficult problem. Reports sometimes indicate that as few as one out of three large software projects can be considered successful, whereas one-third are outright failures, and the remainder are plagued with flaws that demand excessive maintenance or provide a modest/poor level of user satisfaction. It seems unlikely that large-scale games should be any different; at least, until it can be empirically substantiated whether/how game software development is fundamentally different. Computer games are still software applications, so their development is likely similar to other commercial software development efforts.

Engineering scalable software systems is often bracketed as its own family of challenges, and these challenges similarly appear in the development of computer games such as MMORPG, where millions of players are anticipated, with thousands playing concurrently. The CGSE challenges for massively scalable games include how best to (1) design and organize teamwork processes for game development, playtesting, and postdeployment support; (2) divide the CGSE work among developers with different skills across different development sites; (3) organize and enact multisite software project management; (4) design scalable game services and supporting infrastructures that may host multiple server sites; (5) manage concurrent system configurations and product release versions for multiple end-user platforms; (6) manage and secure game-based intellectual property (IP) assets and user-created content; and so forth. Conversely, for MMORPG clients, how are remote game-based middleware services to scaled down or simplified for delivery of real-time game play experience that can fit within the game's client software deployment? In short, research that informs large-scale CGSE projects, as well as scalable game system architectures for integrating remote services, represents an interesting set of challenges likely to be of great interest to game development firms.

Beyond scalability, the world of SE is frequently characterized in modern textbooks as a series of engineering tasks. These SE tasks must be performed systematically, with care, and perhaps even monitored and measured as a continuously improvable set of processes. That's what we teach and what we encourage students and industrial professionals to learn and practice. But many hard and difficult problems arise along the way in many SE projects while performing such tasks, and thus the mainstream SE research community focuses much research attention to advancing knowledge about tools and techniques for addressing or resolving the challenges that arise. As such, we turn to briefly explore other grand challenges of SE, along with modest enumerations of CGSE research opportunities that may follow. The interested reader can undoubtedly identify other R&D opportunities as well.

12.3.2 Game Software Requirements Engineering

Software requirements engineering has been a long-term challenge in SE. It has its own international research conferences and dedicated journals, both of which are intended to complement mainstream research in the field of SE. The existence of both the conferences and journals suggests that international interest in the research and practice of how best to elicit and articulate software functional requirements that may be formalized, as well as what to do with nonfunctional software requirements, is widespread. However, with computer game software, it appears that the practice of game development primarily focuses on creating and satisfying nonfunctional requirements (NFRs) for the game as product, versus the game software's functional requirements that are often tacit and undocumented, or specified in hindsight (Alspaugh and Scacchi 2013). NFRs such as *the game must be fun to play* by a target audience of users/players (e.g., *played by males 18–35 years old* or *gender neutral*) on a target platform (*for play on Microsoft* Xbox One *consoles, browser based, integrated with social media sites such as Facebook* or *mobile devices running iOS or Android operating systems*) at some retail price point or monetization scheme (*free to play, with game-based microtransactions using prepaid user debit accounts* or monthly subscriptions for user accounts) are much more common (Callele et al. 2005). The SE challenge that thus appears is determining what to do during game software development to address or satisfy such NFRs. Alternatively, challenges also exist for finding how best to gamify the requirements engineering and other SE activities (Cooper et al. 2014; Fernandes et al. 2012).

Game developers have learned that merely providing a game whose software functions as intended (i.e., meets its functional requirements) is much less relevant than providing a game that game playtesting (Fullerton et al. 2004) empirically demonstrates satisfying diverse game player focus groups, rather than in-house game developers. In this regard, NFRs for games are testable, but not in the ways clearly aligned with the interests of SE testing research. Instead, it is not surprising to see the industry shifting its focus from large multimillion dollar budget AAA games to games that can be incrementally developed and released with a minimum set of game play features. Early success of a new minimal game with players (e.g., online player reviews, user-created game play videos, and game microtransaction rates of return) will determine whether more features will be added or integrated, thereby realizing that the game system is being developed as an online interactive game play service, rather than just as a software product. Whether such game development prescribes *features* as subject to functional or NFRs is at present an open problem in CGSE, as is the overall game development process that is driven by features that follow from the incremental deployment of testable game feature sets. This is not the same as Scrum or agile development methods, at least, as they have been prescribed in textbooks, but they may represent some linkages to such practices. Therefore, investigating and better understanding the virtues and vices of new game development practices is an open area for future CGSE research.

Another observation on requirements for game development arises with recognition that some game developers are committed end users of the games they play (Scacchi 2011). In such situations, the elicitation of functional requirements can be less complicated compared to traditional SE project situations, where developers and users are distinct groups (Alspaugh and Scacchi 2013). This is primarily the situation for *game modders*, people who intentionally act to modify an existing game, where the released game includes access to a software development kit (SDK) that is pre-configured to afford certain types of changes to the game's appearance, rules of play, play experience, or game purpose (Scacchi 2010b). As modders act as both the developer of (new) game functionality and an end user to be satisfied, there may be no communication/interest gap between developers and users. Thus, there may be no need for traditional requirements elicitation or specification, and instead the developer–user can iteratively explore, try out, and rapidly adapt their needs to what they can accomplish. Therefore, *what is the role or value of requirements engineering in support of game modding as a development modality*, is a question for further investigation and empirical exploration.

12.3.3 Game Software Design

Another classic challenge for SE is determining how best to design a software system to satisfy its requirements or specifications. As noted, computer game requirements may be dominated by NFRs, rather than functional specifications that can be formalized, verified, and validated. Thus, game software design may need to account for such bias or focus.

For students and would-be game developers, many textbooks and practitioner guides target *game design* (e.g., Fullerton et al. 2004; Meigs 2003; Rogers 2010; Schell 2008), rather than *game software* design. Whether such texts should be considered relevant to game software design may hinge on the expectation as to whether prior software design concepts, tools, and techniques are employed or ignored. For example, game design texts often focus attention on how to address NFRs for the appearance and animated *emotional* behavior of in-game characters, choice of game play mechanics well suited for the game's genre, the look and feel of game level or world design, user interface design and overlay, and so forth. As such, these texts say little about the game's software functional requirements.

This, in turn, means that alternatives about game software architecture are unclear, and thus the architectural design of games, and how to make trade-offs therein, remains an open challenge in CGSE. Instead, game designers are assumed or directed to employ a game SDK or development framework (e.g., Construct 2, GameMaker: Studio, GameSalad, Microsoft XNA Game Studio, Project Spark, PyGame, Steam, Unity, and Unreal Development Kit) to realize their game design. However, as many have observed, the selection of a game development environment constrains or predetermines what kind of computer game may be more readily developed. For example, many SDKs primarily support the development of 2D games, but not 3D games; some SDKs feature drag-and-drop game development with little ability to include new source code. Thus, the game development environment encroaches into the functional requirements or NFRs space. This sidesteps the engineering of game software design, and instead replaces it with a development paradigm focused on game design as found in textbooks, rather than on software system design, as found in SE textbooks. Similarly, if an envisioned game to be developed requires unfamiliar or unprecedented game functionality, it may be necessary to develop a game run-time environment (a game engine as a software system application) as well as one or more instances of games that operate with the new game engine.

Next, as multiplayer online games are complex software systems, we can consider how the underlying software architecture facilitates or constrains how the game can be initially designed and configured, built from the existing components, as well as further developed, modded, or evolved. Games are often configured using different middleware libraries or external service components that must be integrated with new game software functions, features, or capabilities. Dragert and colleagues provide a scheme for this in Chapter 10. However, commercial multiplayer games may incorporate 20 or more libraries of external services, including user registration, microtransaction payment, anti-cheating security, in-game or around-game online chat, behavioral character and NPC AI, database management, and others. Further, as some of these capabilities become further specialized, their software give rise to their own autonomous architectural representation. Thus, the challenge arises for how best to mix, match, or reuse heterogeneous game software subsystem architectures in ways that are open to component replacement, architectural reconfiguration, multiversion run-time platforms, and even IP license changes (Scacchi and Alspaugh 2012).

Another matter that arises in game software design is the development and review of game design documents. Oftentimes, the game design document is what is first produced, along with samples of in-game characters, play levels or worlds, narrative storyline for the game (if relevant), description of game play mechanics, embedded challenges or puzzles for players to overcome, and intended game play experience. As before, most of these items do not naturally map into an interconnected configuration of functional system modules, but may be more suggestive of feature-based or event-driven systems. Investigating how game design documents compare to software design documents would be valuable, especially as new generations of students are often eager to engage in game development (Claypool and Claypool 2005). Similar studies may also investigate the role of other online development artifacts widely used in free/open source software (FOSS) development projects, including online chat transcripts and social media, where game/software design rationales are captured, that game developers employ to support their game development projects (Elliott et al. 2007; Huang et al. 2014; Scacchi 2004, 2010a).

12.3.4 Game Software Testing

Given the emerging story of how the development of new computer games will require new methods and technologies for game software requirements and design engineering, so to we should expect game software testing to also evolve and adapt. For example, in Chapter 4, we have already seen Sheth and colleagues demonstrating their HALO approach for software testing that embraces RPG play mechanics, whereas in Chapter 5, Xie and colleagues introduce new ways and means for engaging software developers in peer-to-peer software coding—testing duels. Such approaches might be further explored in the context of software module integration or configuration management game challenges that, in turn, might automatically evaluate whether the resulting system can be automatically built, packaged for remote installation, and regression tested. The Verigames initiative of the Defense Advanced Research Projects Agency (DARPA) (described subsequently) explores the potential for crowdsourcing approaches to testing problems in formal software verification. In Chapter 9, Russell provides examples of how to capture and analyze UX from game play, which can be recognized as a form of game feature acceptance testing by targeted end users. But much still remains to be explored through software testing supporting CG development efforts.

Consider the challenge of addressing how best to validate NFRs for games, such as *the game must be fun to play*, or *operate on PCs, consoles, and mobile devices*. Assessing a game's initial user play experience (Murphy-Hill et al. 2014) and players' experience of fun can entail eliciting end-user opinions, feedback, and concerns about their UX with current game features or capabilities. Approaches like that of Russell may be a starting point. In contrast, validating that a given game can operate on different platforms is a much more operational concept, yet what is to be determined is what game play functionality is common for focused testing, while other functionality such as user interface controls may be specific to the play device platform. An informed game software design may specify where such platform-specific customizations are to be made through functional factoring, so that such design can inform subsequent testing. Formal software architectural designs may also help to facilitate automated testing, as may other techniques, in ways that merit careful empirical study (Murphy-Hill et al. 2014). Similarly, how is game play user experience (UX) to be assessed across platforms, since platform-specific specializations may (or not) affect the end-users play experience. Perhaps game software components and integrated configurations may be subjected to system integration testing duels, following the lead established by Xie and colleagues in Chapter 5. Overall, these options point to the need for one or more alternative schemes for a game software testing and playtesting hybrid regime that can assess common versus platform-specific game functionality, features, and UX, as well as other NFRs.

The last area to address concerns the recent interest in investigating whether computer games can be used to solve difficult problems in software verification. In the United States, DARPA has initiated a research program (informally called *Verigames*) to see what advances can be realized through games designed for play by large distributed and loosely coordinated *crowds* of players. An initial set of games has been developed and deployed on the web (and in one case, exclusively for a mobile platform such as the Apple iPad)—see Verigames project site (2014). Each game takes on an approach that decomposes problems of software verification into simpler ones, such as proving loop invariance properties (Logas et al. 2014). Collectively, these crowdsourced games are envisioned as a fundamentally new approach to the long-standing problem of formal software verification. Of course, the games themselves must be playable, interesting, and fun to the external game players who may have little/no interest in software verification challenges. Said differently, a game that satisfies its functional requirements (e.g., implements a class of loop invariance testing play mechanics) does not necessarily make it interesting and fun to the external users. Conversely, an interesting and a fun game that introduces a new game play mechanic, such as for determining loop invariants, might itself be an innovation in computer games, whether it does or does not solve practical problems in software verification. Nonetheless, the effort to verify large software system elements using a crowdsource approach like Verigames is a bold research undertaking that lies near the center of future CGSE R&D.

12.3.5 Teamwork Processes in CGSE

Many students and independent game developers participate in computer game development competitions or *game jams* (Musil et al. 2010; Preston et al. 2012; Scacchi 2012a; Shin et al. 2012; Zook and Riedl 2013). These jams usually focus on the clean-sheet production of a playable game usually in a limited time frame, such as 24 or 48 hours, though shorter and longer competitions have been engaged. Sometimes, these jams have external for-profit or nonprofit sponsors, who, in turn, may offer financial or technology product rewards. Other times, jams offer no tangible extrinsic rewards, but instead focus on going *for the win*, résumé building, and shared learning experience as the desired outcome. Game jams may also be located in academic settings, so that both *intra-mural* (within school) and *inter-mural* (across schools) game jams can be undertaken in ways that complement SE Education (Claypool and Claypool 2005; Cooper and Longstreet 2014; Scacchi 2012a; Shin et al. 2012; Wang 2014).

An interesting set of research questions arises associated with such jams, perhaps most relevant to empirical studies of alternative game/software development processes, practices, methods, and tools used. For example, for intra-mural game jams, it may be possible to structure and balance the game development teams by team size, game developer role, and SE skill level. This may be done by the participating students indicating their skill level and developer role preference, then have the participants be randomly assigned to teams in ways that balance team size, role, and skill level. This can mitigate against preformed teams with established collaborators, high skill distribution, and relatively mature game development capabilities. Short-duration jams also mitigate against the consequences of team failure or participant dropout and instead make these events more of a CGSE learning experience. In this way, in addition to focusing on game production, the overall game jam serves as a *field site* where selected CG design,

SE processes, and technologies (e.g., Musil et al. 2010; Zook and Riedl 2013) can be comparatively investigated, following empirical SE approaches introduced 30 years ago (cf. Bendifallah and Scacchi 1989; Boehm et al. 1984). Such field sites allow for a careful empirical study of teams using a new game SDK or development technique (e.g., SCRUM, agile development, game modding) versus those who do not, or those who produce traditional SE documents (requirements specifications, architectural designs, and test plans) and follow SE processes for their game versus those who just focus on game design methods. These game jams may, therefore, be better suited for longer durations (e.g., 1–2 weeks). Inter-mural or open-participation game jams may not be so readily structured or balanced at little cost, but instead may address other CGSE questions that better match their natural field organization. These jams may stress short duration and co-location, along with targeted game production on a single randomly chosen topic that is announced at the beginning of the competition.

More generally, game jams offer the opportunity to organize, design, and conduct empirical studies in CGSE that, in turn, may inform both new game design practices or processes and new SE practices and technologies (Dorling and McCaffery 2012). These jams can be used to address CGSE research questions in ways not previously utilized in SE research. Ultimately, this can mean that SE can be viewed as a competitive team-based sport activity that can be fun for students, as well as structured to support a careful empirical study (Scacchi 2012a), rather than SE being a business endeavor to produce application systems hosted on back-end infrastructures accompanied by documents that few will ever read. It also suggests that game jams may be designed as a kind of *meta-game*, so as to structure the outcomes (i.e., the games produced) to embody certain functional features, or the game production process to reward accumulative levels of progress achieved or skills mastered by different teams (*leveling up*), rather than leading to winning and losing teams.

12.3.6 GSD and Global CGSE

GSD focuses attention to challenges that arise when large software development projects are distributed in geographic space across many time zones. GSD often involves software development tasks being performed by teams that are culturally diverse, so that many will not share a first native language, but often may rely on local SE teamwork activities conducted in one's native language, whereas inter-site development activities and project management may be conducted and coordinated in another language (most often English). Yet, many large-budget AAA games are developed in multiple international sites, or for use in global markets with different user language cultures. This implies not just the need for internationalization (or localization) of game user interfaces, but also for international game production management. It should, therefore, be unsurprising that culturally grounded misunderstandings and miscommunication will arise during game software development, much like they do in other GSD projects. Although business efforts to reduce software development costs (e.g., through offshoring certain tasks to lower cost software labor markets) are being tried with both traditional applications and computer games, it is also apparent that critical product design feature choices or system integration activities are closely held by the lead development organization. Therefore, some software product knowledge is purposely withheld in proprietary GSD projects from global collaborators. In contrast, FOSS development of commercial games is not (yet) widely practiced (Scacchi 2004), so it is unclear whether such approaches (Huang et al. 2014; Scacchi 2010a) can overcome the challenges found in proprietary GSD projects (Smite and Wohlin 2011). In sum, most of this is still poorly understood from a research perspective, and a few tools and techniques are being investigated to address cultural challenges in GSD, yet alone in global CGSE.

12.3.7 Game-Based Software Engineering Education

As amply demonstrated by the research efforts presented in Chapters 2 through 6, different ways and means for the engineering of CG software systems is a major focus for software engineering education. To no surprise, we find that other challenges identified for CGSE in Sections 3.1 through 3.6 are appropriate candidates for exploration through software engineering education (SEE) project coursework. Engineering CG software requirements, (architectural) design, testing (including playtesting for UX), teamwork processes, and global CG software development are all open for application and experimentation by SEE innovators. Even large-scale CGSE may be explored through SEE, though this will demand additional expertise by SE educators in knowing how to mobilize software infrastructural services for use within academic SEE coursework. SEE project coursework may be organized and structured about team-based game development competitions. The goal of such competitions is not so much about the determination of winners and losers, but of creating CG development challenges that require, incentivize, or reward the use of SE methods for CG requirements, design, and testing using game SDKs and/or remote middleware services. Similarly, accommodating game development competitions that elicit submissions from international or globally dispersed SEE student project teams might, therefore, also focus comparative assessment on how well student teams practice and demonstrate GSD concepts and techniques through their CG development efforts. Finally, all other areas of SE research and practice, such as configuration management, build and release management, reverse engineering, FOSS development, and agile development, may be seen as potential candidates for gamification in ways that may be engaged through SEE coursework and team projects.

12.4 OTHER RESEARCH OPPORTUNITY AREAS FOR CGSE

One area of CGSE research interest not addressed in this book focuses on the creation of new technologies for (semi)automated generation of computer games (cf. Scacchi 2012b). This kind of research may focus on the invention of new concepts, techniques, and tools for the generation of ready-to-play games based on specifications of game play narrative (such as movie scripts or screenplays), emergent agent-based interaction rules, and functional game software specifications. Such efforts represent a reconstitution of automatic programming or knowledge-based software development approaches once avidly explored in SE research, but now displaced by more conventional programming-centric approaches that average programmers can perform. Although there is an active community of researchers working on computational intelligence, agent-based systems, and procedurally generated worlds for games, much of these efforts are not (yet) being well addressed from a CGSE perspective. For example, current efforts at the procedural generation of game worlds often focuses attention to the generation of visual in-game object models or composed levels, such as automatically generated trees/vegetation, buildings, building interiors, cityscapes, waterways, and geographic/conceptual terrains (Smelik et al. 2014; Smith et al. 2011). However, these efforts do not yet generate in-game characters with complex social behaviors in different roles, nor sociopolitical cultural systems that may/may not feature emergent competitive or combative dynamics, nor utilize engines that provide complex physical or ecosystem simulations (e.g., processes such as digestion, reproduction, speciation, and ecosystem evolution) at different physical scales (from nano to human, or from human to cosmological) (Bartle 2004; Scacchi 2012b). So much innovation is possible in this area of future CGSE research.

In other research, currently outside of CGSE, there is a growing interest in determining whether, or how best, to employ and engineer cloud-based computing infrastructure and services to support online games (Huang et al. 2014; Mishra et al. 2014). Cloud-based software system architectures are recognized to offer scalable services, especially for remote storage, file sharing and content distribution, commercial (purchase) transactions, and remote computation, among others. These architectures may inform the deployment of CG where such scalability is relevant to game publishing business ventures. However, one nagging challenge for CGSE is how best to develop games that can exploit such capabilities, rather than supporting current/legacy games that were developed without the dependence or integration of cloud-based services. For example, cloud-based CG R&D efforts are seeking to host game play computations in the cloud, while streaming visual and audio content updates to remote player clients. This resembles a *fat server, thin client* architectural model that contrasts to the currently *thin server, fat client* model that is more common in networked multiplayer games. Both models, along with others such as massively scaled peer-to-peer or hypergrid architectures (Lopes 2011), represent different assumptions about preferred business models, financial investments, IP protection, network bandwidth and latency quality of service, and anticipated advances in computing technology. Streaming game content is being actively pursued by large IT firms, perhaps inspired by the success of (asynchronous, on-demand) streaming video/audio distribution ventures that are displacing traditional (synchronous, on schedule) media content broadcasters. But game play is interactive and experiential in ways that passive media (films, recorded music, and television programs) are not. Therefore, it is not surprising to see that game play streaming services often provide reduced visual display resolution (to reduce bandwidth and latency) with game content that can be more easily cached (e.g., prerecorded game video content), because wide-area network protocols are not yet developed to meet the performance and *quality of experience* (QoE) requirements that game players expect (Mishra et al. 2014). Thus, the CGSE challenges here include in identifying how best to design games for cloud-based deployment infrastructure, as well as how to design the software infrastructure (including new game networking protocols) for cloud-based games (Huang et al. 2014).

Next, serious games intended specifically for crowdsourced play [sometimes called, *games with a purpose*—GWAP (von Ahn 2006)] are themselves a relatively new capability of interest from a CGSE perspective. In many such games, play is often strongly limited to play mechanics such as 2D/3D puzzle solving, which means these are but one genre of serious games. Many of these *citizen science* games primarily engage puzzle gamers who may or may not care about the underlying purpose or domain for the game. Therefore, it is unclear whether little/no engagement of the game players with the underlying problem domain is a relevant UX factor in game play, or in user satisfaction with a fun and playful game. But the development of GWAP, game-based virtual worlds (Bartle 2004; Scacchi 2010c), or other kinds of serious games in nongame play domains such as protenomics via the *Foldit* game (Cooper et al. 2010), RNA sequencing via the *EteRNA* game (Lee et al. 2014), and mapping the retina or brain connectome via the *EyeWire* game (Frank 2013) may itself represent a new avenue for CGSE research to address—for example, how best to design and software engineer games for different scientific research problem domains (Scacchi 2012b).

The areas identified throughout this chapter for future research in CGSE is a small sample rather than a comprehensive set. CGSE itself represents a new arena for SE research and development. Other CGSE challenges may be found in how best to: (1) engineer cybersecurity software capabilities for multiplayer games, where financial services, user privacy, and anti-cheating requirements must be addressed while insuring online socialization and convivial/competitive game play; (2) integrate CG with social media services and other cloud-based services; (3) develop frameworks or SDKs for implementing games that incorporate heterogeneous devices arising within an Internet of Things; (4) develop automated or semiautomated game production tools that allow nonengineers to rapidly produce and deploy serious games for nonentertainment and scientific research applications (Cooper et al. 2010); (5) engineer remote game client services for display update management and run-time monitoring to improve game QoE; (6) investigate software architectural alternatives for orthogonal, multi-tier middleware services (for game character AI, data analytics, financial payment services, user account management, etc.) developed by independent game service providers; (7) design rapid, iterative, and incremental approaches to minimum playable games (or game feature sets) that allow remote user play to help drive subsequent game play features and functionality, as well as how to adapt such an approach to nongame applications; (8) articulate techniques that combine playtesting with play analytics and visualizations; (9) develop games, game engines, or game development frameworks for educational games in other CS subdisciplines (e.g., serious games for network protocol design, database management, compiler construction, and operating system configuration); and (10) investigate the roles of FOSS tools and techniques for game development in enabling SEE, global knowledge transfer, and socioeconomic development of local game development enterprises.

Last, the concept and the initiative of using games to explore new ways and means for solving long-standing problems in SE is profound, bold, and ambitious. Whether it succeeds is an open issue for now. But whether it can and will be adopted to explore other challenges in SE is, therefore, an opportunity at hand. Similarly, whether such effort can be mobilized and deployed on a regional, national, or global scale without a large government research investment is also a challenge to be addressed. However, we should look for (and perhaps encourage) such efforts to address challenges in CGSE, whereby game development serves game play whose purpose is to inform new ways to develop games.

12.5 FUTURE INVESTMENT OPPORTUNITIES IN CGSE R&D PROGRAMS

It may well be the situation that the mainstream computer game industry has little interest in the pursuit of research in CGSE, as being somehow central to their game product business models or revenue streams. This is not to say that such research may not be beneficial to such business efforts. Instead, such an industry position may instead seek to exploit the spillover benefits that arise from academic research in CGSE that may be supported by government agencies or corporate underwriters. However, Chapters 8, 9, and 5 in this book by Robert Hall, from AT&T Labs, Dan Russell, from Google, and Tao Xie and others, from Microsoft, demonstrate real academic-industrial research interest arising in the arena of CGSE, so perhaps other corporate partners will follow. Similarly, as noted earlier, the DARPA Verigames research initiative in the United States Verigames (2014) is another multiyear effort that essentially is a large investment in the future of CGSE R&D. In contrast, in the United States, the European Union, and elsewhere, (inter)national research programs arise that may represent new opportunities for the collaboration of CGSE researchers and game development students, with domain specialists working in other areas of study.

New distinct research programs are being established (as of 2014) in robotics and brain sciences (e.g., EU Human Brain Project, U.S. BRAIN Initiative). Although both areas have long-standing traditions of R&D, future efforts are focused on producing scientific discoveries, technological breakthroughs, and workforce development. Computer games for teaching robotics, augmented reality games that interact with or employ robots, and game jams that incorporate robotic devices are just a sample of possible avenues for research and study. Similarly, in neuroscience, how best to design and engineer *brain games* (for *neurogaming* studies) and how to engineer multiplayer games for players wearing immersive head-mounted displays or brain–computer interfaces are other examples. Next, how to engineer software systems and infrastructural services that could enable people with limited abilities to control assistive robots through neurotechnologies is yet another example of what such programs may be interested in exploring.

Last, one additional question is how might global CGSE R&D projects develop the software services and playful games that might stimulate scientific discovery (Cooper et al. 2010; Frank 2013; Lee et al. 2014; Scacchi 2012b), workforce development, and knowledge transfer? In particular, how might this occur within domains that are not yet perceived to involve or realize the potential benefits of interdisciplinary research efforts that can be supported and advanced through CGSE? The entertainment-focused game industry is centered in the United States, the European Union, and Asia (principally Japan and South Korea), whereas countries such as Brazil, Russia, India, China, and Singapore are looking for ways to participate in the global game development, services, and publishing business, especially for their domestic markets and emerging skilled workforces. In contrast, the role of such industry in countries in the Middle East, Africa, and Polynesia is unclear and perhaps clouded by other cultural issues. Accordingly, we anticipate and encourage students and researchers to consider opportunities in CGSE research and development within or across these emerging global CGSE R&D markets.

12.6 CONCLUSIONS

Overall, the future of CGSE is filled with many diverse opportunities for research studies and technology development. These opportunities may be of some interest to the extant computer game industry, but the likelihood of interest for the near-term research funds may be found outside of the entertainment-focused computer game studios (Scacchi 2012b). Whether government agencies and corporate sponsors who support high-risk research projects will embrace CGSE as a new opportunity area is an open question, but one that readers of this book may be compelled to advocate and pursue.

Finally, we do not expect the world of SE to suddenly pivot around the emerging area of CGSE, though it might be interesting to see and experience such a transformation. Similarly, it will take time for our colleagues in mainstream computer science to come to recognize how computer games are engaging a new generation of students and researchers, though the emergence of new academic research centers and degree programs for (computer) game science are just beginning to appear. Nonetheless, we believe there is a future to research in CGSE, and this future may need to find its home and advocates in the periphery of disciplines where new lines of research and practice are more likely to emerge. Thus, we encourage you to do so to pursue your interests in CGSE research and practice.

ACKNOWLEDGMENTS

The research of Walt Scacchi was supported by grants #0808783, #1041918, and #1256593 from the U.S. National Science Foundation. No review, approval, or endorsement is implied. Only the authors of this chapter are responsible for statements and recommendations made herein.

REFERENCES

Alspaugh, T.A. and Scacchi, W. (2013). Ongoing Software Development without Classical Requirements, *Proceedings of the 21st IEEE International Conference on Requirements Engineering*, Rio de Janeiro, Brazil, pp. 165–174, July 15–19.

Bartle, R.A. (2004). *Designing Virtual Worlds*, New Riders, Indianapolis, IN.

Bendifallah, S. and Scacchi, W. (1989). Work Structures and Shifts: An Empirical Analysis of Software Specification Teamwork, *Proceedings of the 11th International Conference Software Engineering*, Pittsburgh, PA, ACM and IEEE Computer Society, pp. 260–270, May.

Boehm, B., Gray, T., and Seewaldt, T. (1984). Prototyping versus Specifying: A Multiproject Experiment. *IEEE Transactions on Software Engineering*, **10**(3): 290–303.

Callele, D., Neufeld, E., and Schneider, K. (2005). Requirements Engineering and the Creative Process in the Video Game Industry, *Proceedings of the 13th International Conference on Requirements Engineering*, Paris, France, pp. 240–250, August.

Claypool, K. and Claypool, M. (2005). Teaching Software Engineering through Game Design, *Proceedings of the 10th SIGCSE Conference Innovation and Technology in Computer Science Education*, Caparica, Portugal, pp. 123–127, June.

Cooper, K. and Longstreet, C. (2014) Integrating Learning Objectives for Subject Specific Topics and Transferable Skills, in Cooper, K. and Scacchi, W. (Eds.), *Computer Games and Software Engineering*, CRC Press, Boca Raton, FL.

Cooper, K., Nasr, E., and Longstreet, C.L. (2014). Towards Model-Driven Requirements Engineering for Serious Educational Games: Informal, Semi-formal, and Formal Models. *Proceedings of the 20th International Working Conference on Requirements Engineering: Foundation for Software Quality, Lecture Notes in Computer Science*, Vol. 8396, pp. 17–22.

Cooper, S., Treuille, A., Barbero, J. et al. (2012). The Challenge of Designing Scientific Discovery Games, *Proceedings on Foundations of Digital Games*, Monterey, CA, pp. 40–47, June.

Dorling, A. and McCaffery, F. (2012). The Gamification of SPICE, in *Software Process Improvement and Capability Determination*, Communications in Computer and Information Science, Vol. 290, Springer, pp. 295–301.

Elliott, M.S., Ackerman, M.S., and Scacchi, W. (2007). Knowledge Work Artifacts: Kernel Cousins for Free/Open Source Software Development, *Proceedings of ACM Conference Support Group Work*, Sanibel Island, FL, pp. 177–186, November.

Fernandes, J., Duarte, D., Ribeiro, C. et al. (2012). iThink: A Game-Based Approach Towards Improving Collaboration and Participation in Requirement Elicitation, *Procedia Computer Science*, 15, 66–77, doi:10.1016/j.procs.2012.10.059.

Frank, A. (2013). 70,000+ Have Played "Eyewire" Game that Trains Computers to Map the Brain. *Forbes Online*, http://www.forbes.com/sites/singularity/2013/08/19/70000-have-played-eyewire-game-that-trains-computers-to-map-the-brain/, accessed June 2014.

Fullerton, T., Swain, C., Hoffman, S. (2004). *Game Design Workshop: Designing, Prototyping and Playtesting Games*, CMP Books, San Francisco, CA.

Huang, C.-Y., Chen, K.-T., Chen, D.-Y. et al. (2014). Gaming Anywhere: The First Open Source Cloud Gaming System, *ACM Transactions on Multimedia Computing Communications and Applications*, **10**(1). doi:10.1145/2537855.

Lee, J., Kladwang, W., Lee, M. et al. (2014). RNA Design Rules from a Massive Open Laboratory. *Proceedings of the Academy of Natural Sciences,* 111(6): 2122–2127. doi:10.1073/pnas.1313039111.

Logas, H., Whitehead, J., Mateas, M. et al. (2014), Software Verification Games: Designing Xylem, The Code of Plants, *Proceedings of the 9th International Conference on Foundations of Digital Games*, Ft. Lauderdale, FL, April 3–7.

Lopes, C. (2011). Hypergrid: Architecture and Protocol for Virtual World Interoperability, *IEEE Internet Computing*, **15**(5): 22–29.

Meigs, T. (2003). *Ultimate Game Design: Building Game Worlds*, McGraw-Hill, New York.

Mishra, D., El Zarki, M., Erbad, A., Hsu, C.-H., and Venekatasubramanian, N. (2014). Clouds + Games: A Multifacted Approach, *IEEE Internet Computing*, **18**(3): 20–27.

Murphy-Hill, E., Zimmerman, T., and Nagappan, N. (2014). Cowboys, Ankle Sprains, and Keepers of Quality: How is Video Game Development Different from Software Development? *Proceedings of the 36th International Conference on Software Engineering*, ACM, Hyderabad, India, pp. 1–11, June.

Musil, J. Schweda, A., Winkler, D., and Biffl, S. (2010). Synthesized Essence: What Game Jams Teach about Prototyping of New Software Products, *Proceedings of the 32nd International Conference on Software Engineering*, ACM, Cape Town, South Africa, pp. 183–186, May.

Preston, J. A., Chastine, J., O'Donnell, C., Tseng, T., and MacIntyre, B. (2012). Game Jams: Community, Motivations, and Learning among Jammers. *International Journal on Game-Based Learning*, **2**(3): 51–70.

Rogers, S. (2010). *Level Up!: The Guide to Great Video Game Design*, Wiley, New York.

Scacchi, W. (2004). Free/Open Source Software Development Practices in the Game Community, *IEEE Software*, **21**(1): 59–67.

Scacchi, W. (2010a). Collaboration Practices and Affordances in Free/Open Source Software Development, in I. Mistrík, J. Grundy, A. van der Hoek, and J. Whitehead (Eds.), *Collaborative Software Engineering*, Springer, New York, pp. 307–328.

Scacchi, W. (2010b). Computer Game Mods, Modders, Modding, and the Mod Scene, *First Monday*, **15**(5), May.

Scacchi, W. (2010c). Game-Based Virtual Worlds as Decentralized Virtual Activity Systems, in W.S. Bainbridge (Ed.), *Convergence of the Real and the Virtual*, Springer, New York, pp. 225–236.

Scacchi, W. (2011). Modding as an Open Source Software Approach to Extending Computer Game Systems, *International Journal Open Source Software and Processes*, **3**(3): 36–47, 2011.

Scacchi, W. (2012a). Competitive Game Development: Software Engineering as a Team Sport. Keynote Address, *2nd International Workshop on Games and Software Engineering, International Conference on Software Engineering*, Zurich, Switzerland, May. http://bit.ly/1qLeVZ3.

Scacchi, W. (Ed.), (2012b). *The Future of Research in Computer Games and Virtual Worlds: Workshop Report*, Technical Report UCI-ISR-12-8, Institute for Software Research, University of California, Irvine, CA. http://bit.ly/1tWxUDi.

Scacchi, W. and Alspaugh, T.A. (2012). Understanding the Role of Licenses and Evolution in Open Architecture Software Ecosystems, *Journal of Systems and Software*, **85**(7): 1479–1494.

Schell, J. (2008). *The Art of Game Design: A Book of Lenses*, Morgan Kauffman/Elsevier, Burlington, MA.

Sheldon, L. (2011). *The Multiplayer Classroom: Designing Coursework as a Game*, Cengage Learning PTR, Independence, KY.

Shin, K., Kaneko, K., Matsui, M. et al. (2012). Localizing *Global Game Jam*: Designing Game Development for Collaborative Learning in the Social Context, in Nijholt, A. Romano, T., and Reidsma, D. (Eds.), *Advances in Computer Entertainment, Lecture Notes in Computer Science*, Vol. 7624, Springer, Berlin, Germany, pp. 117–132.

Smelik, R.M., Tutenel, T., Bidarra, R., and Benes, B. (2014). A Survey on Procedural Modelling for Virtual Worlds, *Computer Graphics Forum*, doi:10.1111/cgf.12276.

Smite, D. and Wohlin, C. (2011). A Whisper of Evidence in Global Software Engineering, *IEEE Software*, **28**(4): 15–18.

Smith, G., Whitehead, J., Mateas, M. et al. (2011). Launchpad: A Rhythm-Based Level Generator for 2-D Platformers, *IEEE Transactions on Computational Intelligence and AI in Games*, **3**(1): 1–16.

Verigames (2014). http://www.verigames.com/, accessed June 2014.

von Ahn, L. (2006). Games with a Purpose, *Computer*, **39**(6): 92–94.

Wang, A.I. (2014). The Use of Game Development in Computer Science and Software Engineering Education, in Cooper, K. and Scacchi, W. (Eds.), *Computer Games and Software Engineering*, CRC Press, Boca Raton, FL.

Zook, A. and Riedl, M.O. (2013). Game Conceptualization and Development Processes in the Global Game Jam, *Proceedings on Foundations of Digital Games Workshop on the Global Game Jam*, Crete, Greece.

Index

Note: Locators followed by "*f*" and "*t*" denote figures and tables in the text

A

AAA games, 269, 276
ACM SIGPLAN Conference, 114
Adaptable elements, 145, 149
Adaptable properties, 145
Adaptive serious game, 147
  adaptable properties in, 145–147, 145*t*
  model for content in, 141*f*
Adaptivity process
  definition of, 146–148
  in serious game, 19
  software frameworks for, 134
  types of, 148
ad hoc network, 188, 190
AGoogleADay.com (AGAD) game,
    200–203
  analytics view on New Year's holiday
    2011, 210*f*
  Google search, 201–202
  serious game, 201
  total audience participation, 211*f*
  trivia question game, 201–202
  vs. non-AGAD players, 209*f*
AI modules, 217, 222–226
  definition, 222
  functional groups, 229–230, 231*f*
  interaction, 223–225
  interface, 225–226, 226*f*
  interface for Mammoth Listener, 230,
    230*f*
  reuse, 223–224, 226, 228–229
Android SDK (mobile development
    platform), 48

Application programming interface (API),
    35, 167, 225
Applied CS, 39
  game development in, 43–45, 45*f*, 46*t*
  GDFs used in, 47*f*
  programming languages used to
    teach, 47*f*
Aptitude–treatment interaction
    approach, 148
Art design, difference between game
    design and, 45
Artificial intelligence (AI), 4, 40
  as computational behavior, 218
  layered statechart-based, 219–220
  miscellaneous module properties,
    224–225
  module, 222–226
  Scythe AI tool, 235–237
  for squirrel NPC, 220–222
  in strategy game, 40
Ask Pex! button, 120*f*, 122, 125–126
Assessment situation, 142, 143*f*
Association for Computing Machinery
    (ACM), 38

B

Battleship (game), 101–104
  game interface, 102–103
  location interface, 103
  Othello instead of, 108
  player interface, 104
BetterProgrammers, 119

Blackboard, LMS, 61
Bloom's taxonomy, 69
BlueRose XNA game, screenshots from, 37, 37*f*
Bodies of knowledge (BOKs), 65
Bug Hunt, 109
The Bugslayer, 94
Bug Wars (game), 109
Butterflies game, 188–189
Buzz Aldrin's Race into Space (quest games), 254

C

Caches architectures, 163
CAP theorem, 155
Capture Calculus Toolset (CCT), 194
Carmack, John, 5
CBA (Customer Business Analyst game), 249–250, 249*f*
CCT (Capture Calculus Toolset), 194
Central Intelligence Agency (CIA), 97
   World Factbook, 97–98
CGSE (computer games and software engineering), 262
Challenge class, 69–70
Charles River Media, 5
Client–server architectures, 157, 159, 162
Cloud-based software system, 278
CloudCoder, 117
Cocos2d-x, 193
Codecademy, 118–119
Code Hunt, 18, 126–128
   coding duel in, 128*f*
   example sectors in, 127*f*
   improvements for, 127–128
   main page of, 127*f*
   test generation technologies for, 129
Codelab, 118
CodeWrite, 117
CodingBat, 115–117
Collect Decider statechart, 233, 234*f*
Columbia University
   HALO in, 95
   PSL, 110
   second-level computer science course, 93

Combat-oriented maze games, 4
Commercial-of-the-shelf (COTS), 34
Communication problem, 190
CompuServe, 4
Computer games (CGs), 1, 6–8, 262–263, 267, 272, 280
   field of, 1–3
   in market, 2
   modification of, 5
   practical utility of, 6
   review of, 14
   SE challenges in
      GSD and global CGSE, 275–276
      large-scale software systems, 267–268
      SEE, 276–277
      software design, 270–272
      software requirements, 268–270
      software testing, 272–274
      teamwork processes in CGSE, 274–275
   as software application, 5
   software architecture, 9
   software development, 3–6
   students interest in, 6
   topics in, 6–12
   types of, 2
Computer games and software engineering (CGSE), 3
   challenges for massively scalable games, 268
   emergence of community of interest in, 12–14
   game jams, 275
   GSD and global, 275–276
   need for, 9
   other challenges, 279
   R&D programs, 280–281
   research and practice in, 6
   research areas, 277–280
   teamwork processes, 274–275
Computer science (CS) education, 32, 107, 262
   course
      at Columbia University, 95
      game use in, 109

game development in, 32, 39–45,
41t–42t
applied CS, 43–45, 45f, 46t
experiences from, 49–50
programming languages used to
teach, 47, 47f
promoting or teaching in middle
and high schools, 42, 42t
topics/subjects, 39–40, 40f
gameful approaches for, 105
GDFs used in, 33, 45–48, 47f
programming languages used to
teach, 47f
students thoughts on, 107
COMS 1007: Object Oriented
Programming and Design with
Java, 96–97
Constructivistic–collaborative
approach, 148
Constructivistic theories, 135
Context class, 68–69
Customer Business Analyst (CBA) game,
249–250, 249f

D

Darkstar, 160
Data prioritization techniques, 158
DECENT world, 252–253, 253f, 254f
Defense Advanced Research
Projects Agency (DARPA),
272–273
Desire2Learn, LMS, 61
Device-to-device communication, 21
Dialog Challenge, 70
DinoQuest Online, 244, 245f, 246
Distributed joint state problem, 193
Distributive Interactive Virtual
Environment (DIVE), 157
DOOM, computer game, 4
development of, 5
Drawsome Golf, 100
Dr. Mario (puzzle game), 244–246, 244f
DSG (Distributed Scene Graph),
Intel's, 161
Dynamic symbolic execution
(DSE), 121

E

Eclipse, IDE, 264
Educational games
elements, 66f
field of, 128
Educational software engineering
researchers in, 115
subfield of, 114
typical project on, 115, 121
Edutainment, 61–62
Erikson's developmental stages, 134
EVE Online, 154–155
Experience points (XP), 98
Extensible markup language (XML), 16,
60, 78–79
applications, 79
comprehensive syntax for, 78
documents human legible, 79
formal and concise, 78
partial representation of test game
challenge, 79t–82t
SimSYS, 79, 83
specification for, 78
Eye gaze studies, 204
Eye tracking studies, 22, 204

F

FabLab (games), 247, 248f, 252
Fantastic Voyage (quest games), 254
Feedback and retrospectives for CS
education, students, 105–108
comments, 106
HALO
not beneficial to students, reason,
105, 106f
reason to helped students, 105, 105f
reflections on, 107
reflections on tournaments, 108
thoughts on CS education, 107
Finite state machines (FSMs), 218
First-person shooter (FPS) game,
159, 246
Free/open source software (FOSS), 272,
276, 279
FSMs (finite state machines), 218

Full distribution problem, 190
Functional group, 216, 229–230, 231*f*, 238
    Key Item Tracker, 230, 232
    Wander Move, 232

G

Game-based applications, 2
Game-based virtual worlds, 242–243, 256
    adding Rashomon-style role-play,
        248–251
    meta-problem solving, 254–256
    modding an existing game, 246–248
    producing games, 244–246
    replacing multicharacter dialogs,
        248–251
    resource allocation challenges,
        251–254
Game design document (GDD), 63–64
Game Developers Conference (GDC), 246
Game development
    for advanced programming courses, 40
    in applied CS, 45*f*, 46*t*
    in CS education, 38–50, 40*f*, 41*t*–42*t*
    improper usage of, 49
    to learn, 49
    for promote CS in middle and high
        schools, 42*t*
    in SE education, 38–50, 43*f*
    in software architecture course, 33–38
    for teaching, 32, 39
    use of, 39, 45
Game development framework (GDF), 33
    for CS/SE course, 33
    games in, 51
    licenses and cost of, 52
    programming language used by, 51
    recommendations for use of, 50–52
        educational goal, 50
        programming experience, 50–51
        staff expertise, 51
        subject constraints, 50
        technical environment, 51–52
    technical experience with, 51
    usability of, 51
    used in CS/SE education, 33, 45–48, 47*f*
    XNA and Java, 46

Game elements
    educational, 66*f*, 69–71
    and learning content
        adaptation of, 149
        identified in game, 144
        identified in study, 141*f*
    traditional, 67–69
Game engine, Unity 3D, 46
Game modding, 48
Game play, 73, 77, 245
    descriptions of, 64
    mechanics, 23–24
    repurposing
        case studies in, 243–256
        comparative case analysis, 256–257
        research on, 242–243
    semiformal model, tabular challenge,
        87–89
Game Programming Gems, 5
Games
    AAA games, 269, 276
    AGAD, 200–203
    agnostic, 225, 229
    battleship, 101
    butterflies, 188–189
    CBA, 249, 249*f*
    computer games (CG), 262–263, 267, 272
    design
        designers, 270–271
        difference between art design
            and, 45
        technique, 242
    developers, 269
    engaging properties of, 94
    FabLab, 247, 248*f*
    first-person shooters, 159
    FOSS, 272
    FPS, 246
    game logic, 167
    Geocast, 184–189
    HALO FPS, 250
    iTESS, 185–188
    iTron, 185, 185*f*
    jams, 274–275
    jigsaw puzzle, 168–170
    Mammoth, 226*f*, 230*f*, 237
    modding tools, 243

multiplayer, 253, 271
multiuser, techniques for scaling up,
    156–161
other game-specific techniques, 158–159
*The Residents: Bad Day at the
    Midway*, 250
sample AI for squirrel NPC, 220–222
semiautomated generation, 277
serious, 200–201
servers, 165, 167
software engineering challenges in
    computer, 267–277
Texas Hold'em card, 252–253
trivia question, 201
Unreal Tournament, 49–50
Unreal Tournament 2004 (UT2K4), 246
Unreal Tournament 2007 (UT2K7), 246
video, 184
Warcraft, 48–50
Games and software engineering (GAS)
    workshop, 12–14, 263
Game software
    architecture design, 8–9
    design, 270–272
    online sharing of, 5
    playtesting and user experience, 9–10
    requirements engineering, 8, 268–270
    reuse, 10–11
    testing, 272–274
Games with a purpose (GWAP), 278–279
Gamification, 62
Gamify, 94
GDD (game design document), 63
Geocast games, 184–189
    butterflies, 188–189
    iTESS, 185–188, 187*f*
    iTron, 185, 185*f*
Geocast Games Architecture (GGA), 190,
    194–196
    butterflies, 188–189
    fully distributed architecture, 195
    geographic communications, 195
    iTESS, 185–188
    iTron, 185
    optional long-range extension, 195
    variants, 195–196
Global software development (GSD), 267

Google search, 201–202
Group-private event, 230–231
Guild Wars 2, 159

H

HALO FPS games, 250
HCI (human computer interaction), 201
Hierarchical FSMs (HFSMs), 218
Highly addictive, socially optimized
    (HALO) software, 17, 93
    advantage with, 107
    case study with, 97–100
    gameful testing using, 95–100
    helped students, 105, 105*f*
    not beneficial to students, 105, 106*f*
    plug-in for eclipse, 95, 96*f*
    prototype implementation of, 95
    quests, 98–99
    quests, student-created, 99–100
    reflections on, 107–108
    secret ninja method for, 109
    social nature of, 93
    social rewards in, 94
    software engineering, 94–95
    testing, 95
    uses MMORPG, 93
HTML5 WebSockets, 156
HTML parsing library, 99
HTTP (Hypertext Transfer Protocol),
    155–156
Human computer interaction (HCI), 201
Hypergrid (OpenSim), 252
Hypertext Transfer Protocol (HTTP),
    155–156

I

Id Software, 5
Institute of Electrical and Electronics
    Engineers (IEEE) Xplore, 38
Intellectual property (IP), 268
Intelligent tutoring systems (ITSs), 134
    adaptivity for, 148
Intel's Distributed Scene Graph (DSG), 161
Interactive development environments
    (IDEs), 264

Interest management techniques, 155, 158
Inter-mural game jams, 274–275
International Conference on Software
    Engineering (ICSE), 12–13, 114
Intra-mural game jams, 274
iOS SDK (mobile development platform), 48
iTESS game, 185–188, 187*f*
iTron game, 185, 185*f*
iTron/Parkour game, 185, 186*f*

J

Java (programming language)
    code, 95
    frameworks developed in, 45
    game in, 101
    IDE, 119
    Khepera robot simulator in, 35
    programming exercises in, 115
    XNA and, 46
Jigsaw puzzle game, 20, 168–170, 176–177

K

KeyItemMemorizer module, 225, 226*f*
Key Item Tracker, 230, 232
Khepera robot simulator, 35, 38
Knowledge space theory (KST), 135, 141
KommGame interface, 110
Kyle Wrist Mount, 185

L

Learning management systems (LMS), 61
Learning objectives, integration of, 60, 65
Learning taxonomy, 65–66
Lepidoptera, 207
Live Feed, 123–124, 124*f*
Long-range play problem, 190

M

Macro adaptive approach, 148
Mammoth game, 226*f*, 230*f*, 237
Massively multiplayer online role-playing
    games (MMORPGs), 93, 208,
    264, 268

Massively multiuser online games (MMOs/
    MMOGs), 2, 154, 237, 252
    applications, 154
    architecture for, 20
    CAP theorem, 155
    data prioritization techniques, 158
    description, 154
    EVE Online, 154–155
    The Exiled Realm of Arborea
        (*TERA*), 161
    games launch in, 4
    Guild Wars 2, 159
    HTML5 WebSockets, 156
    interest management techniques, 155
    jigsaw puzzle, 168–170
    REST (representational state transfer),
        155–156, 163
    scalability of, 20
    Second Life, 154–155, 157, 159
    space partitioning, 155, 157, 176–177
    TCP, 168
    tiered architecture, 160–161, 164*f*
    time dilation, 155, 158–159
    WebGL, 156
    web technologies, 154, 156
    World of Warcraft, 154–155, 157, 169
Massively open online courses
    (MOOCs), 115
Meta-design theory, 242–243
Meta-model foundation, 17
Micro adaptive approach, 147
Microsoft Azure, 128
Microsoft Visual Studio, 121, 125
Middleware, 161–162
Mining software repositories, 114
Mission-oriented science projects, 254
Mission planning, 251–253
MMORPGs (massively-multiplayer online
    role-playing games), 93, 208,
    264, 268
MMOs/MMOGs (massively multiuser
    online games), *see* Massively
    multiuser online games
    (MMOs/MMOGs)
Model-driven engineering (MDE), 60
    -based approach, 16
    feature of, 17

Modern serious-game development, goal in, 134
More knowledged other (MKO), 135
    principles of, 147
    role of, 147
    in social development theory, 147
Motivation, 184
Multiplayer online games, 271

N

National Gaming League, 12
.NET (programming language), 120
    tool for, 121
Newell's timescales of human behavior, 203
Nonfunctional requirements (NFRs), 269
Nonplayer characters (NPCs), 11, 67, 216
    AI designed for, 23
    in quiz, 73
    sample AI for squirrel, 220–222
        high-level brain, 222f
        KeyItemMemorizer module, 225, 226f
        overview of, 221f
    trash collector, 231
    variety of, 68
Norwegian University of Science and Technology (NTNU), 32
    software architecture course at, 34

O

Object Constraint Language, 64
Object-oriented design, 43, 52
Object-oriented programming languages, 48, 51
Online programming exercise systems
    BetterProgrammers, 119
    CloudCoder, 117
    Codecademy, 118–119
    Codelab, 118
    CodingBat, 115–117
    gamification of, 18–19, 120–128
    Pex4Fun, 120–128
        Code Hunt, 126–128, 127f, 128f
        educational usage of, 125–126
        gaming in, 122–123

social dynamics in, 123–125
software engineering technologies, 121
user interface, 120, 120f
user ranking in, 124f
Practice-It, 117–118
OpenSim, 252
Open source software (OSS), 252, 257
Othello (game), 108

P

Parlante, Nick, 115
Payloads, 224, 228
Peer-to-peer architectures, 157
Pex4Fun, 18–19, 120–128, 264
    Code Hunt, 126–128, 127f, 128f
    coding duel, 122
    Community link on, 123
    educational usage of, 125–126
    game type in, 121
    gaming in, 122–123
    Live Feed link on, 123
    social dynamics in, 123–125
    software engineering technologies, 121
    test generation technologies for, 129
    type of social games, 123
    types of feedback, 122
    user interface, 120, 120f
    user ranking in, 124f
    users comments on, 126
Pex tool, 121–122
Piaget's stages of cognitive development, 134
Players, scaling up number of, 172–176
    experimental setup, 172–173
    results, 173–176
Practice-It (online platform), 117–118
Pragmatic testing problem, 194
Private event, 227
Program engineering dollars (fictional currency), 110
Programming languages, 3, 15, 18, 21, 35, 45, 120, 229
    to develop games, 45
    use by GDF, 51
    used to teach SE/CS education, 47, 47f

Proxies, 160–161, 165
Proxy and database bottlenecks,
     170–172
Puzzle games
     Dr. Mario, 244–246, 244*f*
     jigsaw, 20
     Tetris, 244–246, 244*f*
     tetrominoes, 244
     tile-matching, 24
Python (programming language), 115,
     166, 177
     free programming classes in, 118

Q

Quality of experience (QoE), 278
Quest games; *see also* Highly addictive,
     socially optimized (HALO)
     software
     Buzz Aldrin's Race into Space, 254
     Fantastic Voyage, 254

R

Rapid recoherence (RRC), 192, 192*f*
Rashomon effect, 250–251
RCAT, *see* Restful client–server
     architecture (RCAT)
RedDwarf, see Darkstar
Representational state transfer (REST),
     155–156
     caches architectures, 163
     cautious MMOs, 163
     client–server architectures, 162
     stateless protocol architectures,
          163
     tiers architectures, 162
     uniform interface architectures,
          163
Repurposing game play mechanics,
     technique of
     case studies, 243–256
          choosing meta-problem solving
               domains, 254–256
          modding existing game, 246–248
          producing functionally similar
               games, 244–246

     recognizing resource allocation
          challenges, 251–253
     replacing multicharacter dialogs
          and adding Rashomon-style
          role-play, 248–251
     comparative case analysis, 256–257
     research on, 242–243
Requirements restriction problem, 193
The Residents: Bad Day at the Midway
     (game), 250
REST (representational state transfer),
     see Representational state
     transfer (REST)
Restful client–server architecture (RCAT),
     20, 161–165
     architecture, 164–165
     components, 166*f*
     jigsaw puzzle, 168–170
     reference implementation, 166–168
     REST, 162–164
     uniform interface architecture, 163
Role-playing game (RPG), 2
Romero, John, 5
RRC (rapid recoherence), 192, 192*f*
Ruby (programming language), 117
     free programming classes in, 118

S

Sakai, LMS, 61
Scalable *Ad Hoc* Geocast Protocol
     (SAGP), 195
Scalable geographic addressing
     framework (SGAF), 195
ScienceDirect, 38
SCXML (Statechart Extensible Markup
     Language), 224
Scythe AI tool, 235–237
     contributions of work, 217
     warnings and errors generated by,
          237, 237*t*
     workflow and key features, 236*f*
          AI construction, 236–237
          importing modules, 235–236
          outputting AI, 237
SDKs (software development kits), 5
Secret ninja formal methods, 92, 109

SEE (Software engineering education),
        6–8, 276–277
    for advance, 7, 13
    game development in, 39–45, 44*t*
        experiences from, 49–50
        programming languages used to
            teach, 47, 47*f*
        topics/subjects, 43
    GDFs in, 33, 45, 47*f*
Semantic validation problem, 194
Serious educational games (SEGs), 16, 62
    challenge for, 66
    creation of, 64
    development of, 16, 64
    high-level model of, 71
    holistic approach to, 66–71
    informal model of, 16, 64
    MDE-based approach for, 65
Serious games, 200
    adaptable properties in, 145–147, 145*t*
    characterize players in, 138–143
    definition of adaptivity, 134–135, 147–148
    development of four, 136–138
        addition and subtraction, 138*f*
        reading numbers, 137*f*
        steps in, 144*f*
        writing numbers, 137*f*
    effects of human tutors in, 134
    future of, 148
    game elements in, 148
    game environment in, 134
    iterative development process for, 140*f*
    provide help in, 143–146
    role of human tutors in, 134–135
    on social development theory, 134
    stages, 19
    study design, 139–140
        domain-specific tasks identified
            in, 142*t*
        game elements and learning
            content identified in, 141*t*
    types of, 148
SE tools, 262
SGAF (scalable geographic addressing
        framework), 195
SIGCSE Technical Symposium, 114
SimSE (game), 7, 109

SimSYS approach, 16, 61, 64, 72*f*
    development of, 61
    formal model
        SimSYS XML, 79, 83
        XML, 78–79, 79*t*–82*t*
    informal model
        example Test Game, 73, 74*f*
        SimSYS storyboard, 73–74
        storyboard, 71, 73
    MDE approach, 71
    use case model, 75–78
        example Test Game, 77, 78*f*
        SimSYS use case, 76–77
        UML, 75–76, 76*f*, 77*f*
SimSYS Game Play Engine, 71, 79, 83
Social development theory, 139, 141,
        146–147
Social reward
    HALO, 94
    for students, 95
Software architecture course, 33–35
    evaluation of, 38
    game development in, 33–38
    at NTNU, 34
Software Architecture in Practice, 33
Software design, 95
    in CS2 class, 110
    principles, 95
    via battleship tournament, 101–104
Software development kits (SDKs), 5, 270
Software engineering (SE), 1, 32
    aspects of, 94
    CGs, challenges in
        GSD and global CGSE, 275–276
        large-scale software systems,
            267–268
        SEE, 276–277
        software design, 270–272
        software requirements,
            268–270
        software testing, 272–274
        teamwork processes in CGSE,
            274–275
    challenges
        architecture, 190
        coding, 193
        design, 191–193

Software engineering (SE) (*Continued*)
  requirements, 193–194
  validation, 194
 data mining for, 114
 education, 6–8, 114
 emergence of, 3
 field of, 1–3
 game development in, 32, 38–50,
   43*f*, 44*t*
 gamification examples in, 124
 GDF for, 33
 GDFs used in, 47*f*
 HALO, 94–95
 programming languages used
   to teach, 47*f*
 project, 7
 topics in, 6–12
Software Hut, 109
Software requirements specification
   (SRS), 63–64
Software testing, 43, 49–50
 basics of, 99
 HALO, 95
 student, 93–94
Space partitioning, 155, 157
 client–server architectures, 157
 DIVE, 157
 dynamic, 157
 MMOs, 155, 157, 176–177
 peer-to-peer architectures, 157
 static, 157
SQLAlchemy (database toolkit), 167
Stack Overflow badges, 124–125
Statechart Extensible Markup Language
   (SCXML), 224
Stateless protocol architectures, 163
Storyboard, 64*f*, 66, 71–73
 SimSYS, 73–74
Student feedback, 105–106
Students
 assignments in HALO, 97
 CodingBat as platform, 117
 -created HALO quests, 99–100
 feedback on CS education, 105–108
  comments, 106
  HALO, reflections on, 105, 105*f*,
   106*f*, 107

 reflections on tournaments, 108
 thoughts on CS education, 107
 game project, 37–38
 player's knowledge in SimSYS, 69
 software architecture course,
   35–37
 software testing, 93–94
Student software testing, 93–94
S-VON network, 161

T

TankBrains (game), 109
TCP (Transmission Control Protocol),
   165, 168
Teaching assistant (TA), 36
TERA (The Exiled Realm
   of Arborea), 161
Test Game
 4 SE Design, 73
 informal model of, 74*f*
 tabular specifications for, 78*f*
 UML use case diagram for, 77*f*
 XML partial representation of, 79*t*–82*t*
Tetris (puzzle game), 49, 94,
   244–246, 244*f*
Tetrominoes (puzzle game), 244
Texas Hold'em card game, 252–253
Tiered architecture, 160–161, 164*f*
Tiered Geocast Protocol, 195
Tiers architectures, 162
Tile-matching puzzle games, 24
Time dilation techniques, 155,
   158–159
Transmission Control Protocol (TCP),
   165, 168
Trash Can Memorizer, 233
Trash collector
 build NPC, 233–234
 case study, 234–235
 specification, 231–232
  collecting trash, 232–233
  exploring, 232
  use trash receptacles, 233
 squirrel, 231–235
Trivia question-style game, 21–22
Two dimension (2D) games, 37, 40

U

UAV (unmanned aerial vehicle),
    186–187
UDP (User Datagram Protocol), 168
UIs (user interfaces), 64, 200, 202
Unified modeling language (UML),
    16, 64
  use case, 75–76
    diagram for Test Game 4, 77*f*
    visual and textual, 76*f*
  variety of, 75
Uniform interface architectures, 163
Unity 3D, 46
Unmanned aerial vehicle (UAV), 186–187
UnrealEd (game level editor), 5, 246, 247*f*
Unreal Tournament 2004 (*UT2K4*)
    games, 246
Unreal Tournament 2007 (*UT2K7*)
    games, 246
User Datagram Protocol (UDP), 168
User experience (UX), 273
User interfaces (UIs), 64, 200, 202
User, views of
  macro level, 204, 208–210
  meso level, 204, 206–208
  micro level, 204–206
  research and design on levels,
    210–211

V

Valve Software, 5
Video games, 184; *see also* Computer
    games (CGs)
Visual programming, 48

Voronoi diagram, 158
Vygotsky's social development theory,
    134–135, 139

W

Web-based programming exercise system,
    117–118
WebGL technology, 156
WebSockets technology, 168
World Factbook, CIA, 97–98
World of Warcraft (computer game),
    93–94, 97, 154–155, 157, 169
World Wide Web, 5, 78

X

XML (extensible markup language), 16,
    60, 78–79
  applications, 79
  comprehensive syntax for, 78
  documents human legible, 79
  formal and concise, 78
  partial representation of test game
    challenge, 79*t*–82*t*
  SimSYS, 79, 83
  specification for, 78
XNA, Microsoft, 36–37

Z

Zone of proximal development
    (ZPD), 135
  definition of, 146
  expand and change over time, 136*f*